The Broadview Pocket Guide
to Writing
revised fourth Canadian edition

A Note on the Cover

For thousands of years humans have been likening the process of writing to the ways in which we interact with the land—ploughing and digging, sowing and reaping. In the early seventh century CE Isadore of Seville tells of how the Romans for their writing used styluses that were at first made of iron, later of bone, and quotes from a now-lost Roman play by the now-unknown playwright Atta: "we shall turn the ploughshares upon wax, and plough with a bone point." Around 1400 the German poet Johannes von Tepl begins his long poem *The Ploughman of Bohemia* with a reference to what he refers to as a well-known maxim of scribes: "the quill is my plough." In some sense the quill or pen is of course like a plough in that it digs into the writing surface. But the digging can also be likened more broadly to what writing does—as Seamus Heaney famously likens it in a 1964 poem about his father's digging and what Heaney himself will do with his "squat pen."

The Broadview Pocket Guide to Writing

revised fourth Canadian edition

*Doug Babington, Don LePan,
Maureen Okun, and Nora Ruddock*

Contributing Editor: Laura Buzzard

broadview press

BROADVIEW PRESS – www.broadviewpress.com
Peterborough, Ontario, Canada

Founded in 1985, Broadview Press remains a wholly independent publishing house. Broadview's focus is on academic publishing; our titles are accessible to university and college students as well as scholars and general readers. With over 600 titles in print, Broadview has become a leading international publisher in the humanities, with world-wide distribution. Broadview is committed to environmentally responsible publishing and fair business practices.

Library and Archives Canada Cataloguing in Publication

Babington, Doug, author
    The Broadview pocket guide to writing / Doug Babington, Don LePan, Maureen Okun, and Nora Ruddock ; contributing editor, Laura Buzzard. — Revised 4th Canadian edition.

Includes bibliographical references and index.
ISBN 978-1-55481-336-0 (paperback)

    1. English language—Rhetoric—Textbooks. 2. English language—Grammar—Textbooks. 3. Report writing—Textbooks. 4. Bibliographical citations—Standards—Textbooks. I. LePan, Don, 1954-, author II. Okun, Maureen, 1961-, author III. Ruddock, Nora, author IV. Buzzard, Laura, editor V. Title. VI. Title: Pocket guide to writing.

LB2369.B24 2016   808'.042   C2016-906254-6

Broadview Press handles its own distribution in North America
PO Box 1243, Peterborough, Ontario K9J 7H5, Canada
555 Riverwalk Parkway, Tonawanda, NY 14150, USA
Tel: (705) 743-8990; Fax: (705) 743-8353
email: customerservice@broadviewpress.com

Distribution is handled by Eurospan Group in the UK, Europe, Central Asia, Middle East, Africa, India, Southeast Asia, Central America, South America, and the Caribbean. Distribution is handled by Footprint Books in Australia and New Zealand.

Broadview Press acknowledges the financial support of the Government of Canada through the Canada Book Fund for our publishing activities.

Design and Typesetting: Eileen Eckert
Cover Design: Lisa Brawn
Proofreading: Joe Davies
Index: Alexandria Stewart

PRINTED IN CANADA

HOW TO USE THIS BOOK AND ITS COMPANION WEBSITE

The goal of *The Broadview Pocket Guide to Writing* is to provide a concise reference text that is easy to use in every respect. We've made the book easy to carry around, and easy to use lying flat on a desk. We've also tried to keep the organization simple so that the book will be easy for you to find your way round in. There are two ways to locate information in the text:

- *index:* Go to the index at the back of the book to find the location in the book for any topic, large or small.
- *page headers:* These list section headings on the left and chapter headings on the right.
- *table of contents:* The detailed table of contents at the beginning of the book sets out the sections, chapters, and headings within chapters.

The purchase price of this book includes free access to *The Broadview Guide to Writing* website, where you will find various sorts of material related to this book. (If you have purchased a used rather than a new copy, you may purchase a passcode online through the main Broadview Press website.) Perhaps most importantly, the companion website includes a wide range of exercises relating to almost every aspect of grammar and usage. Many of these are interactive; you can check immediately if you have answered correctly, and—if you haven't—find an explanation. (Instructors may of course ask that you complete particular exercises and hand in your score sheet to them, but we encourage you to try the exercises on your own as well—especially in areas that the Diagnostic and Review Exercises suggest may not be areas of strength for you.)

You will also find several other sorts of material on *The Broadview Guide to Writing* companion website:

- a selection of expository essays, ranging from Montaigne to the present day, each accompanied by questions and topics for discussion.

- links to a variety of other helpful sites.
- complete sample essays in MLA, APA, Chicago, and CSE formats.

This book does *not* provide certain features that you will find in most other writing guides and handbooks: glossy paper that is both expensive and environmentally unfriendly, and highlighting in many different colours throughout the book. We have added one accent colour, but we have no desire to add more—or to move away from our long-standing policy of using plain (and, as much as possible, recycled) paper stock. That's a choice that's good for the environment—and also one that helps us keep the price of this book at a level little more than half that of most other writing guides or handbooks.

If you have questions or comments about *The Broadview Guide* (or suggestions as to what else we should consider including for future editions, whether on the website or in the bound book), we'd like to hear from you. Just email <customerservice@broadviewpress.com>.

Thank you!

CONTENTS

GRAMMAR

RESEARCH AND DOCUMENTATION

STYLES OF WRITING

1. CHOOSING THE BEST WORDS

1a. Be as Clear and Specific as Possible

In most contexts it is best to use language that communicates your ideas to the reader as clearly as possible. (For more on specific issues relating to academic jargon see the section below on "The Language of Academic Writing" [6a].)

needs checking	Several key components of this issue will be identified in this essay, and various facets of each will be discussed.
revised	This essay will look at three things.
needs checking	They wanted the plan to be optimally functional.
revised	They wanted the plan to work well.
needs checking	In an economic slow down the economy declines.
revised	In an economic slow down the rate of growth in the economy declines.

1b. Watch for Redundancy

Redundancies are words or expressions that repeat in another way a meaning already expressed. Sometimes they may be useful to add emphasis; usually they should be avoided.

needs checking	The house is very large in size.
revised	The house is very large.
needs checking	It would be mutually beneficial for both countries.
revised	It would be beneficial for both countries.

1c. Avoid Wordiness

In groping for ideas at the rough draft stage, writers often latch on to unnecessarily complex or wordy sentence structures.

needs checking	As regards the trend in interest rates, it is likely to continue to be upward.

revised	Interest rates are likely to continue to rise.

needs checking	There are many historians who accept this thesis.
revised	Many historians accept this thesis.

needs checking	Due to the fact that each member of the UN Security Council has a veto, the Council is not infrequently unable to take decisive action.
revised	Since each member of the UN Security Council has a veto, decisive action is rare.

1d. Watch for Missing Parts

It is easy to omit a word or a link in an argument.

needs checking	She told Felicity and about the accident.
revised	She told Felicity and me about the accident.

needs checking	She reminded the conference that just one intercontinental ballistic missile could plant 200 million trees.
revised	She reminded the conference that the money spent on just one intercontinental ballistic missile could be used to plant 200 million trees.

The word *that* should always be included if its omission might lead to confusion.

needs checking	Darwin believed biblical texts such as those dealing with human origins should not be read literally.
revised	Darwin believed that biblical texts such as those dealing with human origins should not be read literally.

Phrases such as *that of* and *those of* must be included in many sentences for the sake of logical clarity.

needs checking	The drives of golfer Mike Weir have never been as long as Tiger Woods or Rory McIlroy.
revised	The drives of golfer Mike Weir have never been as long as those of Tiger Woods or Rory McIlroy.

1e. Choose the Best Verb

If you want to keep the focus on the recipient of an action rather than on its agent, the passive voice is useful. In other situations, the active voice is less wordy and more effective.

needs checking The election was lost by the Premier.
(Passive voice—7 words)

revised The Premier lost the election.
(Active voice—5 words)

needs checking The protestor was killed with a single baton blow to the head.
[Who is responsible for the killing? If the information is known it should generally be given.]

revised One of the soldiers killed the protestor with a single baton blow to the head.

2. CONNECT YOUR IDEAS CLEARLY

The order in which you make your ideas appear and the ways in which you connect them—and show your reader how they connect—are as important to good writing as the ideas themselves.

2a. Paragraphing

There is a degree of flexibility when it comes to the matter of where and how often to start new paragraphs. Sometimes a subtle point in an argument will require paragraph of almost an entire page to elaborate; occasionally a single sentence can form an effective paragraph. Yet separating ideas into paragraphs remains an important aid to the processes of both reading and writing. Following are some guidelines as to when it is appropriate to begin a new paragraph.

i) In narration:

- whenever the story changes direction ("This was the moment Preston Manning had been waiting for...," "When Napoleon left Elba he...")
- when there is a gap in time in the story ("Two weeks later the issue was raised again in cabinet...")

ii) In description:

- whenever you switch from describing one place, person, or thing to describing another ("Even such a brief description as this is enough to give some sense of the city and its pretensions. Much more interesting in many ways are some of British Columbia's smaller cities and towns...")

iii) In persuasion or argument:

- when a new topic is introduced ("There can be little doubt that Austen's asides on the literary conventions of her time provide an amusing counterpoint to her story. But does this running commentary detract from the primary imaginative experience of *Northanger Abbey*?")
- when there is a change in direction of the argument ("To this point we have been looking only at the advantages of a guaranteed annual income. We should also ask, however, whether or not it would be practical to implement.")

iv) When changing from one mode to another:

- Description, narration, and argument are commonly blended together in writing. If, for example, a text moves from describing an experiment to analysing its significance, it's a good time to start a new paragraph. If it moves from telling where Napoleon went and what he did to discussing why events unravelled in this way, the same holds true.

For more on paragraphing, see 5c, *Argument Structure and Paragraphing*, below.

2b. Joining Words

The art of combining correct clauses and sentences logically and coherently is as much dependent on taking the time to think through what we are writing as it is on knowledge of correct usage. It is important to use appropriate joining words to help the reader see how ideas are linked—and important as well not to give too many or contradictory cues to the reader. Almost no writer manages these things (let alone perfect grammar and spelling!) the first time. Good writers typically write at least two or three drafts of any piece of writing before considering it finished.

needs checking   At the end of World War II there was substantial optimism that the application of Keynesian analysis would lead to economic stability and security. Over the post-war period optimistic rationalism weakened in the face of reality.

This passage gives the reader too few cues. It is not immediately clear how the idea of the first sentence is connected to that of the second. The problem is readily solved by the addition of a single word:

revised   At the end of World War II there was substantial optimism that the application of Keynesian analysis would lead to economic stability and security. Over the post-war period, however, optimistic rationalism weakened in the face of reality.

needs checking   A short report in which you request an increase in your department's budget should be written in the persuasive mode. Most reports, however, do not have persuasion as their main objective. Persuasion, though, will often be one of their secondary objectives. In reports like these, some parts will be written in the persuasive mode.

Here, the use of *however* and *though* in consecutive sentences gives the reader the sense of twisting back and forth without any clear sense of direction. This sort of difficulty can be removed by rewording or rearranging the ideas:

> *revised*   A short report in which you request an increase in your department's budget should be written in the persuasive mode. Most reports, however, do not have persuasion as their main objective. Persuasion will thus be at most a secondary objective.

The use of joining words is complicated by grammar; certain joining words are used to show how the ideas of one sentence connect to those of the previous sentence, while others are used to connect ideas in the same sentence. Words commonly used to connect the ideas of different sentences:

as a result,	further,
however,	furthermore,
in addition,	nevertheless,

Words commonly used to connect ideas within the same sentence:

although	though
and	whereas
because	while

(N.B. These lists are far from exhaustive.)

> *needs checking*   There will not be regular delivery service this Friday, however, regular service will resume Monday.
>
> *revised*   There will not be regular delivery service this Friday. However, regular service will resume Monday.
>
> *or*   There will not be regular delivery service this Friday, but regular service will resume Monday.

Additional Material Online
Exercises on joining words may be found at
sites.broadviewpress.com/writing.
Click on **Exercises** and go to
Putting Ideas Together.

Because: The joining word *because* is a particularly trouble-some one. It is easy to become turned around and use *because* to introduce a result or an example rather than a cause.

needs checking	He had been struck by a car because he lay bleeding in the road.
revised	We could infer that he had been struck by a car because we saw him lying bleeding in the road.
	[This follows the causal connections of the writer's thought processes, but is wordy and cumbersome.]
revised	He lay bleeding on the road; evidently he had been struck by a car.
or	He had been struck by a car and lay bleeding on the road.

needs checking	The Suharto regime detained people in jail without trial because it had little respect for the law.
revised	We may conclude that the Suharto regime had little respect for the law because we know it detained people in jail without trial.
	[Again, this follows the causal connections of the writer's thought processes, but is wordy and cumbersome.]
revised	The fact that the Suharto regime detained people for long periods without ever bringing them to trial shows that it had little respect for the law.
or	The Suharto regime in Indonesia showed little respect for the law. It detained people for long periods, for example, without ever bringing them to trial.
or	The Suharto regime in Indonesia had little respect for the law; it detained people for long periods without ever bringing them to trial.

2c. Order and Weight Your Ideas According to Their Importance

The order in which ideas appear in any piece of writing, and the space that is devoted to them, will inevitably send signals to the reader as to their relative importance. For this reason, it is wise to avoid long discussions of matters you consider to be of less importance—or else to relegate them to a note outside the main body of the text. Similarly, it is wise to signal through the amount of space you give to your main ideas your sense of their importance. (Obviously you may also signal this through the use of words and phrases such as most importantly..., crucially....) You should be sure as well to give the reader a clear sense in the opening and closing paragraphs of the direction of the piece of writing.

2d. Watch for Ambiguity

Inappropriate word order may often cause confusion as to how ideas are connected.

needs checking   The macadamia was named for Dr. John MacAdam, an enthusiastic scientist who promoted the nut in its native Australia, and was dubbed "the perfect nut" by Luther Burbank.

revised   The macadamia was named for Dr. John MacAdam, an enthusiastic scientist who promoted the nut in its native Australia. Luther Burbank referred to the macadamia as "the perfect nut."

For more examples, see 1d above and the box below.

Red Tape Holds Up New Bridge

The following are all examples of ambiguity in newspaper headlines. In some cases it may take several moments to decipher the intended meaning.

> Two pedestrians struck by bridge
>
> Man held over giant L.A. brush fire
>
> Illegal aliens cut in half by new law
>
> Passerby injured by post office
>
> Red tape holds up new bridge
>
> Village water holds up well
>
> Jerk injures neck, wins award
>
> Bishop thanks god for calling

(The above examples come courtesy of columnist Bob Swift of Knight-Ridder Newspapers, and Prof. A. Levey of the University of Calgary.)

Here are two gems provided by editor Beth Humphries:

> The fossils were found by scientists
> embedded in red sandstone.
>
> She walked into the bathroom tiled in
> sea-green marble.

And, from a Global News weather telecast, the following prediction:

> "Out west tomorrow, they're going to see the sun,
> as well as Atlantic Canada."

2e. *Illogical or Confused Connections*

Certain words and phrases are particularly likely to lead writers into illogical or confused connections in their writing.

because of the following reasons/the reason is because: The word *because* makes it clear that a cause or reason is being introduced. The addition of a phrase such as *of the following reasons* is redundant. Either use *because* on its own, or use *for the following reasons/many reasons*, etc.

needs checking	During her first few years in New York, Susanna was unhappy because of several reasons.
revised	During her first few years in New York, Susanna was unhappy for several reasons.

Similarly, the phrase *the reason is because* involves repetition; use *that* instead of *because*, or eliminate the phrase completely.

needs checking	The reason ice floats is because it is lighter than water.
revised	The reason ice floats is that it is lighter than water.
or	Ice floats because it is lighter than water.
needs checking	The reason I have come is because I want to apply for a job.
revised	I have come to apply for a job.

is when/is where: Many people use these phrases erroneously when attempting to define something.

needs checking	Osmosis is when a fluid moves through a porous partition into another fluid.
revised	Osmosis occurs when a fluid moves through a porous partition into another fluid.
or	Osmosis is the movement of a fluid through a porous partition into another fluid.

numbers and things: In any sentence about things and numbers associated with those things, it is easy to become tangled up between the things themselves and the measure of number.

Always have this question in the back of your mind: what is the subject of the verb? Here's an example:

needs checking   Delays in new product launches have hammered the company's share price, which started the year at about $60 and now trades at less than $30.

[This sentence may seem fine at first glance; look again. What is the subject of the verb *trades*? It's the noun *price*. But is it in fact the price that trades at under $30? No; it's the shares that trade at less than $30.]

revised   Delays in new product launches have hammered the company's share price, which started the year at about $60 and is now less than $30.

or   Delays in new product launches have hammered the company's shares, which started the year at about $60; now the stock trades at less than $30.

Here are other examples of the same sort of problem:

needs checking   Many people have said that the price of the Tesla is too expensive.

revised   Many people have said that the price of the Tesla is too high.

or   Many people have said that the Tesla is too expensive.

needs checking   The height of the Shanghai Tower rises more than 2,000 feet.

revised   The Shanghai Tower rises more than 2,000 feet.

or   The height of the Shanghai Tower is more than 2,000 feet.

needs checking   The speed of the Sopwith Camel flew at just over 100 miles per hour during WWI.

revised   The Sopwith Camel flew at just over 100 miles per hour during WWI.

or   The maximum speed of the WWI Sopwith Camel was just over 100 miles per hour.

3. MAKING YOUR WRITING CONSISTENT

3a. Agreement among the Grammatical Parts of Your Writing

In order to be consistent, the various parts of your writing must be in agreement grammatically. Fuller treatment of this subject appears below in the section on grammar; here are a few examples of the sorts of problems that can arise:

needs checking   The state of Afghanistan's roads reflect the chaotic situation.

revised   The state of Afghanistan's roads reflects the chaotic situation.

> [Here the writer has made the mental error of thinking of *roads* as the subject of the verb *reflect*, whereas in fact the subject is the singular noun *state*.]

needs checking   A diplomat represents his or her country in its dealings with other countries. They often help to negotiate treaties and other agreements.

revised   Diplomats represent their country in its dealings with other countries. They often help to negotiate treaties and other agreements.

> [The pronoun *they* at the beginning of the second sentence needs to agree grammatically with the noun to which it refers.]

needs checking   We went over to the woman lying on the pavement; she looked either dead or asleep. Suddenly she sits bolt upright.

revised   We went over to the woman lying on the pavement; she looked either dead or asleep. Suddenly she sat bolt upright.

> [The revised passage is written consistently in the past tense.]

needs checking	Unlike the first version of the novel, which appeared in a weekly newspaper, Stowe had a chance to review the galley proofs of the 1852 edition.
revised	Whereas Stowe did not have a chance to proof the first version of the novel, which appeared in a weekly newspaper, she was able to review the galley proofs of the 1852 edition.

> [The grammatical structure of the first of these sentences suggests that a novel can read itself.]

Additional Material Online

For more on consistency when it comes to the grammatical parts of your writing, see **sites.broadviewpress.com/writing**. Click on **Exercises** and go to **"Parts of Speech"** and **"Verbs, Subjects, Modifiers."**

3b. Watch for Mixed Metaphors

Using metaphors can help to convey your ideas more clearly to the reader—and help to make your writing more interesting. A mixed metaphor occurs when we are not really thinking of the meaning of the words we use. "If we bite the bullet we have to be careful not to throw the baby out with the bathwater." "We will leave no stone unturned as we search for an avenue through which the issue may be resolved." As soon as one really thinks about such sentences one realises that the bullet is really better off out of the baby's bathwater, and that the best way to search for an avenue is not to turn stones over.

needs checking	Now the President is out on a limb, and some of his colleagues are pulling the rug out from under him.
revised	Now the President is out on a limb, and some of his colleagues are preparing to saw it off.

4. RHYTHM, VARIETY, BALANCE, AND PARALLELISM

The most predictable syntax in the grammar of English is SUBJECT-PREDICATE, as in the sentence "The effects are disturbing." Upend that predictability, and you are on your way to rhythmical distinctiveness: "Less obvious, but equally disturbing, are the effects this work could have in...."

An important element in rhythmical distinctiveness is balance. Sometimes a pleasing effect may be achieved simply by repeating grammatical structures: "We may not wish to deny Rushton the rights to publish such research. Nor can we deny the harm that it causes." Sometimes balance may be achieved by placing words or phrases in apposition: "Flanagan was Harper's closest confidante, his most influential advisor."

Often paired connectives ("if...then," "either...or," "not only...but also") can help in achieving balance. As always, the writer must be careful to put the words in the right places.

needs checking   Hardy was not only a prolific novelist but wrote poetry too, and also several plays.

revised   Hardy was not only a prolific novelist but also a poet and a dramatist.

needs checking   The experiment can either be performed with hydrogen or with oxygen.

revised   The experiment can be performed with either hydrogen or oxygen.

> [The choice is between the two gases, not between performing and some other thing.]

needs checking   To subdue Iraq through sanctions, he felt, was better than using force.

revised   To subduc Iraq through sanctions, he felt, was better than to use force.

> [The infinitive *to subdue* is balanced by the infinitive *to use*.]

The pairing *both ... and* can also help in achieving balance. But here too, difficulties in getting all the words in the right order can easily arise.

needs checking   As a critic she is both fully aware of the tricks used by popular novelists to score easy successes with readers through stylized depictions of sex and violence, as well as realizing that "serious" novelists are sometimes not above resorting to the very same tricks.

revised   As a critic she is fully aware both of the tricks used by popular novelists to score easy successes with readers through stylized depictions of sex and violence, and of the fact that "serious" novelists are sometimes not above resorting to the very same tricks.

We tend to think of constructions involving words such as *both ... and* and *not only ... but also* when we think of balance and parallelism in written work. But the principles involved extend far more widely. Finding the right order for the words in a long sentence can be surprisingly challenging, even for experienced writers. Keeping words, phrases, and clauses grammatically balanced is less difficult where a pairing of two is concerned—though even here it is easy enough to go astray if you're not careful:

needs checking   This holiday we plan on keeping healthy and we'll get lots of rest.

revised   This holiday we plan on keeping healthy and getting lots of rest.

needs checking   The new government aims to reduce conflict with its neighbours and increasing the rate of economic growth.

revised   The new government aims to reduce conflict with its neighbours and to increase the rate of economic growth.

needs checking   The study concludes that Facebook use is associated with declines in subjective measures of well-being, and the more people use Facebook, the worse they tend to feel.

revised   The study concludes that Facebook use is associated with declines in subjective measures of well-being, and that the more people use Facebook, the worse they tend to feel.

> [Repetition of the function word *that* makes clear to the reader how the second part of the sentence is connected to the first; the sentence's second part reports another of the same study's conclusions.]

When it is a matter of keeping three or more elements parallel or in balance, everything becomes more difficult.

needs checking   His accomplishments included a succession of strategic successes during World War II, helping to revive Europe after the war, and he founded an important new international organization.

revised   His accomplishments included a succession of strategic successes during WWII, a plan to revive Europe after the war, and the foundation of an important new international organization.

or   He is remembered for his strategic successes during WWII, for his plan to revive Europe after the war, and for the foundation of an important new international organization.

> [These are only two of many ways in which the sentence might be revised so as to make its three parts grammatically parallel.]

needs checking   A plant-based, whole foods diet is associated with improvements in heart condition, greater life expectancy, diabetes is reduced, lowering of cancer rates, less chance of Alzheimer's, and also there are other health benefits.

revised　A plant-based, whole foods diet is associated with improvements in heart condition, greater life expectancy, lower rates of diabetes, lower incidence of cancer, lower incidence of Alzheimer's, and many other health benefits.

or　A plant-based, whole foods diet typically improves heart condition; increases one's life expectancy; significantly lowers one's chances of being afflicted with diabetes, heart disease, cancer, or Alzheimer's; and is associated with many other health benefits as well.

> [Again, these are only two of many ways in which the problem of the sentence's faulty parallelism may be corrected.]

In the above examples parallelism is a matter of grammatical structure first and foremost. But (as we touched on in the first section of this book) the importance of balance and parallelism to writing is not only a matter of grammar. Sentences that are balanced and that include parallel structures tend to be both more comprehensible and more pleasing to the reader. In the following examples the initial sentence is not grammatically incorrect; the revisions are a matter of style rather than of correctness. You may judge for yourself as to how they compare in terms of the reader's experience.

worth checking　Teams with very low payrolls are unlikely to achieve much success, even in the regular season, and very unlikely to be able to win in the postseason against teams who are able to afford the best-paid stars. The Oakland As are often cited as an exception to the rule that low budget teams are unlikely to succeed in baseball, and it's true that they have enjoyed a surprising degree of success in the regular season. Perhaps inevitably, however, they have not enjoyed much success in the postseason.

revised　Teams with very low payrolls are likely to struggle in the regular season, and to struggle even more if they reach the playoffs and face teams who can afford the best-paid stars. If the Oakland As's low payroll makes their regular season success seem surprising, it also makes their postseason failures seem inevitable.

Additional Material Online

Exercises on balance and parallelism may be found at **sites.broadviewpress.com/writing**. Click on **Exercises** and go to **"Style."**

worth checking   What Marianne and her mother conjectured one moment as perhaps being possible, the next moment they believed to be probable. Anything they wished might happen they soon found themselves hoping for, and soon after that the hope would become an expectation.

revised   What Marianne and her mother conjectured one moment, they believed the next; with them, to wish was to hope, and to hope was to expect.

(Jane Austen, *Sense and Sensibility*)

worth checking   Our nation is made up of people of all sorts of religious beliefs. Many Americans are Christians but we also have Jews, Muslims, and Hindus among us, and there are also many American nonbelievers. America has also been shaped by many languages and cultures, from all over the world.

revised   We are a nation of Christians and Muslims, Jews and Hindus, and nonbelievers. We are shaped by every language and culture, drawn from every end of this earth.

(Barack Obama, First Inaugural Address)

In most cases, revising to strengthen parallel structures in your writing will have the happy byproduct of making it more concise. But that's not always the case; the second sentence from the Obama passage quoted above is longer than it need be, but a pleasing instance of parallelism nonetheless.

Even careful balancing cannot make a steady diet of long sentences palatable; a rich source of rhythm in any well written essay is the short sentence. When revising their work, careful writers look to balance long sentences and short ones—and to notice such things as a preponderance of "there is..." and "it is..." sentences.

needs checking   It is important to consider the cultural as well as the economic effects of globalization. In the past few years there have been many people who have argued that these would be even more significant, and would inevitably cause the disappearance of many nations as distinct cultural entities.

revised   Globalization has cultural as well as economic effects. In the past few years many have argued that these are even more significant, and that they will eventually cause the disappearance of many nations as distinct cultural entities.

CONTEXTS OF WRITING

5. ACADEMIC WRITING: ESSAYS AND ARGUMENTS

5a. From Topic to Thesis Statement

Each writer requires a purpose, one that is more than the mere desire to earn this month's salary or this term's B+ in history.

The stated assignment is an obvious place to begin. "Discuss the rise to power of Francisco Franco." Or "Thoroughly explain the advances in medical imaging since the beginning of this century." Or "Analyse the connections between Margaret Atwood's poetry and her novels." Very few writers are absolutely free to devise their own purposes.

But it's important for all writers to become engaged with the topic they are writing about. What if (returning to Francisco Franco) a prospective writer is bothered by the whole notion of "power" in the world of Spanish politics and warfare? Ignoring that abstract and difficult word might very well short-circuit her ability to handle the assignment—whereas grappling with its definition might provide sufficient purpose to set her writing in gear. Rather than half-heartedly narrate a string of events from the 1930s or merely list the political parties of that era, she would be motivated to write by the tension and ambiguity surrounding a single word in the assignment. Focusing on the nature of power might lead the writer to her thesis statement:

- Like most fascists, Franco saw power as an end in itself, not merely as a means to achieving other ends.

Unlike the topic, the **thesis statement** expresses an argumentative purpose and a point of view. It should be meaningful, clear, and concise—typically, according to most authorities, no more than a sentence or two. In certain contexts, however (such as when complex and subtle arguments are being expressed), it may be helpful to extend the "thesis statement" over a full paragraph, setting out a series of claims.

Thesis Statements: Some Examples

needs checking   Art is important to society in many ways, and I will talk about them in this essay. One of the artists I will focus on is Robert Mapplethorpe, the subject of much controversy over many years.

(Yawn. The statement is too general and too vague to have significance.)

revised   The art of Robert Mapplethorpe deserves to be exhibited—and at public expense—even if most people find it abhorrent.

(This statement is more precise, more limited, more interesting.)

needs checking   In this paper I will examine various reasons for launching the war in Kosovo in 1999.

(This is a statement of topic rather than of thesis.)

revised   The moral case for the US and its allies to wage a bombing-only war against Yugoslavia in 1999 was stronger than the strategic one; air attacks alone had never before been enough to win a war.

(Suddenly an argument is being made.)

needs checking   The purpose of this essay is to explore the interplay between poetry and the novel. I will demonstrate that good poets don't usually write good novels and vice versa.

(Full points for ambition, but it's the subject for a book, not a term paper. At most, a short paper might justifiably speculate about such a large question in its conclusion; the main focus should be much narrower. Also, the statement is far too bold in its generalization. "What about Thomas Hardy?" the professor will ask. "What about Boris Pasternak?")

revised   Ondaatje's characters seem thin and unreal to the reader—alternately brittle and transparent. Paradoxically, however, it may be precisely these qualities that allow the poetic power of his prose—at once brutal and fragile—to strike the reader with full force.

(A much narrower but still controversial thesis exploring the connections between poetry and prose.)

A thesis statement need not declare anything earth-shattering, but it should not be trivial or self-evident. Effective thesis statements are moulded to fit both the length of the essay and the expertise of its writer. There is no logical sense in asserting, at the outset of a 3,000-word history paper, that *every military leader since Attila the Hun has repeated his mistakes*. The vocabulary of absolutes (*every, all, best, only*, etc.) commits a writer to universal coverage—and authoritative knowledge—of the topic. Strength in argumentative writing often comes from a willingness to qualify assertions and to acknowledge that contrary points of view are, if not convincing, at least intelligent and comprehensible. Words such as *often*, *usually*, and *largely*, and phrases such as *for the most part*, and *to a great extent* are not necessarily signs that the writer lacks the courage of her convictions; more frequently they are indications that she is careful.

5b. The Nature of Argument

When people use the noun *argument* in everyday speech, of course, they tend to use it in this sense: *a heated exchange of opposing views*. This type of argument tends to be angry and loud and not very well reasoned. To speak of the argument of an essay, however, or of an argument presented in a debate, is to use the noun *argument* in a different sense: *a reason or set of reasons presented in order to persuade others*.

Here is the beginning of an argument in the first sense:

"I can't believe marijuana is still illegal; our government is really stupid!"

"You're stupid to smoke it! You just want everyone to be as stupid as you are."

"You're stupid if you think marijuana makes a person stupid."

"Oh, go ahead: smoke your brain out. See if I care."

Notice that neither person here is advancing arguments in the second sense of that word. They are making assertions, they are hurling insults at each other, and they are ascribing motivations for the views the other person is asserting. But they are not providing reasons for what they believe—let alone putting a series of reasons together into a coherent whole.

For the sort of argument that is a reason or set of reasons presented in order to persuade others, then, it is not enough simply to assert what you feel. An argument in this sense may be passionately advanced, or even scathing, but it is not angry; it aims to bring light, not heat. An argument explains; draws distinctions; considers possible exceptions to generalizations; provides evidence; asks questions, suggests answers—and responds to objections. An argument is alert for ambiguities and contradictions. An argument tries to consider a range of different possibilities—often including hypothetical possibilities that may help to clarify the ideas involved. But an argument in this sense is never open-ended: it must always lead to a conclusion.

How does one construct this sort of argument in writing? There are many ways in which that question can be answered; a little further on we will discuss at some length various modes of thought that may be involved in constructing arguments (*cause and effect, classification, generalization,* and so on). But in another sense there is a two-word answer to the question *How does one construct an argument?*—with paragraphs.

5c. Argument Structure and Paragraphing

On what basis is writing divided into paragraphs? We should be careful to note that different principles apply to narrative, descriptive, and persuasive writing (see 2a, above). But most essay writing for undergraduates is persuasive writing—writing that aims to present an argument. As it happens, it's with persuasive writing that the structuring of paragraphs is both most difficult and most important. The paragraph is the structural unit of argument in an essay of this sort. And in such essays paragraphs come in three basic types: body paragraphs, which comprise the bulk of the essay; introductory paragraphs; and concluding paragraphs. In order to keep things clear both in the mind of the writer (as the essay is being composed) and in the mind of the reader (as the essay is being read), each of the paper's significant points should have its own body paragraph. But how many significant points should an essay include? In practice, that depends less on the subject of the essay than on the length of the essay. Let's say you have been asked to write a paper of 1,000 to 1,500 words arguing either for or against legalizing marijuana in your state or province. That's a topic on which it's possible to make a case very concisely in a sentence or two, and just as possible to make a book-length case of 100,000 words or more. How many significant points should you try to make in an essay of 1,000 to 1,500 words?

The short answer in most cases is four or five. As writers, we are often told that in the interests of variety and freshness it's good to vary the lengths of paragraphs—as it is to vary the lengths of sentences. That's absolutely true, but it's also true that extremely short or extremely long paragraphs should generally be avoided in academic essay writing. It's all too easy for writers to lose their focus in writing an extremely long paragraph—and for readers to lose their focus as they try to wade through it. At the other extreme, the one-sentence paragraph is only rarely appropriate to academic writing. It is a punchy form that may have the force of an exclamation mark in certain styles of journalistic writing; like the exclamation mark itself, though, it very rarely serves to further the flow of an argument in academic writing.

The *average* length of a paragraph, then, tends to be in the range of 150 to 250 words. Some significant points can be made in a couple of sentences, and some may require a full page or more to elaborate properly, but in most cases 150–250 words will be an appropriate amount of space to devote to introducing, clarifying, and dealing with a significant point in the paper.

Let's take the marijuana topic as an example. Say you decide to argue in favour of legalization. An essay of between 1,000 and 1,500 words has room for six or seven paragraphs— an introductory paragraph, a concluding paragraph, and four or five paragraphs that make significant points. Here's what a simple paragraph plan for an essay of between 1,000 and 1,500 words might look like:

First paragraph: Introduction: sketch of the historical and contemporary background; thesis statement

Second paragraph: Illegal marijuana sales help to finance organized crime

Third paragraph: Enforcing marijuana laws is too expensive

Fourth paragraph: Taxes on marijuana would be a source of revenue

Fifth paragraph: Marijuana use is not that harmful; compare with other legal substances

Sixth paragraph: Rebut counter argument that legalization will lead to an increase in hard drug use

Seventh paragraph: Conclusion

As everyone knows, there is more than one side to every argument. Let's say you'd prefer to argue against legalization. Then your plan might look like this:

First paragraph: Introduction: sketch of the historical and contemporary background; thesis statement

Second paragraph: Take issue with the argument that marijuana is less harmful than other legal substances

Third paragraph: Legalization could lead to increase in drug use

Fourth paragraph: Specific harms from smoking and from eating marijuana or its byproducts

Fifth paragraph: Marijuana is a gateway drug

Sixth paragraph: Rebut counter argument that marijuana should be treated the same way as alcohol

Seventh paragraph: Conclusion

The above outlines give a sense of how an argument might be formed on two directly opposing viewpoints. Often, of course, there are more than two possibilities. One important lesson in developing thesis statements for arguments of your own is to try to resist habits of binary thinking—of thinking that there can be two and only two possibilities. On a topic such as this one, one might also, for example, argue one of the following positions:

- Where there are good arguments from opposing sides of an issue, searching for a middle way is often the best course; marijuana should be decriminalized, but not legalized.

- It is almost as bad where harmful substances are concerned to let corporate interests play a leading role as it is to let organized crime play a leading role; our goal should be to make marijuana legal, safe, and not very popular. The best way to accomplish that goal is for the government to take full control—for government rather than for-profit corporations to grow and process the plants, to operate non-glamorous retail outlets in out-of-the-way locations, to package the drug in plain wrappings, and to allow no advertising.

- With some North American jurisdictions now experimenting with different approaches to legalization, the safe course for other jurisdictions to follow is to wait until conclusive results are in from those experiments—which may take a decade or more.

Organizing paragraphs in longer essays

The paragraph structure of longer essays tends to be more complex than in the two examples provided above. It is often helpful to think of such structures in terms of paragraph clusters as well as individual paragraphs and to formulate an outline that includes groups of subordinate paragraphs. It's important to be aware, though, that any paragraph outline you develop during the planning and writing process should be regarded as subject to change as you move forward. Such a document is an important step in the process—but even at later stages you may well find that you need to make structural adjustments. You may decide that a paragraph is really expressing two important ideas instead of one, and should be split in two. You may decide that a couple of paragraphs represent an unnecessary digression, and should simply be cut. Or you may decide that one or more paragraphs would be more effective if they were moved to a different position in the essay. Like so many other things, it's virtually impossible to get all this right in your first draft; paragraphing should be something you pay almost as much attention to in the revision process as you do during the planning process.

Topic Sentences: Each paragraph should not only have a topic; it should have a point to make. To make sure it does, you may find it helpful to compose a ***topic sentence*** for each paragraph—a sentence in which you set out clearly what you intend the paragraph to show. (Sentences of this sort might well be called thesis statements at the paragraph level; by convention, though, the term *thesis statement* is reserved for the statement of the argument of the full essay.)

Many writers find it helpful to draft topic sentences when they make outlines for their papers. This takes a little bit more time up front, but often saves quite a lot of time later; when you go to write the first draft, you can use them as the first or second sentence of each paragraph, and they will help you—and, later, your reader—keep track of the structure of your argument. To return to the essay in favour of marijuana legalization we outlined above, an outline that uses topic sentences would look something like this:

First paragraph: Introduction leading to thesis statement: In both financial and social terms, the costs to society of enforcing the current marijuana laws far outweigh the benefits.

Second paragraph: Making marijuana illegal has the effect of encouraging more serious crime; the activities of organized crime are often largely financed with revenues from the sale of marijuana.

Third paragraph: Enforcing the marijuana laws is a poor way to spend taxpayers' money; huge unnecessary costs are incurred on police resources, the courts, and the correctional system.

Fourth paragraph: In addition, making marijuana legal and taxing its sale (as we do with alcohol) would provide substantial funding for all sorts of good purposes.

Fifth paragraph: The harm caused by marijuana smoking is far, far less than that caused by substances which are already legal—notably alcohol.

Sixth paragraph: Those who claim that legalizing marijuana would lead to greater use of more dangerous drugs are committing the slippery slope fallacy.

Seventh paragraph: Conclusion: On balance, the benefits of legalizing marijuana far outweigh the risks....

A similar outline for the essay against legalization would look something like this:

First paragraph: Introduction leading to thesis statement: The risks to society of legalizing marijuana far outweigh the potential benefits.

Second paragraph: Much as it is often argued that marijuana isn't *very* harmful, or isn't *as* harmful as alcohol or *as* harmful as heroin, no one has ever suggested that marijuana is not to some degree a harmful drug.

Third paragraph: If marijuana is legalized and thereby made more widely available, it stands to reason that this harmful drug will become more widely used than it is today.

Fourth paragraph: If marijuana is smoked, it causes harm to the lungs (in addition to the chemical changes brought about by the action of THC in the brain); if it is eaten, there is a severe danger of overdose when those who do not fully appreciate its effects fully consume more than the recommended maximum dose.

Fifth paragraph: There is abundant evidence that many users of marijuana move on to other, more dangerous, "hard" drugs; if society were to give marijuana use its blessing, that drug will likely become a stepping stone to hard drug use for more and more people.

Sixth paragraph: The most common argument in favour of legalizing marijuana is that it's less dangerous than alcohol and alcohol is already legal. But if both are harmful, why should we add to the harmful temptations that people are already exposed to?

Seventh paragraph: Conclusion: From all the angles discussed, the risks to society of legalizing marijuana far outweigh the potential benefits....

Implied Topic Sentences: Just as beginners do, many experienced writers try to include in almost every paragraph a topic sentence to make it clear just what that paragraph is arguing. They don't *always* do that, though; indeed, some highly accomplished writers only rarely include explicit statements in each paragraph of the paragraph's purpose. But that doesn't mean the underlying structure isn't there. One interesting exercise is to go through an essay by an experienced writer and for each paragraph either identify the topic sentence or—where the topic is implied rather than expressly stated in a topic sentence—compose the "missing" topic sentence.

For more on using paragraphs to structure arguments, we recommend Ian Johnston's *Essays and Arguments: A Handbook on Writing* (revised edition 2015); it's a text that has a proven track record of improving students' skills in formulating written arguments.

Additional Material Online
Exercises on paragraphing may be found at
sites.broadviewpress.com/writing.
Click on **Exercises** and go to
"Putting Ideas Together."

5d. Your Arguments, Others' Arguments

Another way to look at the organization of arguments is in terms of one's own ideas and those of others. When the concepts of plagiarism and of "original work" are discussed, it is rightly emphasized that any essay (or article, or web posting, or full-length book) should present one's own ideas, not simply regurgitate the ideas of others. But does that mean one's own work has to be written without reference to that of others? No—far from it. Nor does "original" in the context of academic writing mean that an essay or academic book has to present ideas no one has thought of before. It simply means that the ideas put forward should be thought through and synthesized by you as an individual—that you should not simply borrow someone else's thinking.

That process of thinking-through, synthesizing, and developing an argument cannot and should not be done in a vacuum. An essay in which you try to think through a topic entirely on your own, without reference to the arguments others have made, tends to be far less interesting than an essay that draws on others' arguments for support, and also that engages directly with opposing arguments. The importance of engaging in this way with the arguments of others is the central point of one of the past generation's most influential books about the nature of academic argument, Gerald Graff and Cathy Birkenstein's *They Say / I Say*. As they point out,

> the underlying structure of effective academic writing—
> and of responsible public discourse—resides not just in
> stating your own ideas, but in listening closely to others
> around us, summarizing their views in a way they will
> recognize, and responding with our own ideas in kind….
> [T]o argue well you need to do more than assert your own
> ideas. You need to enter a conversation, using what others
> say (or might say) as a launching pad or sounding board
> for your own ideas. (3)

Engaging with the arguments of others is important as a means of helping your reader to locate what you are saying in a broader context. But it is also important in helping you to formulate your own arguments for the reader. Obviously it can be helpful to draw on the arguments of others to support the views you are trying to convince your reader to adopt. By citing the arguments others have made—and, where appropriate, by summarizing or quoting from those arguments in support of your own—you can often make the points in your argument more persuasive.

Even more important is to come to grips with what those who oppose the arguments you wish to make have said. Crafting strong arguments often entails pointing out weaknesses in the arguments of those who argue opposing positions—but it also entails seeking out the strongest points that have been made against the position you have adopted. If you're arguing in favour of legalizing marijuana, you might well want to refer to (or quote from) the substantial series of articles and editorials that the *New York Times* ran in favour of legalization in late July and early August of 2014, but you would also be well advised to look at some of the strongest arguments made on the other side—by the American Medical Association, for example. If you are arguing against legalization, of course you may want to cite the AMA in support of your argument—but it may also be advisable to try to counter some of those *New York Times* arguments.

What if you aren't able to find strong arguments that challenge the points you wish to make? That may be a sign of several things. First of all, you should ask yourself if you have chosen a sufficiently interesting and challenging topic. If you are thinking of writing an essay arguing that men and women should receive equal pay for equal work, or that racism is bad, you're not likely to find strong and interesting opposing views to come to grips with. (For a discussion of how to formulate appropriate topics and thesis statements, see above, "From Topic to Thesis Statement.")

But what if you are thinking of writing an essay arguing a particular position about a newly published short story, or about a very recent political development, or about a philo-sophical position that has recently been advanced for the first time? You may not be able to find strong and interesting opposing views to come to grips with in those sorts of cases either—but that doesn't mean you've chosen a poor topic. So what should you do—just state your own views and not worry about opposing arguments? Here's a better way: invent as strong a set of opposing arguments as you can. You should try to anticipate the strongest possible argument you can imagine might be made by someone taking an opposing position. If you can persuasively counter any such arguments, you will have surmounted an important test—and written a first-rate essay.

In this connection it is worth drawing attention to the phrase in parentheses in the passage from Graff and Birkenstein quoted above: "You need to enter a conversation, using what others say (or might say) as a launching pad or sounding board for your own ideas." There are many ways in which writers introduce what others might say into their arguments. Sometimes these will merely be straw person arguments, but in many cases they represent a genuine effort on the part of the writer to imagine and to counter the strongest possible case that might be made against one's own position. Here are some ways in which ideas of this sort can be introduced:

> An opponent might argue that.... But that would be to....

> On the other side, it could be suggested that.... But in that case....

> We may well imagine the counter argument to this—that.... But this counter argument does not hold up to close scrutiny....

The discussions of integrating quotations and using signal phrases (pages 187–89, 251–54) may also be helpful in this connection.

6. STYLES AND DISCIPLINES

6a. The Language of Academic Writing

Academic writing often depends upon the use of academic jargon; much as the term *jargon* is often used pejoratively, its core meaning is *specialized language used by a particular group (whether academic or professional)*. Such language may sometimes be used in ways that are overblown or unnecessarily wordy. But it is important to remember that, properly used, academic or professional jargon is a means of communicating more economically than would be possible with less specialized language. Here is an example, drawn from the academic discipline of philosophy:

> When it comes to particular cases, is it possible for a consequentialist to respond in any coherent fashion to deontological arguments? Or for the deontologist to respond in any coherent fashion to consequentialist arguments? Inevitably, the two will talk past each other.

> When it comes to particular cases, is it possible for someone who believes that whether an action is right or wrong depends largely on the consequences it produces to respond in any coherent fashion to the arguments of someone who believes that the rightness or wrongness of actions must be based on those actions possessing inherent qualities according to which each action is required, permitted, or forbidden? Or for the latter to respond in any coherent fashion to the arguments of the former? Inevitably, the two will talk past each other.

The first of these, in which the specialized jargon of academic philosophy is used, is obviously far more economical. To be sure, *consequentialist* and *deontologist* are terms to be avoided if you are writing for an audience with no philosophical background. But if you are writing for an audience of philosophers or philosophy students, such terms are essential tools of the trade.

In everyday usage, of course, *jargon* is often used as a synonym for **unnecessarily** *technical or difficult language.* Language of that sort is indeed to be avoided:

needs checking   In order to ensure that the new delivery structure for regional renal care will be optimally functional, there must be accessibility for populations throughout the region to interdigitated modalities of care.

revised   If the new system of regional renal care is to work well, hospitals and clinics must be located in or near the main population centres.

needs checking   Our plan is more philosophical than operational in terms of framework.

revised   We are at the idea stage; our plan hasn't been tested yet.

The goal in academic writing, then, is to balance the requirements of the academic discipline with those of communication—to write in a varied and flexible style, using everyday words and expressions when appropriate, and using academic terms when those are the most effective and economical means of expression.

Additional Material Online
For more on the conventions of writing in different academic disciplines, go to **sites.broadviewpresscom/writing**. Click on **Academic Writing** and go to **"Across the Disciplines."**

The tone of academic writing is typically one of careful argument. The aim is to persuade the reader through logic and through the marshalling of evidence (rather than, for example, through attempting to exhort or entertain the reader). It is thus always important when writing in an academic context to provide support for whatever claims you make, and to be careful in how you phrase those claims. Almost all academic writers rely heavily on words and on phrases such as *for the most part*, *mainly*, *tends to...*, and so on, in order to ensure that the claims they are making allow for some exceptions. Conversely, they generally avoid words such as *always* and *never*, which would leave their arguments open to being refuted through a single exception. Most academic essays are formal pieces of writing, and should be approached as such. Readers expect a calm and disinterested tone, free of extreme emotion and of slang or conversational usage. That should not be taken to imply that thinking rigorously about a topic precludes feeling strongly about it—or conveying to the reader how the writer feels. But usually it is advisable to try to do this without employing first-person singular pronouns; most academic writers use I or me infrequently, if at all. Most academic writers aim to succeed in persuading their readers by letting the evidence speak for itself. Thus, many instructors advise their students to entirely avoid the use of first-person pronouns.

As with all guidelines to style and tone, though, this one should not be regarded as written in stone. George Orwell, often praised as the finest essayist of the twentieth century, uses I and me frequently.

6b. Writing about Literature / Writing about Texts

One sort of convention in academic writing that can take some getting used to is the way in which verb tenses are used. Many students find writing about literature particularly challenging in this respect; its conventions present fundamental problems for the student at the level of sentence structure.

The past tense is, of course, normally used to name actions which happened in the past. But when one is writing about what happens in a work of literature, convention decrees that we use the simple present tense.

| *needs checking* | Romeo fell in love with Juliet as soon as he saw her. |
| *revised* | Romeo falls in love with Juliet as soon as he sees her. |

needs checking   In her short stories, Alice Munro explored both
the outer and the inner worlds of small town life.

revised   In her short stories, Alice Munro explores both the
outer and the inner worlds of small town life.

If literature in its historical context is being discussed, however, the simple past tense is usually the best choice:

needs checking   Shakespeare writes *Romeo and Juliet* when he was
about thirty years of age.

revised   Shakespeare wrote *Romeo and Juliet* when he was
about thirty years of age.

needs checking   Alice Munro wins the Governor General's Award
for the first time in 1968, for her collection *Dance
of the Happy Shades.*

revised   Alice Munro won the Governor General's Award
for the first time in 1968, for her collection *Dance
of the Happy Shades.*

In some circumstances either the past or the present tense may be possible in a sentence, depending on the context:

correct   In her early work Munro often explored themes
relating to adolescence.

[appropriate if the focus is on historical developments relating to the author]

also correct   In her early work Munro often explores themes
relating to adolescence.

[appropriate if the focus is on the work itself]

Notice that if the subject of a sentence is the work itself, the present tense is required:

needs checking   Munro's early work often explored themes relating
to adolescence.

revised   Munro's early work often explores themes relating
to adolescence.

Often in an essay about literature the context may require shifting back and forth between past and present tenses. In the following passage, for example, the present tense is used except for the sentence that recounts the historical fact of Eliot refusing permission:

T.S. Eliot's most notorious expression of anti-Semitism is the opinion he expresses in *After Strange Gods* that in "the society that we desire," "any large number of free-thinking Jews" would be "undesirable" (64). Tellingly, Eliot never allowed *After Strange Gods* to be reprinted. But his anti-Semitism emerges repeatedly in his poetry as well. In "Gerontion," for example, he describes...

In such cases even experienced writers have to think carefully during the revision process about the most appropriate tense for each verb. Note in the following example the change in verb tense from *was* to *is*.

needs checking   In *The Two Gentleman of Verona* Shakespeare exhibited a degree of technical accomplishment unprecedented in the English drama. He still had much to learn as a dramatist and as a poet; in its wit or its power to move us emotionally *The Two Gentlemen of Verona* was at an enormous remove from the great works of a few years later. But already, in 1592, Shakespeare had mastered all the basic techniques of plot construction that were to sustain the structures of the great plays.

revised   In *The Two Gentleman of Verona* Shakespeare exhibits a degree of technical accomplishment unprecedented in the English drama. He still had much to learn as a dramatist and as a poet; in its wit or its power to move us emotionally *The Two Gentlemen of Verona* is at an enormous remove from the great works of a few years later. But already, in 1592, Shakespeare had mastered all the basic techniques of plot construction that were to sustain the structures of the great plays.

consistency in verb tense when integrating quotations: If one is writing about literature the writing will usually be in the present tense, but the quotations one wishes to use are likely to be in the past tense. Often it is thus necessary, if you are incorporating a quotation into a sentence, to rephrase and/or adjust the length of the quotation in order to preserve grammatical consistency. If a quotation is set apart from the body of your own writing, on the other hand, you do not need to (and should not) rephrase.

needs checking Emma Bovary lives largely through memory and fantasy. She daydreams frequently, and, as she reads, "the memory of the Vicomte kept her happy" (244).

[The past tense *kept* is inconsistent with the present tense *reads* and *daydreams*.]

revised Emma Bovary lives largely through memory and fantasy. She daydreams frequently, and, as she reads, the "memory of the Vicomte" (244) keeps her happy.

or Emma Bovary lives largely through memory and fantasy. She daydreams frequently, and blends fact and fiction in her imaginings: "Always, as she read, the memory of the Vicomte kept her happy. She established a connection between him and the characters of her favorite fiction" (244).

For more on integrating quotations, see MLA Style, below, pages 187–88.

The same principles that are used in writing about literature often apply in certain other disciplines when you are writing about texts. In many other disciplines the present tense is the tense most commonly used in such circumstances, if you are treating the ideas you are discussing as "live" ideas:

needs checking In an important recent book, Nelly Ferguson surveyed the history of the decline of empires, and predicted that during the course of the twenty-first century China will replace the United States as the world's leading power.

revised In an important recent book, Nelly Ferguson surveys the history of the decline of empires, and predicts that during the course of the twenty-first century China will replace the United States as the world's leading power.

needs checking	In their 2015 paper Smith and Johnson suggested that parental influence is more important than that of peers, even for adolescents. This essay will examine these claims and assess their validity.
revised	In their 2015 paper Smith and Johnson suggest that parental influence is more important than that of peers, even for adolescents. This essay will examine these claims and assess their validity.

It is important to remember that the use of the present tense in academic writing is not dependent on how recently the ideas being discussed were first put forward; the key thing is whether or not you are discussing them as live ideas today. You may use the present tense when discussing a paper written six months ago—but you may also use the present tense when discussing a text dating from twenty-four centuries ago. Just as you may say when writing about literature that Shakespeare *explores* the potentially corrosive effects of ambition, so too you may say that Aristotle *approaches* ethical questions with a view as much to the virtue of the doer as to the rightness of the deed, and that Marx *values* highly the economic contribution of labour—even though Shakespeare and Aristotle and Marx are themselves long dead. As with the text of a story or poem, the writings of dead thinkers may be discussed as embodying live thoughts—ideas that may retain interest and relevance.

Conversely, if the ideas you are discussing are being considered historically rather than as of current relevance, you should not use the present tense.

needs checking	The renowned astronomer Fred Hoyle advances arguments against the big bang theory of the origin of the universe. Hoyle suggests that the universe perpetually regenerates itself.
	[Hoyle's arguments have now been refuted.]
revised	The renowned astronomer Fred Hoyle advanced arguments against the big bang theory of the origin of the universe. Hoyle suggested that the universe perpetually regenerates itself.

As is the case with writing about literature, academic writing in disciplines such as history or philosophy or political science may often look at a text both from a historical perspective and from the perspective of the live ideas that are put forward within it. In such circumstances the writer needs to be prepared to shift verb tenses depending on the context:

purely historical context

Darwin finally published his theory only after an article by Alfred Wallace advancing a similar theory had been published. The central element in Darwin's theory was the concept of natural selection. Unlike Wallace, Darwin had become convinced that...

historical context + live ideas

Darwin finally published his theory only after an article by Alfred Wallace advancing a similar theory had been published. The central element in Darwin's theory is the concept of natural selection; according to Darwin's theory, all organisms are...

purely historical context

Hobbes believed that the tragic upheaval of the English civil war had been caused by the spread of dangerous beliefs about humans and human society. Hobbes's view was that humans require a structure of government to enforce a structure of laws; otherwise, he felt, they would revert to a state of nature in which life would be "nasty, brutish, and short." Hobbes's opponents did not disagree with the substance of this notion. But because he had argued from first principles rooted in human realities rather than in any divine ordering, he was accused of atheism, and threatened with prosecution...

historical context + live ideas

Hobbes firmly believed that the tragic upheaval of the English civil war had been caused by the spread of dangerous beliefs about humans and human society. Hobbes's view is that humans require a structure of government to enforce a structure of laws; otherwise they revert to a state of nature in which life will be "nasty, brutish, and short." That central notion still lies at the core of much political theory today...

Additional Material Online
An extended discussion of Writing about Literature /
Writing about Texts may be found at
sites.broadviewpress.com/writing.
Click on **Academic Writing** and go to
"Writing about Texts."

6c. Writing about Science

The many academic forms of writing about science include the review article (in which a writer surveys and assesses evidence on a particular topic from various sources); the research or experimental report, usually in the form of an article (in which a researcher writes up the results of an experiment of specific scope—lab reports are good practice for articles of this kind); the conference presentation or a poster board (in which scientists report in a limited or abbreviated fashion about specific research); the abstract (in which scientists provide a brief summary of the findings of a report or research paper); and the funding application, generally intended for a national or commercial grant or funding body (which usually includes an abstract and a statement of the importance of the research, along with a costing breakdown for the research).

i) Structure of the research paper

The research article is in many ways the paradigmatic type of scientific writing. Unlike articles in the humanities, research articles in the sciences are generally organized into specific sections that usually appear in a set order: Introduction, Methods, Results, and Discussion. The opening section of the article, the *Introduction,* tells the reader the purpose and nature of the study. How does it fit in with previous research? What has it been designed to show? What was the hypothesis? The norm is to keep the introduction fairly brief; normally, it explains a bit about the background to the paper and indicates why the research was undertaken. The paper's introduction may, in fact, include a background section or be called *Background.*

While it is appropriate to position the paper in the larger context of previous research here, extended discussion of that larger picture is not normally included in the introduction.

The *Methods* section is often very detailed. An important principle is that the paper should provide enough information about how the research was set up and conducted that other researchers can replicate the results. The reader also needs enough information to be able to understand the rationale for each step in the process.

The *Methods* section in a scientific research paper is always written in the past tense. When you are conducting your own research, however, it can be helpful to set out the details of the process beforehand in the present and/or future tenses, and then read over your notes with a view to the larger picture. Is the research being set up in the most unbiased way possible? Can the proposed method truly be expected to provide evidence one way or the other as to whether the hypothesis is valid? Are the most useful statistical methods being used to assess the data?

The *Results* section, as its name suggests, details the results at length. It often includes tables, charts, and graphs as a way of visually presenting these results.[1] The *Discussion* section provides an analysis of the meaning of those results, both in terms of the particular experiment and in terms of past experiments in the same area. Do the results confirm or refute the original hypothesis? What questions are left unanswered? What significance does the data have in the context of other research in this area? In what ways is the research subject to drawbacks (e.g., small sample size, indeterminate findings, confounding elements, short timeframe)? Do the results prompt any recommendations for the future?

Finally, scientific papers are almost always accompanied by an abstract, which comes before the actual paper. The *Abstract* summarizes the entire paper in no more than one

---

1   *Results* and *Discussion* are usually treated as separate sections of a paper; some journals, however, will ask that they be combined into one section of the paper.

or two paragraphs (usually 250 words or less); it is meant to convey the essence of the research to those who may not have time to read the entire paper, or who may be trying to determine if the entire paper will be of interest to them. Abstracts are often included in searchable databases for this latter purpose.

ii) Scientific tone and stylistic choices

Most contemporary natural sciences writers strive for objectivity of tone, while writers in the humanities and social sciences may foreground their own subject positions and sometimes adopt a less formal tone. Look, for example, at the way in which anthropologist Emily Martin opens her classic article on "The Egg and the Sperm":

> As an anthropologist, I am intrigued by the possibility that culture shapes how biological scientists describe what they discover about the natural world.... In the course of my research I realized that the picture of egg and sperm drawn in popular as well as scientific accounts of reproductive biology relies on stereotypes central to our cultural definitions of male and female. The stereotypes imply not only that female biological processes are less worthy than their male counterparts but also that women are less worthy than men. Part of my goal in writing this article is to shine a bright light on the gender stereotypes hidden within the scientific language of biology. Exposed in such a light, I hope they will lose their power to harm us.

Martin acknowledges at the outset that she occupies a specific position in relation to her research, and she uses the first person frequently ("I am intrigued," "I realized," "my goal"). Moreover, she acknowledges that her motive for conducting and publishing her research is not merely to expand objective knowledge about the world; she aims not only to shine a bright light on gender stereotypes, but also to reduce "their power to harm us." And yet, at its core, Martin's article is an example of careful scientific inquiry: she conducted a thorough survey of relevant scientific literature, her assessment of it follows scientific standards of objectivity, and she makes a strong argument based on clear and well-documented evidence.

Academics writing in natural science disciplines such as biology, chemistry, and physics, as well as those writing in the behavioural sciences (e.g., psychology, anthropology, sociology), all value scientific standards of objectivity and strive to make strong arguments based on strong evidence. However, differences in style and tone can be very noticeable, with the natural science disciplines tending towards a more formal and impersonal style than Martin adopts. But tone varies widely within the behavioural sciences as well; compare Martin's discussion of egg and sperm representations with the following behavioural science abstract for a 2012 scientific article that received a great deal of attention in general-interest media, "Facebook Use Predicts Declines in Subjective Well-Being in Young Adults":

> Over 500 million people interact daily with Facebook. Yet, whether Facebook use influences subjective well-being over time is unknown. We addressed this issue using experience-sampling, the most reliable method for measuring in-vivo behavior and psychological experience. We text-messaged people five times per day for two-weeks to examine how Facebook use influences the two components of subjective well-being: how people feel moment-to-moment and how satisfied they are with their lives. Our results indicate that Facebook use predicts negative shifts on both of these variables over time. The more people used Facebook at one time point, the worse they felt the next time we text-messaged them; the more they used Facebook over two-weeks, the more their life satisfaction levels declined over time. Interacting with other people "directly" did not predict these negative outcomes. They were also not moderated by the size of people's Facebook networks, their perceived supportiveness, motivation for using Facebook, gender, loneliness, self-esteem, or depression. On the surface, Facebook provides an invaluable resource for fulfilling the basic human need for social connection. Rather than

enhancing well-being, however, these findings suggest that Facebook may undermine it.

There are obvious differences in tone between this passage and that by Martin quoted above. Most obviously, the writers employ terminology specific to the academic discipline in which the authors are writing: "subjective well-being," "predicts," "moderated by," and "negative outcomes." More generally, the abstract is much more impersonal in tone than the first paragraph of Martin's paper; the reader is not told of any moment of realization which led to these researchers' work, or of what effects they hope their research will have. Instead, the passage provides a summary of the reasons for the study, the nature of the study, the main results, and some sense of their significance—all in reasonably direct and specific prose.

Notice the relative brevity of the sentences used as the abstract opens—the first is only eight words long. Long sentences are certainly sometimes appropriate (and indeed necessary)—but in scientific writing as in other sorts, varying sentence lengths is a good way to help maintain reader interest.

Expressing ideas concisely and varying sentence length are two ways of making your writing clear and readable. Using parallel or balanced sentence structures is another. Notice how the parallel grammatical structures in the following sentence (*the more ... the worse ...; the more ..., the more...*) emphasize the study's findings: "The more people used Facebook at one time point, the worse they felt the next time we text-messaged them; the more they used Facebook over two weeks, the more their life satisfaction levels declined over time."

It is often imagined that complex and difficult-to-read sentence structures strike an appropriately academic tone—that direct sentences and rhetorical balance are for journalists or novelists, not students and scholars. If scientific research is important, however, then surely it's worthwhile to communicate that research in clear and readable prose.

iii) The first person and the active voice

Students writing in disciplines such as biology, physics, psychology, or engineering are often advised to avoid grammatical structures associated with what might seem a subjective approach—most notably, the first person (*I* or *we*). Such advice is often also given to students writing English or history papers, and the reason is much the same: instructors want to discourage students from thinking of the writing of an academic paper as an exercise in expressing one's likes or dislikes. Unsubstantiated opinions are not appreciated in any of the academic disciplines. But how well one has supported one's argument bears no necessary relation to whether or not one has used the first person. In the Emily Martin example quoted above, Martin uses the first person extensively, but she doesn't just express an opinion; her study is supported using a lot of evidence, and the discussion itself is objective in nature.

Similarly, the abstract of the paper about Facebook by Ethan Kross et al. does not achieve its more formal and impersonal tone by avoiding the first person. Quite the contrary: Kross et al. use the first person twice in the first three sentences of the abstract: "We addressed," "We text-messaged."[1] Scientific objectivity, then, is not a matter of avoiding the first person; it is rather a matter of avoiding bias when framing one's research questions, of designing research projects intelligently and fairly, and of interpreting the results ethically.

Discussions of impersonality and objectivity in scientific writing have also often been framed in terms of the question of whether to use the active or the passive voice. For most of the twentieth century, many instructors in the natural sciences tried to train students to use the passive voice[2]—to write things like "*It **was decided** that the experiment **would be conducted** in three stages*" and "*These results **will be discussed** from several*

---

[1]   In the case of group authorship, which is very common in the sciences, the plural must, of course, be used.

[2]   As Randy Moore and others have pointed out, nineteenth-century scientists used the active voice and the first person freely. The active voice and "first-person pronouns such as *I* and *we* began to disappear from scientific writing in the United States in the 1920s."

perspectives" in order to convey a more impersonal and objective tone. In the late twentieth century, however, the scientific community began to swing around to the view that, much as the passive might sometimes have its place, the active voice should be the default writing choice. Here is Randy Moore, writing in *The American Biology Teacher* in 1991:

> The notion that passive voice ensures objectivity is ridiculous[;] objectivity has nothing to do with one's writing style or with personal pronouns. Objectivity in science results from the choice of subjects, facts that you choose to include or omit, sampling techniques, and how you state your conclusions. Scientific objectivity is a personal trait unrelated to writing.

The 1990s saw heated debates in the pages of certain scientific journals on the matter of whether the active or the passive should be the default. But in the end the decision was clear: the active voice was the best choice. Nearly every major scientific journal now recommends that its authors use the active voice in most situations—and that they use the first person where appropriate as well.

The various *Nature* journals, the American Chemical Society Style Guide, and the American Society of Civil Engineers Style Guide are representative. The following instructions are from their respective websites:

> *Nature* journals prefer authors to write in the active voice ("we performed the experiment ...") as experience has shown that readers find concepts and results to be conveyed more clearly if written directly.

> Use the active voice when it is less wordy and more direct than the passive.... Use first person when it helps to keep your meaning clear and to express a purpose or a decision.

> Wherever possible, use active verbs that demonstrate what is being done and who is doing it....

Instead of: Six possible causes of failure were identified in the forensic investigation.

Use: The forensic investigation identified six possible causes of failure.

Though the active voice is better as a default choice, the passive voice can be useful in many ways, including as a way of shifting attention away from the researcher to the experiment itself. The following statements, for example, all make effective use of the passive:

- The cooling process was completed in approximately two hours.

- This compound is made up of three elements.

- Phenomena of this sort may be seen only during an eclipse.

6d. Business and Professional Writing

Tone may be the most important aspect of business and professional writing. The adjective *businesslike* conjures up images of efficiency and professional distance, and certainly it is appropriate to convey those qualities in most business reports, memos, and correspondence. In a great deal of business and professional writing, however, it is also desirable to convey a warm, personal tone; striking the right balance between the personal and the professional is at the heart of the art of business writing. Here are some guidelines.

Consult your colleagues. Circulate a draft of any important document to others and ask their opinion. Is the tone too cold and formal? Is it too gushy and enthusiastic? Is it too direct? Or not direct enough?

Be careful about suggesting you are speaking for your entire organization. Unless you are sure, you are well advised to qualify any extreme statements.

| *needs checking* | Our organization underprices every competitor. |
| *revised* | In my experience our prices are lower than those of major competitors. |

| *needs checking* | There is no way we would ever cut back on research and development. |
| *revised* | As an organization we have a strong commitment to research and development. |

Given that most business and professional communication operates within a hierarchical power structure, it is particularly important to foreground consideration in memos, letters, and emails. Avoid direct commands wherever possible; give credit to others when things go right; and take responsibility and apologize when things go wrong.

| *needs checking* | Here is the material we spoke of. Send the report in by the end of the month to my attention. |
| *revised* | I enclose the material we spoke of. If you could send in the report by the end of the month to my attention, I'd be very grateful. |

| *needs checking* | I am writing in response to your complaint. We carry a large number of products with similar titles, and sometimes errors in shipping occur. Please in future specify the ISBN of the item you are ordering, as that will help keep errors to a minimum. |
| *revised* | Thank you for your letter—and my sincere apologies on behalf of our company for our mistake. As you may know, we carry a large number of products with similar titles, and (particularly in cases where our customer service department is not able to double check against an ISBN) errors do sometimes occur. But that is an explanation rather than an excuse; I do apologize, and I have asked that the correct item be shipped to you immediately. Thank you for drawing this matter to my attention. |

6e. Slang and Informal English

Many words and expressions often used in conversation are considered inappropriate in academic, business, or professional writing. Here is a short list of words and expressions to avoid in formal writing:

AVOID	REPLACE WITH
anyways	anyway
awfully	very, extremely
boss	manager, supervisor
bunch	group
(except for grapes, bananas etc.)	
buy	bargain
(as a noun—"a good buy")	
go (to mean "say")	say
have got	have, own
kid	child, girl, boy
kind of, sort of	rather, in some respects
lots of	a great deal of
mad	angry
(unless to mean "insane")	

All contractions (it's, he's, there's, we're, etc.) should generally be avoided in formal writing, as should conversational markers such as *like* and *well*.

needs checking	Let's say for example unemployment got much worse, the government would need to act.
revised	If, for example, unemployment became much worse, the government would need to act.

7. THE SOCIAL CONTEXT

7a. Gender

The healthy revolution in attitudes towards gender roles in recent generations has created some awkwardness in English usage—though not nearly so much as some have claimed. *Chair* is a simple non-sexist replacement for *chairman*, as is *business people* for *businessmen*. Nor is one forced into *garbage-person* or *policeperson*; *police officer* and *garbage collector* are entirely unobjectionable even to the linguistic purist. *Fisher* is a good replacement for *fisherman*; here again, there is no need for the *-person* suffix.

The use of *mankind* to mean *humanity*, and of *man* to mean *human being*, have for some years been rightly frowned upon. (Ironically enough, *man* originally had *human being* as its **only** meaning; in Old English a *werman* was a male adult human being, a *wifman* a female.) A remarkable number of adults still cling to sexist usages, however, and even still try to convince themselves that it is possible to use *man* in a gender-neutral fashion.

Well, why **can't** *man* be gender neutral? To start with, because of the historical baggage such usage carries with it. Here, for example, is what the best-selling novelist Grant Allen had to say on the topic in a magazine called *Forum* in 1889:

> In man, I would confidently assert, as biological fact, the males are the race; the females are merely the sex told off to recruit and reproduce it. All that is distinctly human is man—the field, the ship, the mine, the workshop; all that is truly woman is merely reproductive—the home, the nursery, the schoolroom.

But the baggage is not merely historical; much of the problem remains embedded in the language today. A useful litmus test is how sex and gender differences are approached. Look, for example, at this sentence from an issue of *The Economist*:

> One of the most basic distinctions in human experience—
> that between men and women—is getting blurrier and
> blurrier.

Now let's try the same sentence using *man's* instead of *human*:

> One of the most basic distinctions in man's experience—
> that between men and women—is getting blurrier and
> blurrier.

In this sort of context we are all forced to sense that something is amiss. We have to realise when we see such examples that *man* and *he* and even *mankind* inevitably carry with them some whiff of maleness; they can never fully and fairly represent all of humanity. (If they didn't carry with them some scent of maleness it wouldn't be possible to make a joke about the difficulty of turning *men* into *human beings*.) Most contexts are of course more subtle than this, and it is thus often easy for humans—but especially for men—not to notice that the male terms always carry with them connotations that are not gender-neutral. *Humanity, humans, people*—these words are not in any way awkward or jargon-ridden; let's use them.

To replace *man* with *humanity* is not inherently awkward to even a slight degree. But the pronouns are more difficult. Clearly the consistent use of *he* to represent both sexes is unacceptable. Yet *he/she, s/he*, or *he or she* are undeniably awkward. *S/he* is quite functional on the printed page, but defies translation into oral English. Another solution is to avoid the singular pronoun as much as possible either by repeating nouns ("An architect should be aware of the architect's clients' budgets as well as the architect's grand schemes") or by switching to the plural ("Architects should be aware of their clients' budgets as well as their own grand schemes"). Of these two the second is obviously preferable. In longer works some prefer a third strategy that eliminates awkwardness entirely: to alternate between the masculine pronoun *he* and the feminine pronoun *she* when referring to a single, generic member of a group. Using *she* to refer to, say, an architect, or a professor, or a sports star, or a prime minister can have the salutary effect of reminding readers or listeners that there is nothing inherently male in these occupations. In a short piece of writing, however, it can be distracting to the reader if there are several bounces back and forth between female and male in the same paragraph. And a cautionary note should accompany this strategy even when it may conveniently be employed; be **very** careful not to assign *he* to all the professors, executives, or doctors, and *she* to all the students, secretaries, or nurses.

Pronouns: Undoubtedly the most troublesome questions for those who are concerned both about gender equality and about good English arise over situations involving singular pronouns such as *everyone, anyone, anybody, somebody, someone, no one, each, either, neither*. It can be difficult enough to re-cast sentences involving such words so that everything agrees, even before the issue of gender enters the picture.

> Everybody felt that the film was better than any other they had seen that year.

According to the rules most of us have been taught, that sentence is wrong; *everybody* is singular, and *they* must therefore be changed:

> Everybody felt that the film was better than any other she had seen that year.

> Everybody felt that the film was better than any other he had seen that year.

> Everybody felt that the film was better than any other she or he had seen that year.

But, as many have pointed out, the insistence on the singularity of such pronouns is a relatively recent phenomenon, dating from the codification of English grammar that took root in the eighteenth century. Before that time Chaucer, Shakespeare, Swift, and the rest had no qualms about using *they* or *their* to refer to *anyone* and *everyone*. When alternatives are either awkward or sexist, it may be best to return to the ways of Chaucer and Shakespeare:

awkward   Everyone will have a chance to express his or her views before the meeting is over.

gender neutral   Everyone will have a chance to express their views before the meeting is over.

Questions relating to pronouns and to gender issues are not restricted to pronouns such as *everyone* and *everybody*; they are also a matter of when to choose *we* and *us* or *they* and *them*. It is always good to think about the first or third person pronouns one is using, and who they may include or exclude. In some cases it may be better to repeat a noun than to replace it with a pronoun.

worth checking   The twentieth century brought a revolution in the roles that women play in North American society; in 1900 they still were not allowed to vote in any North American jurisdiction.

[If the writer is male and addressing an audience of both women and men, it is more inclusive to avoid using the third person "they."]

revised   The twentieth century brought a revolution in the roles that women play in North American society; in 1900 women still were not allowed to vote in any North American jurisdiction.

or   The twentieth century brought a revolution in gender roles in North American society; in 1900 women still were not allowed to vote in any North American jurisdiction.

Of course issues of gender are not confined to the right word choice. Consider the following descriptions of political candidates with essentially the same backgrounds:

• Carla Jenkins, a lawyer and a school board trustee, is also the mother of three lovely daughters.
• George Kaplan, a lawyer and a school board trustee, has a long record of public service in the region.
• George Kaplan, a lawyer and a school board trustee, is also the father of three lovely daughters.

- Carla Jenkins, a lawyer and a school board trustee, has a long record of public service in the region.

The impression left in many minds by such phrasings is that the person described as having a long record of public service is well suited to public office, while the person whose parenting is emphasized may be better suited to staying at home.

Some may feel that parenthood is relevant in such cases; if you do, be sure to mention it both for women and for men. The general rule should be that, when describing a person, you should mention only the qualities you feel are relevant. And be sure to describe women and men with the same lens: if you feel it necessary to refer to relationship status or physical appearance, be sure to do so for men as well as women; if you mention degree qualifications or career achievements, be sure to do so for women as well as men.

7b. Race and Ethnicity, Class, Religion, Sexual Orientation, Disability, etc.

The issues discussed above regarding when to use *we* and *us* or *they* and *them* apply just as much where matters of race or religion or sexual orientation are concerned as they do to matters of gender:

worth checking   In the late twentieth and early twenty-first centuries several rulings by the Supreme Court altered the landscape considerably where Canada's Aboriginal peoples are concerned. They now have much greater leverage when it comes to natural resource issues than they did before the Court's Delgamuukw and Tsilhqot'in decisions.

[If the writer is not Aboriginal and is addressing an Aboriginal audience or an audience of both Aboriginal and non-Aboriginal people, it is more inclusive to avoid using the third-person "they" and "them."]

revised   In the late twentieth and early twenty-first centuries several rulings by the Supreme Court altered the landscape considerably where Canada's Aboriginal peoples are concerned. First Peoples now have much greater leverage when it comes to natural resource issues than was the case before the Court's Delgamuukw and Tsilhqot'in decisions.

worth checking   I would like to conclude my remarks with a prayer that has meant a great deal to me. We all know how God can bring light into our lives; certainly He has done so for me.

> [appropriate if the speaker is addressing a crowd that she knows is entirely made up of fellow believers—but inappropriate if the speaker is addressing a mixed crowd of believers, agnostics, and atheists]

revised   I would like to conclude my remarks with a prayer that has meant a great deal to me. Many of you may have experienced the feeling of God bringing light into your life; certainly He has done that for me.

> [appropriate if the speaker is addressing a mixed crowd of believers, agnostics, and atheists]

Another important principle is to avoid the use of unnecessary racial or religious identifiers. As with gender, mentioning a person's race, religion, or sexual orientation in connection with occupation is a common habit, but one that reinforces stereotypes as to what sort of person one would naturally expect to be a lawyer or a doctor or a nurse. Unless race or gender or religion is in some way relevant to the conversation, it is inappropriate to refer to someone as a male nurse, or a Jewish doctor, or a Native lawyer. Nor is it generally appropriate to stereotype members of particular groups even in ways that one considers positive; by doing so one may fail to give credit for individual achievement, while leaving the harmful impression of the group possessing qualities that are essential to it.

needs checking	Of course she gets straight As in all her subjects; she's from Hong Kong.
revised	It's no wonder she gets straight As in all her subjects; her parents have given her a great deal of encouragement, and she works very hard.

Many other issues of bias in language are specific to particular categories; the discussion below is of course far from comprehensive.

race: As with gender or disability or sexual orientation, one should not foreground racial or cultural background unless it is clearly relevant to what is being discussed. The more we foreground a person's race or gender when it is *not* a characteristic relevant to the discussion, the more we encourage people to emphasize race or gender rather than focusing on other human attributes.

worth checking	I was given a ticket for speeding last week; a black police officer pulled me over just after I'd crossed the Port Mann bridge. So I had to pay the bridge toll *and* an eighty dollar fine!
revised	I was given a ticket for speeding last week; a police officer pulled me over just after I'd crossed the Port Mann bridge. So I had to pay the bridge toll *and* an eighty dollar fine!
worth checking	I've heard that Professor Andover's course in Canadian literature is very interesting. She's of Asian background from the look of her; she just joined the department this year. Apparently she's an expert on Leonard Cohen and the connections between literature and music.

> [It may not be immediately apparent to some readers that there is anything odd or problematic about this example. Substitute "She's white—of Caucasian racial background from the look of her" and the point may become more clear; the racial or cultural background of Professor Andover is not relevant here.]

revised   I've heard that Professor Andover's course in Canadian literature is very interesting. She just joined the department this year; apparently she's an expert on Leonard Cohen and the connections between literature and music.

nigga/nigger: Almost everyone knows that *nigger* is a highly derogatory term that was once very widely used in North America; that the term conveyed a presumption that black people were inferior to whites—and that the term was frequently employed as an expression of blatant hatred and contempt. In the mid twentieth century the word *nigger* began to be acknowledged as racist and hence utterly unacceptable, and it disappeared from respectable publications and from polite conversation. But it never went away: the forbidden term continued to be used in certain less polite circles as an expression of racism—and it still continues to be so used today.

In the late twentieth century, as a gesture of resistance in the face of the continuing oppression of black people in the United States, some groups of young African Americans began to "reclaim" the term *nigger* (or *nigga*) as their own, using it defiantly among themselves to refer to one another. That remains common practice today—and as a result, some young people of other backgrounds now sometimes wonder why they too shouldn't be allowed to use the "forbidden" term. The reason is simple: it remains tainted by the history of oppression with which it is associated. It is one thing for members of a group that has been on the receiving end of oppression to embrace such a term as an expression of solidarity among themselves. It is quite another for those belonging to other groups to presume to do the same.

Indian/First Nations/Aboriginal: In Canada the word *Indian* has become tainted by centuries of history in which those who had taken the land from the indigenous peoples used the word *Indian* to denigrate those peoples. It's not uncommon for some First Nations people to refer to one another informally or ironically as *Indians*. If you hear an Aboriginal person calling another Aboriginal person *Indian*, does that mean it's all right for every Canadian to do that? Emphatically not: given that many First Nations people consider the term offensive, other Canadians should avoid using it. (One exception is discussions of individuals or groups who embrace the term because of the political rights it connotes; the word *Indian* is still used by the Canadian government to indicate *Indian status*.)

The most widely accepted terms used to refer to indigenous Canadians are *Aboriginal people* and, less often, *First Peoples*. Canada's Aboriginal peoples can be divided into three large groups—*First Nations*, *Inuit*, and *Métis*—and these terms should be used when you are referring to one group specifically. Be careful not to make the common mistake of using *First Nations* when you really mean *Aboriginal people* more generally:

needs checking	In the past decade, government policies have reflected a change in attitude toward First Nations rights in Canada, from the Far North to the Great Lakes.
revised	In the past decade, government policies have reflected a change in attitude toward Aboriginal rights in Canada, from the Far North to the Great Lakes.

Whenever you can, the best thing to do is refer to a specific tribe or Nation:

worth checking	Neal McLeod is a First Nations painter, poet, and Indigenous Studies teacher.
revised	Neal McLeod is a Cree painter, poet, and Indigenous Studies teacher.

African American/black: For the past two or three generations *black* and (in the United States) *African American* have both been widely considered appropriate terms. The latter, of course, is only appropriate if one is referring to an American:

needs checking	Nelson Mandela is widely considered to have been the greatest leader of his generation—not just the

> greatest African-American leader, but the greatest leader, period.

revised   Nelson Mandela is widely considered to have been the greatest leader of his generation—not just the greatest black leader, or the greatest African leader, but the greatest leader, period.

Terms with offensive history: A few racial and cultural terms are so deeply encoded in the language that people may use them without being aware of their underlying meaning.

needs checking   I'm convinced that the shopkeeper tried to gyp me. [*Gyp* originated in the prejudice that Roma were congenital cheats.]

revised   I'm convinced that the shopkeeper tried to cheat me.

class: Another example of a widely used expression that is strongly coloured with bias is the expression *white trash*. The implications of the expression are brought forward in the following passage:

> The [Jerry Lee] Lewis and [Jimmy] Swaggart clans were, in the harsh modern parlance, white trash. They lived in the black part of town, and had close relations with blacks. Mr. Swaggart's preaching and Mr. Lewis's music were strongly influenced by black culture. "Jimmy Swaggart was as black as a white man can be," said black elders in Ferriday. (*The Economist*, April 15, 2000)

This passage brings out the implication of the expression; the 'trashiness' that is the exception for white people is implicitly regarded as the norm for black people.

The expression "that's so ghetto" brings together class and race in a similar way. Used to describe something that is makeshift or shoddily put together, the expression carries the implication that such is the norm for African Americans living in poor neighbourhoods. It's an expression that's derogatory both towards poor people and towards black people, and it should be avoided.

The inappropriateness of expressions such as "white trash" and "that's so ghetto" is often acknowledged. Less widely understood is the degree to which various expressions that are often used to describe wealthy people carry class baggage. Think, for example, of expressions such as these:

- She comes from a good family.
- He's making a good income now.
- By some definitions the couple may not be rich, but they are certainly well-off.

A centuries-old tradition among the rich and the middle class in North American and European culture holds that it is vulgar to refer to oneself or to friends and acquaintances as rich. For generations it has been accepted among the wealthy (and among many who aspire to wealth) that in most situations one should use euphemisms when referring to wealth and income. Many euphemisms do no harm, of course. But when one uses phrases such as *good family* to mean *rich family*, one is subtly colouring the financial with the moral. By implication, such phrasings further disadvantage those already disadvantaged by poverty, lending it a taint of a moral as well as a financial shortfall.

worth checking	The novel focuses on a woman who comes from a good family in New York; when the family falls on hard times, she faces difficult choices.
revised	The novel focuses on a woman who has moved in high society in New York; when her family falls on hard times, she faces difficult choices.

Even when you are using accepted terminology to discuss class, it is good to keep in mind the effects your word choice might have. *Lower class*, for example, is a widely used term that suggests a negative value judgement; descriptors such as *working class* (where appropriate) and *low-income* may be preferable.

religion: Given the generally high level of awareness in Western society of the evils of anti-Semitism it is extraordinary that *jew* is still sometimes used in casual conversation as a verb in the same way that *gyp* is used—and that *Jewish* can still sometimes be encountered as a synonym for *stingy*. These are usages that have their roots in a long tradition of anti-Jewish prejudice—in the many centuries during which most Christian societies prohibited Jews from entering most respectable occupations, leaving Jews little choice but to provide services such as moneylending that Christians needed but for various reasons did not want to provide themselves. Moneylending then became part of the vicious stereotyping that surrounded Jews. Like other extremely offensive terms discussed in this book, terms that preserve old anti-Semitic prejudices should never be allowed to go unchallenged. When they are challenged, speakers will often realize they have been unthinkingly using a coinage learnt in childhood—and will change.

A difficult issue is how to refer to extremists affiliated with a particular religion. Should those who profess faith in Islam but believe it is acceptable to kill and maim vast numbers of civilians who are associated with organizations they despise (Osama bin Laden's followers killing 2,996 people on September 11, 2001, followers of the Islamic State movement killing thousands in Iraq and Syria) be called Islamic fundamentalists, or Islamists, or jihadis, or terrorists, or simply mass killers? If someone claims to be following the Islamic faith and commits extreme acts of horrendous violence against unarmed civilians in the name of his faith, many argue that it's entirely fair to describe that person as an Islamic extremist. But fair to whom? When the two words are brought together, inevitably something of the one rubs off on the other, leaving some suggestion in the minds of those reading or hearing the term that extremism comes naturally to Muslims. Many North Americans may appreciate this point more clearly if we think of the phrase *Christian extremist*. Would it seem appropriate to use that term to describe one of the murderers of a dozen or more workers in abortion clinics in North America in the 1980s and 1990s (most of whom professed to be inspired by their Christian faith)? Probably not: a strong argument can be made that no religion deserves to be identified through the actions of its most violent and unprincipled adherents.

The best way to approach such questions may be to be as specific as possible—and to try to use language that cannot be taken to equate the beliefs of an entire religion with those of extremists on the fringes of that religion.

worth checking	Hindu terrorists killed over a thousand Muslims in the violence in India's Gujarat state in 2002.
revised	Extremists believed to be associated with the Vishva Hindu Parishadm (VHP) killed over a thousand Muslims in the violence in India's Gujarat state in 2002.

sexual orientation: There remains a great deal of confusion in North America over what constitutes acceptable language regarding sexual orientation. We can start with those very words—*sexual orientation*. That term has for the most part now replaced *sexual preference* when it comes to describing gay, lesbian, bisexual, heterosexual, and other sexualities—and for a good reason. The word "preference" carries with it a connotation of choice—the notion that one *chooses* whether or not to be gay. It was on that sort of presumption that past generations tried to "cure" people of same-sex desires. It's on that presumption too that some still refer to a "gay lifestyle," as if sexual orientation were akin to deciding either to settle down in a quiet, leafy suburb or travel round the world as a backpacker. In fact, of course, gay, lesbian, and bisexual people choose from among just as many lifestyles as do heterosexual people. And, as a great many scientific studies have shown, most gays and lesbians no more "choose" to be attracted to members of the same sex than most heterosexuals "choose" to be attracted to members of the opposite sex. Nor do bisexuals typically choose to be bisexual; they simply find themselves being attracted to individuals of either sex.

gay/homosexual: The term *gay* is now preferred to the term *homosexual*; why is that? Because of its history, is the short answer. The term *homosexual* was for so many generations used as a term of abuse—and, in the medical profession, as a term naming a form of mental illness—that it has now become tainted. That said, there are still a variety of contexts in which the word may (and should) still be used.

needs checking Wilde was said to have had a gay relationship with Lord Douglas.

> [A term such as "gay relationship" is anachronistic when applied to events in other historical eras—such as the famous trial of Oscar Wilde in the 1890s—and "homosexual" may better reflect the terminology and cultural categories of the time.]

revised Wilde was said to have had a homosexual affair with Lord Douglas.

> [However, in some contexts, it may be possible or even preferable to avoid using homosexual while still reflecting historical realities:]

or Following his romantic affair with Lord Douglas, Wilde was charged with the crime of "gross indecency."

needs checking Male bonobos typically engage in a wide variety of gay sex.

> ["Gay" is generally used only where human sexuality is concerned; "homosexual" remains the prevalent term when one is writing of non-human species.]

revised Male bonobos typically engage in a wide variety of homosexual activity.

"That's so gay": Soon after the word *gay* came to be recommended in the late twentieth century as the preferred non-pejorative term for same-sex sexual orientation, the expression "that's so gay" began to be widely used in conversation by young people. Its meaning? "That's really stupid," or "That's weak and ineffectual." Inevitably such usages connect at some level with other meanings; it's impossible if you use such a term to avoid a broader association of what is gay with what is

stupid, weak, and ineffectual. (Imagine if people started to use the expression "that's so white" or "that's so black" or "that's so Christian" to mean "that's really stupid.") Much as many have protested that "that's so gay" is an "innocent expression," it's not. The cumulative repetition of this and similar colloquial expressions does a great deal to reinforce human prejudice against gays, lesbians, and bisexuals, and to make it more diffi-cult for those who are gay to be open about it, and proud of it.

Additional Material Online
Exercises on bias-free language may be found at
sites.broadviewpress.com/writing.
Click on **Exercises** and go to **"Style."**

7c. Bias-free Vocabulary: A Short List

actress	actor
alderman	councillor
anchorman	anchor/news anchor
Asiatic	Asian
bad guy	villain
bellboy	bellhop
bogeyman	bogey monster
brotherhood	fellowship, community

(when not speaking of all-male situations)

businessman	businessperson, entrepreneur
caveman	cave-dweller
chairman	chair
cleaning lady	cleaner
clergyman	minister, member of the clergy
common man	common person, average person, ordinary person
congressman	representative
con-man	con-artist

draftsman	drafter
Eskimo	Inuit

(Note: Some Alaskan groups still prefer *Eskimo*.)

farmer's wife	farmer
fireman	firefighter
fisherman	fisher
forefathers	ancestors
foreman	manager, supervisor
freshman	first-year student
frontman	figurehead, front
garbageman	garbage collector
grandfather	grandparent

(Note: As in "Those currently covered by the old provisions will be grandfathered in.")

gunman	shooter
gyp	cheat, con
Gypsies	Roma

(Note: When a nomadic people from India began to appear in Britain in the late medieval period, they were thought to have come from Egypt and were termed *'gypcian*. Over the centuries, however, *Gypsies* was very frequently used in a derogatory way; the term *Roma* has now come to be generally accepted as the best term for those outside the culture to use. *Gypsy* may still be a useful term of self-description for some of Roma background.)

Indian	Aboriginal, First Nations, First Peoples

(Note: As with *Eskimo/Inuit* and *African American/black*, the key consideration is sensitivity to audience. If you do not belong to the group but you know that the people you are writing about prefer a particular designation, that is the one to use. The above references current Canadian usage; in the United States, *American Indian* and *Native American* remain commonly used.)

infantryman	footsoldier
insurance man	insurance agent

layman	layperson
longshoreman	shiploader, stevedore
maid	housekeeper
mailman	letter carrier, mail carrier
male nurse	nurse
man	humanity
man (an exhibit)	staff
man (a barricade)	fortify, occupy
man (a ship)	crew
man enough	strong enough
man hours	staff time, work time
manhandle	rough-up, maul
manhole	sewer hole, access hole
manhole cover	sewer cover
mankind	humankind, people, humanity, humans
manly	self-confident, courageous, straightforward
manmade	handmade, human-made, constructed
middleman	intermediary, go-between
mother tongue	native language
mothering	parenting
negro	black, African American
niggardly	stingy

(Note: The word *niggardly* has no etymological connection with *nigger*. Since the one suggests the other to many minds, however, it is safer to avoid using it.)

Oriental	Asian, Middle Eastern
policeman	police officer
postman	letter carrier, mail carrier
salesman, saleslady	salesperson, sales clerk, sales representative
snowman	snowbody (rhymes with *nobody*)
spokesman	representative, spokesperson, agent
sportsman	sportsperson

stewardess	flight attendant
thinking man	intellectual, thinking person
unsportsmanlike	unsporting
waitress	server
weatherman	weather forecaster
womanly	warm, tender, nurturing, sympathetic
workman	worker, labourer, wage earner

GRAMMAR

8. BASIC GRAMMAR: AN OUTLINE

8a. Parts of Speech

● Nouns

Nouns are words that name people, things, places, or qualities. Some examples follow:

- names of people: *boy*, *John*, *parent*
- names of things: *hat*, *spaghetti*, *fish*
- names of places: *Saskatoon*, *Zambia*, *New York*
- names of qualities: *silence*, *intelligence*, *anger*

Nouns can be used to fill the gaps in sentences like these:

- I saw _____ at the market yesterday.
- He dropped the _____ into the gutter.
- Has learning Italian taken a lot of _____ ?
- Hamilton is a _____ with several hundred thousand people living in it.
- _____ is my favourite ski resort.

Some nouns (e.g., *sugar*, *milk*, *confusion*) are uncountable—that is, we cannot say *a milk*, *two milks*, or *three milks*.

● Pronouns

Pronouns replace or stand for nouns. For example, instead of saying, *The man slipped on a banana peel* or *George slipped on a banana peel*, we can replace the noun *man* (or the noun *George*) with the pronoun *he* and say *He slipped on a banana peel*.

personal and indefinite pronouns: Whereas a personal pronoun such as *he* or *she* refers to a definite person, the words *each*, *every*, *either*, *neither*, *one*, *another*, and *much* are indefinite. They may be used as pronouns or as adjectives; in either case, a singular verb is needed.

- Each player wants to do her best.

> (Here the word *each* is an adjective, describing the noun *player*.)

- Each wants to do her best.

> (Here the word *each* is a pronoun, acting as the subject of the sentence.)

- Each of the players wants to do her best.

> (The word *each* is still a pronoun, this time followed by the phrase *of the players*. But it is the pronoun *each* that is the subject of the sentence; the verb must be the singular *wants*.)

possessive pronouns and adjectives: See under "Adjectives" below.

relative pronouns: These pronouns relate back to a noun that has been used earlier in the same sentence. Consider how repetitious these sentences sound:

- I talked to the man. The man wore a red hat.

We could of course replace the second *man* with *he*. Even better, though, is to relate or connect the second idea to the first by using a relative pronoun:

- I talked to the man who wore a red hat.
- I found the pencil. I had lost the pencil.
- I found the pencil that I had lost.

The following are all relative pronouns:

who	whose (has other uses too)
which	that (has other uses too)
whom	

Try replacing the second noun in the pairs of sentences below with a relative pronoun, so as to make only one sentence out of each pair:

- I polished the table. I had built the table.
- Premier Wall is vacationing this week in Quebec's Eastern Townships. The premier cancelled a planned holiday last fall.

- The word *other* is often used by literary theorists when speaking of a sense of strangeness in the presence of cultural difference. *Other* is usually preceded by the definite article when so used.

pronouns acting as subject and as object: We use different forms of some pronouns depending on whether we are using them as subjects or objects and whether they are singular or plural.

	singular	*plural*
Subject Pronouns	I	we
	you	you
	he/she/it	they
	who, what, which	who, what, which

	singular	*plural*
Object Pronouns	me	us
	you	you
	him/her/it	them
	whom, what, which	whom, what, which

- She loves Frankie.

    (Here the pronoun *she* is the subject of the sentence.)
- Frankie loves her.

    (Here the word *her* is the object; *Frankie* is the subject.)
- That's the woman who loves Frankie.

    (Here the pronoun *who* is the subject of the clause *who loves Frankie*.)
- That's the woman whom Frankie loves.

    (Here the pronoun *whom* is the object of the verb *love*; *Frankie* is the subject of the clause *whom Frankie loves*.)

The distinctions between *I* and *me* and between *who* and *whom* are treated more fully under Subject and Object Pronouns, pages 118–19.

● Articles

Articles (determiners often classed as a form of adjective) are words used to introduce nouns. There are only three of them: *a*, *an*, and *the*. Articles show whether or not one is drawing attention to a particular person or thing.

For example, we would say *I stood beside a house* if we did not want to draw attention to that particular house, but *I stood beside the house that the Taylors used to live in* if we did want to draw attention to the particular house. *A* (or *an* if the noun following begins with a vowel sound) is an indefinite article—used when you do not wish to be definite or specific about which thing or person you are referring to. *The* is a definite article, used when you do wish to call attention to the particular thing or person, and when a noun is followed by a specifying phrase or clause (such as *used to live in*, which follows the noun *Taylors*). Remember that if you use *the*, you are suggesting that there can be only one or one group of what you are referring to.

Choose the appropriate article (*a*, *an*, or *the*):

- _____ moon shone brightly last night.
- She had _____ long conversation with _____ friend.
- Have you ever driven _____ car?
- Have you driven _____ car that your wife bought on Monday?

● Adjectives

Adjectives are words used to tell us more about (describe or modify) nouns or pronouns. Here are some examples of adjectives:

big	good	heavy
small	bad	expensive
pretty	careful	healthy
quick	slow	unexpected

- The small boy lifted the heavy table.

> (Here the adjective *small* describes or tells us more about the noun *boy*, and the adjective *heavy* describes the noun *table*.)

- The fast runner finished ahead of the slow one.

> (*Fast* describes *runner* and *slow* describes *one*.)

Notice that adjectives usually come before the nouns that they describe. This is not always the case, however; when the verb *to be* is used, adjectives often come after the noun or pronoun, and after the verb:

- That woman is particularly careful about her finances.

> (*Careful* describes *woman*.)

- It is too difficult for me to do.

> (*Difficult* describes *it*.)

Adjectives can be used to fill the gaps in sentences like these:

- This _____ sweater was knitted by hand.
- As soon as we entered the _____ house we heard a clap of _____ thunder.
- Those shoes are very _____.
- Derrida's argument could fairly be described as _____.

Some words can be either adjectives or pronouns, depending on how they are used. That is the case with the indefinite pronouns (see above), and also with certain possessives (words that show possession):

	singular	*plural*
Possessive	my	our
Adjectives	your	your
	his/her	their
	whose	whose
Possessive	mine	ours
Pronouns	yours	yours
	his/hers	theirs
	whose	whose

- I have my cup, and he has his.

        (Here the word *his* is a pronoun, used in place of the noun *cup*.)

- He has his cup.

        (Here the word *his* is an adjective, describing the noun *cup*.)

- Whose book is this?

        (Here the word *whose* is an adjective, describing the noun *book*.)

- Whose is this?

        (Here the word *whose* is a pronoun, acting as the subject of the sentence.)

● Verbs

Verbs are words that express actions or states of affairs. Most verbs can be conveniently thought of as "doing" words (e.g., *open, feel, do, carry, see, think, combine, send*), but several verbs do not fit into this category. Indeed, the most common verb of all—*be*—expresses a state of affairs, not a particular action that is done. Verbs are used to fill gaps in sentences like these:

- I _____ very quickly, but I _____ not _____ up with my brother.
- She usually _____ to sleep at 9:30.
- Stephen _____ his breakfast very quickly.
- They _____ a large farm near Chicago.
- There _____ many different languages that people _____ in India.

One thing that makes verbs different from other parts of speech is that verbs have tenses; in other words, they change their form depending on the time you are talking about. For example, some present tense forms of the verb *to be* are as follows: *I am, you are, he is*, etc.; these are some past tense forms: *I was, you were, he was*, etc. If you are unsure whether or not a particular word is a verb, one way to check is to ask if it has different tenses. For example, if you thought that perhaps the word *football* might be a verb, you need only ask yourself if it would be correct to say, *I footballed, I am footballing, I will football,* and so on. Obviously it would not be, so you know that *football* is the noun that names the game, not a verb that expresses an action. See the next chapter in this book for a discussion of verb tenses.

● Adverbs

These words are usually used to tell us more about (describe or modify) verbs, although they can also be used to tell us more about adjectives or about other adverbs. They answer questions such as *How ...?, When ...?,* and *To what extent ...?,* and often they end with the letters *ly.* Here are a few examples, with some adjectives also listed for comparison:

Adjective	*Adverb*
careful	carefully
beautiful	beautifully
thorough	thoroughly
sudden	suddenly
slow	slowly
easy	easily
good	well

- He walked carefully.
  > (The adverb *carefully* tells us how he walked; it describes the verb *walked*.)
- He is a careful boy.
  > (The adjective *careful* describes the noun *boy*.)
- My grandfather died suddenly last week.
  > (The adverb *suddenly* tells how he died; it describes the verb *died*.)
- We were upset by the sudden death of my grandfather.
  > (The adjective *sudden* describes the noun *death*.)
- She plays the game very well.
  > (The adverb *well* tells us how she plays; it describes the verb *plays*. The adverb *very* describes the adverb *well*.)

- She played a good game this afternoon.

  (The adjective *good* describes the noun *game*.)
- She played a very good game.

  (The adverb *very* describes the adjective *good*, telling us how good it was.)
- Our friends will meet the new baby soon.

  (The adverb *soon* describes the verb *will meet*, telling when the action will happen.)

Choose adverbs to fill the gaps in these sentences:

- Ralph writes very _____.
- The judge spoke _____ to her after she had been convicted on six counts of stock manipulation and fraud.
- They were _____ late for the meeting this morning.

● Prepositions

Prepositions are joining words, normally used before nouns or pronouns. Some of the most common prepositions are as follows:

about	across	after
at	before	for
from	in	into
of	off	on
over	to	until
with		

Choose prepositions to fill the gaps in these sentences:

- I will tell you _____ it _____ the morning.
- Please try to arrive _____ eight o'clock.
- He did not come back _____ Toronto _____ yesterday.
- I received a letter _____ my sister.

ending a sentence with a preposition: Some authorities have argued that it is poor English to end a sentence with a preposition. The best answer to them is Winston Churchill's famous remark upon being accused of ending with a preposition: "This is the sort of pedantic nonsense up with which I will not put." Obviously such awkwardness as this can be avoided only by ending with a preposition. It is surely true that in many other cases ending sentences with prepositions is awkward. In practice, however, these are situations that we are already likely to avoid. The following dialogue (a version of which was passed on to me by Prof. A. Levey of the University of Calgary) provides in dramatic form another demonstration of the absurdity of strictures against ending with prepositions:

"Where do you come from?"
"From a place where we don't end sentences with prepositions."
"Let me rephrase. Where do you come from, you stupid pedant?"

● Conjunctions and Conjunctive Adverbs

Conjunctions and conjunctive adverbs are normally used to join groups of words together, and in particular to join clauses together. Conjunctions can be divided into three types: coordinating, subordinating, and correlative.

coordinating conjunctions: Coordinating conjunctions join parallel groupings of words. Since there are only seven such conjunctions in English, they can be memorized easily. Some people use the acronym *FANBOYS* as a memory aid:

> **F**or
> **A**nd
> **N**or
> **B**ut
> **O**r
> **Y**et
> **S**o

- Carmen thought the movie was silly, but we really liked it.
> (The coordinating conjunction *but* joins the main clauses *Carmen thought the movie was silly* and *we really liked it*. Note that a comma precedes a coordinating conjunction used in this way.)

- His anxiety about public performance made him uncomfortable yet improved his playing.

  > (The coordinating conjunction *yet* joins the verb phrases *made him uncomfortable* and *improved his playing*.)

- The novel was short, dense, and gripping.

  > (The coordinating conjunction *and* joins the adjectives *short*, *dense*, and *gripping*—as it does in this sentence! When joining more than two words or phrases, a coordinating conjunction may be preceded either by a comma or not, as long as the choice is consistent in a single piece of writing.)

subordinating conjunctions: Subordinating conjunctions join subordinate clauses to main clauses. Any clause beginning with a subordinating conjunction is a subordinate clause. English has many subordinating conjunctions; here is a partial list of commonly used ones (note that some are groups of words):

after	although	as	as long as
as though	because	before	even though
if	in order that	since	so that
unless	until	whereas	while

- They stopped playing because they were tired.

  > (The subordinating conjunction *because* joins the clauses *They stopped playing* and *they were tired*, making the second of these subordinate.)

- I will give her your message if I see her.

  > (The subordinating conjunction *if* joins the clauses *I will give her your message* and *I see her*, making the second of these subordinate.)

conjunctive adverbs: Conjunctive adverbs, as their name suggests, are adverbs that join word groups as well as modifying them. Conjunctive adverbs can join main clauses together or join a stand-alone main clause to a previous sentence; either way, and unlike other types of conjunctions, conjunctive adverbs need not appear exactly at the beginning of the word groups they join. Wherever it appears, a conjunctive adverb must be set off with commas or preceded by a semi-colon if (and only if) it joins two clauses in one sentence. Here are some common conjunctive adverbs (note that some of them are phrases):

alternatively	certainly	furthermore
however	indeed	in fact
in other words	likewise	meanwhile
moreover	nonetheless	on the other hand
otherwise	similarly	that is
therefore	thus	unfortunately

- Miss Polly was busy hiding the silverware. Meanwhile, the Foley brothers arrived at the ranch.

  > (*Meanwhile* links the two sentences by indicating the time relationship between them.)

- That new tablet is fantastic. No one, however, will want to pay such a high a price for it.

  > (*However* signals a contrast between the two points made by the two sentences, and so is a transition joining them. Because it is embedded in its sentence, *however* is set apart with commas.)

- I have excellent reasons for abandoning this project; unfortunately, the others on my team disagree with me.

  > (*Unfortunately* joins the two main clauses of one sentence, and so is preceded by a semi-colon and followed by a comma.)

correlative conjunctions: Correlative conjunctions come in pairs and can join single words or word groups. Here are some examples:

both ... and	either ... or
neither ... nor	not only ... but also
so ... that	such ... as

Whatever is joined by correlative conjunctions must have the same grammatical structure, as in the examples below:

- That dishcloth is both smelly and unsanitary.

  > (*Both* and *and* join the adjectives *smelly* and *unsanitary*.)

- Neither the dollar nor the economy will fare well if oil prices drop any lower.

  > (*Neither* and *nor* join the noun phrases *the dollar* and *the economy*.)

- Not only is our candidate well educated but she is also personable.

  > (*Not only* and *but also* join the clauses *our candidate is well educated* and *she is personable*. Note that when joining clauses, *not only* requires that the usual order of subject and verb in the following clause be reversed—and *but also* is split by the following clause's subject and verb.)

Many conjunctions can also act as other parts of speech, depending on how they are used. Notice the difference in each of these pairs of sentences:

- He will not do anything about it until the morning.

  > (Here *until* is a preposition joining the noun *morning* to the rest of the sentence.)

- He will not do anything about it until he has discussed it with his wife.

  > (Here *until* is a subordinating conjunction introducing the clause *he has discussed it with his wife*.)

- I slept for half an hour after dinner.

  > (Here *after* is a preposition joining the noun *dinner* to the rest of the sentence.)

- I slept for half an hour after they had gone home.

  > (Here *after* is a subordinating conjunction introducing the clause *they had gone home*.)

- She wants to buy that dress.

  > (Here *that* is an adjective describing the noun *dress*: "*Which dress?*" "*That dress!*")

- George said that he was unhappy.

  > (Here *that* is a subordinating conjunction introducing the clause *he was unhappy*.)

Choose conjunctions to fill the gaps in the following sentences:

- We believed _____ we would win.
- They sat down in the shade _____ it was hot.
- My father did not speak to me _____ he left.

8b. Parts of Sentences

● Subject

The subject is the thing, person, or quality about which something is said in a clause. The subject is usually a noun or pronoun.

- The man went to town.
  > (The sentence is about the man, not about the town; thus, the noun *man* is the subject.)
- Groundnuts are an important crop in Nigeria.
  > (The sentence is about groundnuts, not about crops or about Nigeria; thus, the noun *groundnuts* is the subject.)
- Nigeria is the most populous country in Africa.
  > (The sentence is about Nigeria, not about countries or about Africa; thus, the noun *Nigeria* is the subject.)
- He followed me up the stairs.
  > (The pronoun *He* is the subject.)

core subject: The core subject is the single noun or pronoun that forms the subject.

complete subject: The complete subject is the subject together with any adjectives or adjectival phrases modifying it:

- The woman in the huge hat went to the market to buy groceries.
  > (The core subject is the noun *woman* and the complete subject is *the woman in the huge hat*.)

● Object

An object is something or someone towards which an action or feeling is directed. In grammar an object is the thing, person, or quality affected by the action of the verb. (To put it another way, it receives the action of the verb.) Like a subject, an object normally is made up of a noun or pronoun.

direct object: The direct object is the thing, person, or quality directly affected by the action of the verb. A direct object usually answers the question *What?* or *Who?* Notice that direct objects are not introduced by prepositions.

indirect object: The indirect object is the thing, person, or quality that is indirectly affected by the action of the verb. All indirect objects could be expressed differently by making them the objects of the prepositions *to* or *for*. Instead, the prepositions have been omitted. Indirect objects answer the questions *To whom?* and *For whom?*

* McGriff hit the ball a long way.
> (What did he hit? The ball. *The ball* is the direct object of the verb *hit*.)
* She threw me her hat.
> (What did she throw? Her hat. *Her hat* is the direct object. To whom did she throw it? To me. *Me* is the indirect object. Note that the sentence could be rephrased: *She threw her hat to me*.)
* They gave their father a watch for Christmas.
> (The direct object is *watch*, and the indirect object is *father*.)

● Predicate

The predicate is everything that is said about the subject. In the example under "Subject," *The woman in the huge hat went to the market to buy groceries*, *went to the market to buy groceries* is the predicate. A predicate always includes a verb.

● Clauses and Phrases

A clause is a distinct group of words that includes both a subject and a predicate. Thus a clause always includes a verb.

A phrase is a distinct group of words that does *not* include both a subject and a verb. Examples:

Clauses	*Phrases*
because he is strong	because of his strength (no verb)
before she comes home	before the meeting (no verb)
the professor likes me	from Halifax
a tree fell down	at lunch
who came to dinner	in the evening

Types of clauses

main clause (or **independent clause**): A main clause is a group of words that is, or could be, a sentence on its own.

subordinate clause (or **dependent clause**): A subordinate clause is a clause that could not form a complete sentence on its own.

Except for the coordinating conjunctions (*and*, *but*, *or*, *nor*, *for*, *yet*, and *so*), conjunctions do not introduce main clauses, so if a clause begins with a word such as *because*, *although*, or *if*, you can be confident it is a subordinate clause. Similarly, relative pronouns introduce subordinate clauses—never main clauses.

- She lives near Victoria.

    (One main clause forming a complete sentence. The pronoun *She* is the subject, *lives* is the verb, and the preposition *near* and the noun *Victoria* together form a phrase.)

- He danced in the street because he was feeling happy.

    main clause: He danced in the street

    subject: _____

    predicate: _____

    subordinate clause: because he was feeling happy

        subject: _____
        predicate: _____

- Mavis has a cat who likes to drink from the kitchen faucet.
        main clause: Mavis has a cat
        subject: _____
        predicate: _____
        subordinate clause: who likes to drink from the
          kitchen faucet
        subject: _____
        predicate: _____

Subordinate clauses may be further subdivided as follows:

adjectival subordinate clause: a subordinate clause that tells us more about a noun or pronoun. Adjectival clauses begin with relative pronouns such as *who, whom, whose, which,* and *that.*

adverbial subordinate clause: a subordinate clause that tells us more about the action of the verb—telling *how, when, why,* or *where* the action occurred.

noun subordinate clause: a clause that acts like a noun to form the subject or object of a sentence.

Examples:

- He talked at length to his cousin, who quickly became bored.
        (*Who quickly became bored* is an adjectival subordinate
        clause, telling us more about the noun *cousin.*)
        subject of subordinate clause: the pronoun *who*
        verb in subordinate clause: _____
        subject of main clause: the pronoun *He*
        verb in main clause: _____
- My husband did not like the gift that I gave him.
        (*That I gave him* is an adjectival subordinate clause
        telling us more about the noun *gift.*)
        subject of subordinate clause: the pronoun *I*
        verb in subordinate clause: _____
        subject of main clause: _____
        verb in main clause: _____

- The boy whom she wants to marry is very poor.

    (*Whom she wants to marry* is an adjectival subordinate clause telling us more about the noun *boy*. Notice that here the subordinate clause appears in the middle of the main clause, *The boy is very poor.*)
    subject of subordinate clause: _____
    verb in subordinate clause: _____
    subject of main clause: _____
    verb in main clause: _____

- I felt worse after I had been to the doctor.

    (*After I had been to the doctor* is an adverbial subordinate clause telling us when I felt worse.)

- He could not attend because he had broken his leg.

    (*Because he had broken his leg* is an adverbial subordinate clause telling us why he could not attend.)

- She jumped as if an alarm had sounded.

    (*As if an alarm had sounded* is an adverbial subordinate clause telling us how she jumped.)

- What he said was very interesting.

    (*What he said* is a noun clause acting as the subject of the sentence, in the same way that the noun *conversation* acts as the subject in *The conversation was very interesting.*)

- Sue-Ellen told me that she wanted to become a lawyer.

    (*That she wanted to become a lawyer* is a noun clause acting as the object, in the same way that the noun *plans* acts as the object in *Sue-Ellen told me her plans.*)

Types of phrases

adjectival phrase: a phrase that tells us more about a noun or pronoun.

adverbial phrase: a phrase that tells us more about the action of a verb, answering questions such as *When ...?*, *Where ...?*, *How ...?*, and *Why ...?*

- The boy in the new jacket got into the car.

    (*In the new jacket* is an adjectival phrase telling us more about the noun *boy.*)

- I drank from the cup with a broken handle.

    (*With a broken handle* is a phrase telling us more about the noun *cup*.)

- We went to the park.

    (*To the park* is an adverbial phrase telling where we went.)

- They arrived after breakfast.

    (*After breakfast* is an adverbial phrase telling when they arrived.)

Distinguishing phrases and clauses

- They were late because of the weather.

    (*Because of the weather* is an adverbial phrase telling us why they were late. It has no verb.)

- They were late because the weather was bad.

    (*Because the weather was bad* is an adverbial clause telling us why they were late.)

    subject: _____

    verb: _____

- The man at the corner appeared to be upset.

    (*At the corner* is an adjectival phrase telling us more about the noun *man*.)

- The man who stood at the corner appeared to be upset.

    (*Who stood at the corner* is an adjectival clause telling us more about the noun *man*.)

    subject: _____

    verb: _____

● Parts of Speech and Parts of the Sentence

- After the generous man with the big ears has bought presents, he will quickly give them to his friends.

    ### Parts of speech:

    after: *conjunction*   the: *article*

    generous: _____   man: _____

    with: _____   the: _____

big: _____ ears: _____

has bought: _____ presents: _____

he: _____ will give: _____

quickly: _____ them: _____

to: _____ his: _____

friends: _____

Parts of the sentence:

main clause: He will quickly give them to his friends.

subject: _____

predicate: _____

verb: _____

direct object: _____

indirect object: _____

subordinate clause: After the generous man with the big ears has bought presents,

Is this an adjectival or an adverbial subordinate clause?

core subject: the noun _____

complete subject: _____

adjectival phrase: with the big ears

this phrase tells us more about the noun: _____

predicate: _____

direct object: _____

Additional Material
A discussion of run-on sentences and sentence fragments ("incomplete sentences") may be found on **pages 120–24**.

9. VERBS AND VERB TENSE DIFFICULTIES

9a. The Infinitive

The infinitive is the starting point for building a knowledge of verb tenses; it is the most basic form of the verb. Some examples of infinitives are *to go, to be, to do, to begin, to come, to investigate*. The infinitive form remains the same whether the action referred to happens in the past, the present, or the future.

The most commonly made mistake involving infinitives is the colloquial substitution of *and* for *to*, especially in the expression *try and do it* for *try to do it*. The great issue in this area among grammarians, however, is the **split infinitive**—the infinitive which has another word or words inserted between to and the verb: *to quickly go; to forcefully speak out; to thoroughly investigate*. Some authorities argue that it is always grammatically incorrect to break up the infinitive in this way. Most, however, see the matter as one of awkwardness rather than incorrectness. In most cases a sentence with a split infinitive will sound more awkward than one without—but this is not a firm and fast rule.

9b. The Simple Present Tense

	SINGULAR	PLURAL
1st person	I say	we say
2nd person	you say	you say
3rd person	he, she, it says	they say

9c. Subject-Verb Agreement

Almost all of us occasionally have problems in writing the third person of the simple present tense correctly. All too often the letter *s* at the end of the third person singular is left out. The simple rule here is that whenever you use a verb in the third person singular of the simple present tense, it *must* end in *s*.

> *needs checking*   The compound change shape when heated.
>
>   *revised*   The compound changes shape when heated.
>
>   [*Compound*, which is the subject, is an *it* and therefore third person singular.]

It is not particularly difficult to make the subject agree with the verb in the above example, but even professional writers often have trouble with more complex sentences. Two common categories of subject-verb agreement errors are discussed below.

i) The subject and verb are separated by a long phrase or clause.

> *needs checking*   The recent history of these African nations illustrate a variety of points.
>
>   *revised*   The recent history of these African nations illustrates a variety of points.

Here the writer has made the mental error of thinking of nations as the subject of the verb *illustrate*, whereas in fact the subject is the singular noun *history*. "The history illustrate..." would immediately strike most people as wrong, but the intervening words have in this case caused grammatical confusion.

> *needs checking*   As the statement by Belgium's Prime Minister about his country's deficit and unemployment problems indicate, many nations are in the same shape, or worse.
>
>   *revised*   As the statement by Belgium's Prime Minister about his country's deficit and unemployment problems indicates, many nations are in the same shape, or worse.
>
>   [The subject is the singular noun *statement*, so the verb must be *indicates* rather than *indicate*.]

needs checking   Courses offered range from the history of the Greek and Roman world to the twenty-first century, and covers Britain, Europe, North America, Africa, and the Far East. (History Dept. Prospectus, Birkbeck College, University of London)

revised   Courses offered range from the history of the Greek and Roman world to the twenty-first century, and cover Britain, Europe, North America, Africa, and the Far East.

Sometimes a long sentence can in itself throw off a writer's sense of subject-verb agreement, even if subject and verb are close together. In the following example the close proximity of the subject *simplifications* to the verb has not prevented error:

needs checking   The decline in the quality of leadership is mirrored in the crude simplifications which characterizes the average person's view of the world.

revised   The decline in the quality of leadership is mirrored in the crude simplifications which characterize the average person's view of the world.

ii) The error of using *there is* instead of *there are* when the subject is plural has become more and more frequent in writing as well as in speech.

When these two expressions are used, remember that the subject comes after the verb; use *is* or *are* depending on whether the subject is singular or plural:

needs checking   There's many more opportunities of that sort than there used to be.

revised   There are many more opportunities of that sort than there used to be.

Additional Material Online
Exercises on subject-verb agreement may be found at
sites.broadviewpress.com/writing.
Click on **Exercises** and go to
"Verbs, Subjects, Modifiers."

9d. Historical Present

To use the "historical present" is to use the present tense in a narrative set in the past. In many medieval histories the narrative alternates frequently between the present tense and the past tense, but from the sixteenth century until the late twentieth century most narratives of past action were recounted using the past tense. The historical present was used on a very selective basis by some historians and journalists (and by a few writers of fiction), the purpose being to lend a sense of immediacy to particular scenes that the writer wanted to express with memorable vividness.

In the twenty-first century the historical present has become much more commonly used in a wide variety of contexts. Many works of fiction are now written entirely in the present tense. Many works of history shift back and forth continually between the past tense and the historical present. Even newscasts now use the historical present frequently. As in earlier eras, the aim is presumably to impart a greater sense of immediacy and interest to what is being recounted. It is all too easy in such circumstances, however, to create a sense of confusion rather than a sense of immediacy in the reader's mind—particularly given that the present tense is often also used idiomatically to refer to future events (e.g., *We arrive at 9:00 in the morning* rather than *We will arrive at 9:00 in the morning*). It is essential, then, to pay careful attention to what tenses are being used.

needs checking Throughout the day, shells fall on the city. Dozens are killed. The President, however, refused to authorize a ceasefire. The Cabinet holds an emergency meeting tonight.

[The passage begins in the historical present, but then switches to the past tense. The fourth sentence shifts back to present tense— but it is not clear what time is being referred to. Is the emergency meeting also in the past (and the report being filed late at night)? If so, what was the outcome of the meeting? Or is the report being filed before "tonight"—in which case the emergency meeting is still in the future.]

revised Throughout the day, shells fell on the city. Dozens were killed. The President, however, refused to authorize a ceasefire. The Cabinet will hold an emergency meeting tonight.

or Throughout the day, shells fall on the city. Dozens are killed. The President, however, refuses to authorize a ceasefire. The Cabinet will hold an emergency meeting tonight.

9e. Survey of Verb Tenses

1st PERSON:

the present progressive (or continuous) tense	I am finishing
the simple past tense	I finished
the past progressive (or continuous) tense	I was finishing
the simple future tense	I will finish
the future progressive (or continuous) tense	I will be finishing
the present perfect tense	I have finished
the past perfect tense	I had finished
the future perfect tense	I will have finished
the conditional	I would finish
the past conditional	I would have finished
the present perfect continuous	I have been finishing
the past perfect continuous	I had been finishing
the future perfect continuous	I will have been finishing
the conditional continuous	I would be finishing
the past conditional continuous	I would have been finishing

9f. Voice

Most verbs have both an **active** and a **passive** voice. The active is used when the subject of the verb is doing the action, whereas the passive is used when the subject of the verb is receiving the action or being acted on.

Some examples:

ACTIVE	PASSIVE
I did it.	It was done.
She hit him.	He was hit.
They will give a speech.	The speech will be given.

(See also 1e and 6c.)

9g. Mood

Most sentences in English are in the *indicative mood*, which is used when we are expressing facts and opinions or asking questions. We use the *imperative mood* when giving orders or advice, and we use the *subjunctive mood* to denote actions that are wished for or imagined, or would happen if certain conditions were met. Some examples:

> If I were you, I would do what she says.

> The doctor advises that he stop smoking immediately.
> (not *that he stops*)

needs checking   If a bank was willing to lend money without proper guarantees, it would go bankrupt very quickly.

revised   If a bank were willing to lend money without proper guarantees, it would go bankrupt very quickly.

For more on conditions see pages 128–30.

COMBINING VERB TENSES: SOME CHALLENGES

9h. The Past Perfect Tense

The chief use of the past perfect tense is to show that one action in the past was completed before another action in the past began:

> I told my parents what <u>had happened</u>.
> [The happening occurred before the telling.]

> She thought very seriously about what he <u>had said</u>.
> [The saying occurred before the thinking.]

The past perfect is particularly useful when the writer wishes to flashback, or move backwards in time:

needs checking   The tail was still moving, but the snake itself was quite dead. It crawled out from under a rock and slowly moved towards me as I was lowering the canoe at the end of the portage.

revised   The tail was still moving, but the snake itself was quite dead. It had crawled out from under a rock and had moved slowly towards me as I had been lowering the canoe at the end of the portage.

The past perfect is frequently used when we are reporting speech indirectly:

> She said that she had finished the work, and we asked him when he had known of the diversion of funds.

9i. Combining Tenses—Quoted Material

It is often difficult to achieve grammatical consistency when incorporating quoted material in a sentence:

needs checking   Prime Minister Wilson admitted at the time that "such a policy is not without its drawbacks."
[The past tense *admitted* and the present tense *is* do not agree.]

There are two ways of dealing with a difficulty such as this:

(a) Change the sentence so as to set off the quotation without using the connecting word *that*. Usually this can be done with a colon.

(b) Use only that part of the quotation that can be used in such a way as to agree with the tense of the main verb.

revised	Prime Minister Wilson did not claim perfection: "such a policy is not without its drawbacks," he admitted.
or	Prime Minister Wilson admitted at the time that such a policy was "not without its drawbacks."

9j. Irregular Verbs

The majority of verbs in English follow a regular pattern—I *open* in the simple present tense, I *opened* in the simple past tense, I *have opened* in the present perfect tense, and so forth. Most of the more frequently used verbs, however, follow different patterns. For example, we say *I went* instead of *I goed*. Here is a list of irregular verbs in English:

BASE FORM	SIMPLE PAST	PAST PARTICIPLE
arise	arose	arisen
awake	awoke/awaked	awoken/awaked/woken
be	was/were	been
bear	bore	borne
beat	beat	beaten
become	became	become
begin	began	begun
bend	bent	bent
bite	bit	bitten
bleed	bled	bled
blow	blew	blown
break	broke	broken
bring	brought	brought
build	built	built
burn	burned/burnt	burned/burnt
burst	burst	burst
buy	bought	bought
can	could	been able
catch	caught	caught
choose	chose	chosen
cling	clung	clung
come	came	come

dig	dug	dug
dive	dived/dove	dived
do	did	done
drag	dragged	dragged
draw	drew	drawn
dream	dreamed/dreamt	dreamed/dreamt
drink	drank	drunk
drive	drove	driven
eat	ate	eaten
fall	fell	fallen
feel	felt	felt
fight	fought	fought
find	found	found
fit	fitted or fit (US)	fitted
flee	fled	fled
fling	flung	flung
fly	flew	flown
forbid	forbade	forbidden
forecast	forecast	forecast
forget	forgot	forgotten
forgive	forgave	forgiven
freeze	froze	frozen
get	got	got
give	gave	given
go	went	gone
grind	ground	ground
grow	grew	grown
hang	hanged/hung	hanged/hung
have	had	had
hear	heard	heard
hide	hid	hidden
hold	held	held
hurt	hurt	hurt
keep	kept	kept
kneel	knelt	knelt
know	knew	known
lay	laid	laid
lead	led	led

lean	leaned/leant	leaned/leant
leap	leaped/leapt	leaped/leapt
learn	learned/learnt	learned/learnt
leave	left	left
lend	lent	lent
let	let	let
lie	lay	lain
light	lighted/lit	lighted/lit
lose	lost	lost
make	made	made
may	might	
mean	meant	meant
meet	met	met
must	had to	had to
pay	paid	paid
prove	proved	proven/proved
put	put	put
read	read	read
ride	rode	ridden
ring	rang	rung
rise	rose	risen
run	ran	run
saw	sawed	sawed/sawn
say	said	said
see	saw	seen
seek	sought	sought
sell	sold	sold
sew	sewed	sewed/sewn
shake	shook	shaken
shall	should	
shine	shone	shone
shoot	shot	shot
show	showed	showed/shown
shrink	shrank	shrunk
shut	shut	shut
sing	sang	sung
sink	sank	sunk
sit	sat	sat

sleep	slept	slept
smell	smelled/smelt	smelled/smelt
sow	sowed	sowed/sown
speak	spoke	spoken
speed	speeded/sped	speeded/sped
spell	spelled/spelt	spelled/spelt
spend	spent	spent
spill	spilled/spilt	spilled/spilt
spin	spun	spun
spit	spat	spat
split	split	split
spread	spread	spread
spring	sprang	sprung
stand	stood	stood
steal	stole	stolen
stick	stuck	stuck
sting	stung	stung
strike	struck	struck
swear	swore	sworn
sweep	swept	swept
swim	swam	swum
swing	swung	swung
teach	taught	taught
tear	tore	torn
tell	told	told
think	thought	thought
throw	threw	thrown
tread	trod	trodden/trod
understand	understood	understood
wake	waked/woke	waked/woken
wear	wore	worn
weep	wept	wept
win	won	won
wind	wound	wound
wring	wrung	wrung
write	wrote	written

needs checking	A problem had arose even before the discussion began.
revised	A problem had arisen even before the discussion began.
needs checking	In 1948 Newfoundlanders choose to join Canada.
revised	In 1948 Newfoundlanders chose to join Canada.
needs checking	Thucydides analized the events that lead to the Peloponnesian war.
revised	Thucydides analized the events that led to the Peloponnesian war.
needs checking	The report laid on her desk until Thursday afternoon.
revised	The report lay on her desk until Thursday afternoon.
needs checking	The government's majority shrunk in the election.
revised	The government's majority shrank in the election.
needs checking	Pictures were taken while the royal couple swum in what they had thought was a private cove.
revised	Pictures were taken while the royal couple swam in what they had thought was a private cove.

10. DANGLING CONSTRUCTIONS

Participles, infinitives, and gerunds may all be used to introduce phrases within sentences. With phrases of this sort, it is important to make sure that the participle, infinitive, or gerund relates grammatically to the subject of the adjacent main clause.

needs checking	Waiting for a bus, a brick fell on my head. [Bricks do not normally wait for buses.]
revised	While I was waiting for a bus, a brick fell on my head.

In sentences such as this one the absurdity is easy to notice; it is much more difficult to do so with longer and more complex sentences.

needs checking   Considering all the above-mentioned studies, the evidence shows conclusively that smoking can cause cancer.

revised   Considering all the above-mentioned studies, we conclude that smoking causes cancer.

better   These studies show conclusively that smoking can cause cancer.

needs checking   Turning for a moment to the thorny question of Joyce's style, the stream of consciousness technique realistically depicts the workings of the human mind.

     [The stream should not be doing the turning.]

revised   Turning for a moment to the thorny question of Joyce's style, we may observe that his stream of consciousness technique realistically depicts the workings of the human mind.

better   Joyce's style does not make *Ulysses* easy to read, but his stream of consciousness technique realistically depicts the workings of the human mind.

needs checking   Considered from a cost point of view, Combo Capital Corporation could not really afford to purchase Skinflint Securities.

     [Combo is not being considered; the purchase is.]

revised   Considered from the point of view of cost, the purchase of Skinflint Securities was not a wise move by Combo Capital Corporation.

better   Combo Capital Corporation could not really afford to buy Skinflint Securities.

needs checking   Once regarded as daringly modern in its portrayal of fashionable *fin de siècle* decadence, Wilde draws on traditional patterns to create a powerful Gothic tale.

     [The novel is an "it"; Oscar Wilde was a "he."]

revised	*The Picture of Dorian Gray* was once regarded as daringly modern in its portrayal of fashionable *fin de siècle* decadence. In the novel Wilde draws on traditional patterns to create a powerful Gothic tale.
needs checking	To conclude this essay, the French Revolution was a product of many interacting causes.
	[The French Revolution concluded no essays.]
poor	To conclude this essay, let me say that the French Revolution was a product of many causes.
better	The explanations given for the French Revolution, then, are not mutually exclusive; it was a product of many interacting causes.
needs checking	In reviewing the evidence, one point stands out plainly.
	[A point cannot review evidence.]
poor	In reviewing the evidence, we can see one point standing out plainly.
better	One point stands out plainly from this evidence.

Notice that the best way to eliminate the problem of dangling constructions is often to dispense with the original phrase entirely.

11. NOUNS AND PRONOUNS

(See also pages 82–84.)

Nouns are words that name people, things, places, or qualities. The following words are all nouns: *boy, John, spaghetti, Zambia, silence, anger.*

Pronouns replace or stand for nouns. For example, instead of saying "The man slipped on a banana peel" or "George slipped on a banana peel," we can replace the noun *man* (or the noun *George*) with the pronoun *he* and say "He slipped on a banana peel." A discussion of some problems commonly experienced with nouns and pronouns follows.

Additional Material Online

A full discussion of the category **dangling construction** (including how it relates to the category **dangling modifier**) is provided alongside a range of relevant exercises at **sites.broadviewpress.com/writing**. Click on **Exercises** and go to **"Verbs, Subjects, Modifiers"** and **"Understanding Dangling Constructions and Dangling Modifiers."**

11a. Singular and Plural Nouns

Some nouns are unusual in the way that a plural is formed. Here is a list of some that frequently cause mistakes:

appendix	appendixes or appendices
attorney general	attorneys general
bacterium	bacteria
basis	bases
court martial	courts martial
crisis	crises
criterion	criteria
curriculum	curricula
datum	data
ellipsis	ellipses
emphasis	emphases
erratum	errata
father-in-law	fathers-in-law
focus	focuses or foci
governor general	governors general
index	indexes or indices
matrix	matrixes or matrices
medium	media
millennium	millennia
nucleus	nuclei
parenthesis	parentheses
phenomenon	phenomena
referendum	referenda or referendums
runner-up	runners-up
stratum	strata
symposium	symposia
synthesis	syntheses
thesis	theses

needs checking	The chief criteria on which an essay should be judged is whether or not it communicates clearly.
revised	The chief criterion on which an essay should be judged is whether or not it communicates clearly.
needs checking	This data proves conclusively that the lake is badly polluted.
revised	These data prove conclusively that the lake is badly polluted.
needs checking	The media usually assumes that the audience has a very short attention span.
revised	The media usually assume that the audience has a very short attention span.
needs checking	The great popularity of disco music was a short-lived phenomena.
revised	The great popularity of disco music was a short-lived phenomenon.

11b. Singular Pronouns

The pronouns *anybody, anyone, each, each other, either, every, neither, nobody, no one, one another* are all singular. In order to be grammatically correct, they should therefore take singular verbs.

needs checking	According to a poll of the electorate and the party, neither seem satisfied with the leader's performance.
revised	According to a poll of the electorate and the party, neither seems satisfied with the leader's performance.

The particular case of balancing grammatical agreements, syntactical awkwardness, and issues of gender is dealt with above, pages 65–67.

Following is a list of common indefinite pronouns:

> always plural: *both*, *many*
>
> always singular: *another*, *anybody*, *anyone*, *anything*, *each*, *either*, *every*, *everybody*, *everyone*, *everything*, *neither*, *nobody*, *no one*, *nothing*, *one*, *somebody*, *someone*, *something*
>
> singular or plural, depending on the context: *all*, *any*, *more*, *most*, *none*, *some*

- Some of the house is painted blue.
- Some of the houses on this street are painted blue.

11c. Unreferenced or Wrongly Referenced Pronouns

Normally a pronoun must refer to a noun in the previous sentence or clause.

needs checking	A herbalist knows a lot about the properties of plants. They can often cure you by giving you medicine.
revised	A herbalist knows a lot about the properties of plants. He can often cure you by giving you medicine.
better	Herbalists know a lot about the properties of plants. They can often cure you by giving you medicine.

Confusion can result if there is more than one possible referent for a pronoun.

needs checking	My father and my brother visited me early this morning. He told me that something important had happened.
revised	My father and my brother visited me early this morning. My father told me that something important had happened.

needs checking   The deficit was forecast to be $2 billion, but turned out to be over $20 billion. This reflected the government's failure to predict the increase in interest rates and the onset of a recession.

> [This *what*?]

revised   The deficit was forecast to be $2 billion, but turned out to be over $20 billion. This vast discrepancy reflected the government's failure to predict the increase in interest rates and the onset of a recession.

11d. Subject and Object Pronouns

Different forms of certain pronouns are used depending on whether we are using them as a subject or an object. *I, we, he/she/it, they*, and *who* are subject pronouns, whereas *me, us, him/her/it, them*, and *whom* are object pronouns.

> He shot the sheriff.
>> [Here the pronoun *he* is the subject of the sentence.]
>
> The sheriff shot him.
>> [Here the word *him* is the object; the *sheriff* is the subject.]
>
> That is the man who shot the sheriff.
>> [Here the pronoun *who* is the subject of the clause *who shot the sheriff*.]
>
> That is the man whom the sheriff shot.
>> [Here the pronoun *whom* is the object; the *sheriff* is the subject.]

Perhaps as a result of the slang use of me as a subject pronoun ("Me and him got together for a few beer last night"), the impression seems to have lodged in many minds that the distinction between **I** and **me** is one of degree of politeness or formality rather than one of subject and object.

needs checking	There is no disagreement between you and I.
revised	There is no disagreement between you and me.
	[Both *you* and *I* are here objects of the preposition *between*. "Between you and I" is no more correct than is "I threw the ball at he."]

Though the grammatical distinction between **who** and **whom** is in theory just as clear as the distinction between *I* and *me* or the distinction between *she* and *her*, in common usage it is much more blurred. The subject-object distinction in this case has largely broken down; the grammatically correct form often sounds awkward, and many authorities no longer insist on the distinction always being maintained. For example, even grammatical purists sometimes find themselves saying "I didn't know who I was talking to," even though the rules say it should be *whom* (subject—*I*; object—to *whom*).

12. ADJECTIVES AND ADVERBS

Adjectives are words used to tell us more about (*describe* or *modify*) nouns or pronouns. *Big*, *small*, *good*, *careful*, and *expensive* are all examples of adjectives. Adverbs are usually used to tell us more about (*describe* or *modify*) verbs, although they can also be used to modify adjectives or other adverbs. *Carefully*, *expensively*, *suddenly*, and *slowly* are all examples of adverbs. In conversation adjectives are often substituted for certain adverbs, but this should not be done in formal writing.

needs checking	She did good on the test.
revised	She did well on the test.
needs checking	He asked them not to talk so loud.
revised	He asked them not to talk so loudly.
needs checking	The governors thought it should be worded different.
revised	The governors thought it should be worded differently.

needs checking	They promised to do the job cheaper, easier, and quicker.
revised	They promised to do the job more cheaply, more easily, and more quickly.

12a. Comparatives and Superlatives

Most adjectives and adverbs have comparative and superlative forms; the comparative is used when comparing two things, the superlative when comparing three or more.

needs checking	Smith was the most accomplished of the two.
revised	Smith was the more accomplished of the two.

Always be careful not to construct double comparisons:

needs checking	Gandalf is much more wiser than Frodo.
revised	Gandalf is much wiser than Frodo.

13. INCOMPLETE SENTENCES

incomplete sentences (sentence fragments): An incomplete sentence (or sentence fragment) is a group of words that has been written as if it were a complete sentence, but that, as a matter of grammatical correctness, needs something else to make it complete. The group of words *When the meeting ends*, for example, cannot form a complete sentence on its own; grammatically, it is structured as a subordinate clause (see page 96). To form a complete sentence, one can either transform it into an independent clause (*The meeting will end tomorrow*) or attach it as a subordinate clause to a separate, independent clause (*When the meeting ends tomorrow, we should have a comprehensive agreement*).

Focusing on the word *fragment*, some people imagine that incomplete sentences are always very short. That's not the case. Whether a sentence is complete or not is a matter of grammatical correctness, not of sentence length. For example, the short group of words *Marina walked to the sea* can form a complete sentence, but this much longer group of words is a sentence fragment:

needs checking	While Marina was walking to the sea and thinking of her father and the sound of a wood thrush.
revised	While Marina was walking to the sea, she heard the sound of a wood thrush and thought of her father.
needs checking	Unemployment was a serious problem in Britain in the 1990s. In fact, throughout the world.
revised	Unemployment was a serious problem in the 1990s, not just in Britain but throughout the world.

The three words that most frequently lead students to write incomplete sentences are *and*, *because*, and *so*; each is discussed below.

Although there are certain cases in which it is possible to begin a sentence with *and*, these are difficult to sense. It is usually better for all except professional writers not to begin sentences with *and* if they wish to avoid incomplete sentences.

| *worth checking* | For this crop you should add Compound 'D' fertilizer to the soil. And you should add top dressing a month later. |
| *revised* | For this crop you should add Compound 'D' fertilizer to the soil, and top dressing a month later. |

In order to prevent young children who have difficulty in writing long sentences from writing incomplete sentences, many elementary school teachers wisely tell their pupils not to begin sentences with *because*. In fact it is not incorrect to begin with *because*, so long as the sentence is complete. The rule to remember is that any sentence with *because* in it must mention both the cause and the result. Whether the word *because* comes at the beginning or in the middle of the sentence does not matter; what is important is that the sentence has two parts.

needs checking	In the early 1980s Sandinista leaders told their people to be ready for war. Because the United States had been trying to destabilize Nicaragua.
revised	In the early 1980s Sandinista leaders told their people to be ready for war, because the United States had been trying to destabilize Nicaragua.

The word *so* is probably the biggest single cause of incomplete sentences. As is the case with *and*, there are certain situations in which professional writers manage to get away with beginning sentences with *so*, but normally this should not be attempted in formal academic writing. *So* should be used to join ideas together into one sentence, not to separate them by starting a new sentence.

needs checking	The dish was too heavily spiced. So most of it had to be thrown away.
revised	The dish was too heavily spiced, so most of it had to be thrown away.

When writing informally, experienced writers sometimes intentionally write sentences that are grammatically incomplete. Normally this is done as a means of adding emphasis:

In the end she was convinced it was the best way. The only way.

At first the police believed it to be a simple case of mistaken identity. But not for long.

14. RUN-ON SENTENCES

The most important mark of punctuation is the full stop (or period), which is used to separate one complete sentence from another. But what constitutes a complete sentence? What constitutes a run-on sentence, or a sentence fragment? These questions are complex ones, involving the structures of English grammar (Section 8b) and the conventions governing the use of various joining words, as well as the rules governing the use of periods, commas, and semicolons.

A run-on sentence is a sentence that continues running on and on when, as a matter of grammatical correctness, it should be broken up into two or more sentences. Sometimes people use the expression *run-on sentence* loosely to refer to a sentence that is simply very long, regardless of whether or not it is grammatically correct. A well-constructed long sentence, though, can be an excellent means of expressing complex ideas; for the sake of clarity, then, it's important not to confuse the idea of a long sentence with the idea of a run-on sentence. The term *run-on sentence* should be used only when issues of grammatical correctness are involved.

One variety of run-on sentence (a **fused sentence**) occurs when independent clauses (see page 96) are not separated by any punctuation.

needs checking	Early last Thursday we were walking in the woods it was a lovely morning.
revised	Early last Thursday we were walking in the woods. It was a lovely morning.

A second (and more common) variety of run-on sentence occurs when a comma (rather than a period or a semi-colon) is used between independent clauses, without the addition of any coordinating conjunction. This type of run-on sentence is called a **comma-splice**.

needs checking	It was a lovely morning, we were walking in the woods.
revised	It was a lovely morning. We were walking in the woods.
or	It was a lovely morning, and we were walking in the woods.

In simple examples such as those above, the matter may seem straightforward. Sometimes, though, it is not so simple. The conventions of English dictate that only certain words may be used to join two independent clauses into one sentence; the seven coordinating conjunctions (*and, but, or, for, nor, so,* and *yet*) may be used to join independent clauses.

needs checking   The temperature stayed below freezing, therefore the ice did not melt.

revised   The temperature stayed below freezing. Therefore, the ice did not melt.

or   The temperature stayed below freezing, so the ice did not melt.

> [The word *therefore* is not a coordinating conjunction, and thus may not be used to join independent clauses. The word *so* is a coordinating conjunction, and may thus be used to join independent clauses—provided that a comma is used as well.]

Another class of joining words is the conjunctive adverb. Some of the words most commonly used as conjunctive adverbs are *also, hence, however, moreover, nevertheless, otherwise,* and *therefore.* When used as conjunctive adverbs, these words typically indicate how the main idea in one sentence relates to the main idea of a previous sentence. In such cases a period (or a semi-colon) should separate the ideas from each other. They should not be "spliced" together with a comma:

needs checking   During the rainy season more water flows over Victoria Falls than any other, however several other falls are higher than Victoria.

revised   During the rainy season more water flows over Victoria Falls than any other. However, several other falls are higher than Victoria.

Unlike *when, then* should not be used to join two clauses together into a single sentence. *And then* may be used, or a semi-colon, or a new sentence may be begun.

needs checking   On June 10, 1999 Yugoslav troops began withdrawing, then the NATO bombing was suspended and the war in Kosovo ended.

revised   On June 10, 1999 Yugoslav troops began withdrawing. The NATO bombing was then suspended and the war in Kosovo ended.

15. EAL: FOR THOSE WHOSE NATIVE LANGUAGE IS NOT ENGLISH

The fact that different languages have different grammatical and syntactical conventions creates particular problems for anyone learning a new language. This section focuses on some of the peculiarities of English that are particularly likely to present difficulties to those learning English as an additional language.

15a. Articles

Articles are words used to introduce nouns. Unlike many other languages, English often requires the use of articles:

needs checking	We are interested in house with garage.
revised	We are interested in a house with a garage.

There are only three articles—*a*, *an*, and *the*. Articles show whether or not one is drawing attention to a <u>particular</u> person or thing. For example, we would say "I stood beside a house" if we did not want to draw attention to that particular house, but "I stood beside the house that the Taylors used to live in" if we wanted to draw attention to the particular house.

A (or *an* if the noun following begins with a vowel sound) is an <u>indefinite</u> article—used when you do not want to be definite or specific about which thing or person you are referring to. *The* is a <u>definite</u> article, used when you do wish to call attention to the particular thing or person. Remember that if you use *the* you are suggesting that there can be only <u>one</u> of what you are referring to.

In order to use articles properly in English it is important to understand the distinction English makes between nouns naming things that are countable (*houses, books, trees,* etc.) and nouns naming things that are not countable (*milk, confusion,* etc.). Some non-count nouns name things that it does seem possible to count: *sugar, grass, furniture,* etc. In such cases counting must in English be done indirectly: *a grain of sugar, two grains of sugar, three blades of grass, four pieces of furniture,* and so on.

Distinguishing between count and non-count nouns is inevitably a challenge for those whose first language is not English. A dictionary such as *The Oxford Advanced Learner's Dictionary* can be very helpful; unlike most dictionaries it indicates whether or not each noun is a count noun.

needs checking	They bought a nice furniture for the living room.
revised	They bought a nice piece of furniture for the living room.

15b. Frequently Used Non-count Nouns

Abstractions: advice, anger, beauty, confidence, courage, employment, fun, happiness, hate, health, honesty, information, intelligence, knowledge, love, poverty, truth, wealth, wisdom.

To eat and drink: bacon, beef, beer, bread, broccoli, butter, cabbage, candy, cauliflower, celery, cereal, cheese, chicken, chocolate, coffee, corn, cream, fish, flour, fruit, ice, ice cream, lettuce, margarine, meat, milk, oil, pasta, pepper, rice, salt, spinach, sugar, tea, water, wine, yogurt.

Other substances, things, and actions: air, cement, clothing, coal, dirt, equipment, furniture, gas, gasoline, gold, grass, homework, jewellery, luggage, lumber, machinery, mail, metal, money, music, paper, petroleum, plastic, poetry, pollution, research, scenery, silver, snow, soap, steel, timber, traffic, transportation, violence, weather, wood, wool, work.

NB The plural of many of these non-count nouns may be employed when you want to denote more than one type of the substance. *Breads*, for example, refers to different sorts of bread; *coffees* refers to different types of coffee, and so on.

Articles are not used in English to the same extent that they are used in some other languages; nouns can frequently stand alone without their article, particularly when they are being used in a general, non-specific sense. When used in this way, non-count and plural count nouns need no article.

needs checking	If the English is to be spoken correctly, the good grammar is important.
revised	If English is to be spoken correctly, good grammar is important.

needs checking	The freedom is something everyone values.
revised	Freedom is something everyone values.

In most cases no article is necessary before a noun that is capitalized:

needs checking	They were strolling through the Stanley Park.
revised	They were strolling through Stanley Park.

15c. Continuous Verb Tenses

In English the continuous tenses are not normally used with many verbs having to do with feelings, emotions, or senses. Some of these verbs are *to see, to hear, to understand, to believe, to hope, to know, to think* (meaning *believe*), *to trust, to comprehend, to mean, to doubt, to suppose, to wish, to want, to love, to desire, to prefer, to dislike, to hate.*

needs checking	He is not understanding what I mean.
revised	He does not understand what I mean.

needs checking	At that time he was believing that everything on Earth was created within one week.
revised	At that time he believed that everything on Earth was created within one week.

15d. Omission or Repetition of the Subject

With the exception of imperatives (e.g. *Come here! Don't stop!*), where *you* is understood to be the subject, English requires that the subject of the sentence be stated. Some other languages permit the omission of the subject in various circumstances where the subject may be inferred. English does not.

needs checking   The protesters demonstrated peacefully; stood quietly outside the gates of the Prime Minister's residence.

revised   The protesters demonstrated peacefully; they stood quietly outside the gates of the Prime Minister's residence.

If the subject appears after the verb, a frequent requirement in English is for *there* or *it* to be added as an expletive before the verb *to be*.

needs checking   Is not possible to finish the job this week.
revised   It is not possible to finish the job this week.

needs checking   By the end of the twentieth century, were almost one million more people in Houston than there had been in 1980.

revised   By the end of the twentieth century, there were almost one million more people in Houston than there had been in 1980.

Within a single clause English does not permit the repetition of either the subject or the object.

needs checking   The line that is longest it is called the hypotenuse.
revised   The line that is longest is called the hypotenuse.

needs checking   The members of the cast loved the play that they were acting in it.
revised   The members of the cast loved the play that they were acting in.

15e. The Conditional

Particular rules apply in English when we are speaking of actions which *would happen if* certain conditions were fulfilled. Here are some examples.

If I *went* to Australia, I *would have* to fly.

If I *drank* a lot of gin, I *would be* very sick.

I *would lend* Joe the money he wants if I *trusted* him.

Each of these sentences is made up of a main clause in which the conditional *would have*, *would be*, etc. is used, and a subordinate clause beginning with *if*, with a verb in the simple past tense (*went*, *drank*, *trusted*). In all cases the action named in the *if* clause is considered by the speaker to be unlikely to happen, or quite impossible. The first speaker does not really think that she will go to Australia; she is just speculating about what would be necessary if she did go. Similarly, the second speaker does not expect to drink a lot of gin, and the third speaker does not trust Joe. Situations like these, which are not happening and which we do not expect to happen are called *hypothetical situations*; we speculate on what *would* happen *if* but we do not expect the *if* to come true.

If we think the *if* is indeed likely to come true, then we use the future tense instead of the conditional in the main clause, and the present tense in the subordinate *if* clause, as in these examples:

If I drink a lot of gin I will be very sick.

> [The speaker thinks it quite possible that he will drink a lot of gin.]

If I go to Australia, I will have to fly.

> [The speaker thinks that she may really go.]

Some writers mistakenly use the conditional or the present tense (instead of the past tense form) in the *if* clause when they are using the conditional in the main clause:

needs checking   If I want to buy a car, I would look carefully at all the models available.

revised   If I wanted to buy a car, I would look carefully at all the models available.

> [The speaker does not want to buy a car.]

or   If I want to buy a car, I will look carefully at all the models available.

> [The speaker may really want to buy a car.]

needs checking   If the authorities would find out what happened, both boys would be in serious trouble.

revised   If the authorities found out what happened, both boys would be in serious trouble.

or   If the authorities were to find out what happened, both boys would be in serious trouble.

Similar problems occur with the past conditional:

needs checking   If the Titanic would have carried more lifeboats, hundreds of lives would have been saved.

revised   If the Titanic had carried more lifeboats, hundreds of lives would have been saved.

Additional Material Online

Exercises on the conditional may be found at **sites.broadviewpress.com/writing**. Click on **Exercises** and go to **"Conditional Constructions."**

PUNCTUATION

16. THE PERIOD

The period (or full stop) is used to close sentences that make statements. Common difficulties with run-on sentences and incomplete sentences are discussed above in the section on grammar.

Notice that when a question is reported in indirect speech it has the form of a statement, and the sentence should therefore be closed with a period:

needs checking	He asked what time it was?
revised	He asked what time it was.

The period is also used to form abbreviations (*Mr.*, *Ms.*, *Hon.*, *Ph.D.*, *A.M.*, *P.M.*, *Inc.*, etc.). If you are in any doubt about whether or not to use a period in an abbreviation, or where to put it, think of the full form of what is being abbreviated.

needs checking	Jones, Smithers, et. al. will be there in person.
	[*et al.* is short for the Latin *et alia*, "and others."]
revised	Jones, Smithers, et al. will be there in person.

17. THE COMMA

The comma is used to indicate pauses, and to give the reader cues as to how the parts of the sentence relate to one another.

needs checking	Because of the work that we had done before we were ready to hand in the assignment.
revised	Because of the work that we had done before, we were ready to hand in the assignment.

The omission or addition of a comma can completely alter the meaning of a sentence—as it did in the Queen's University Alumni letter that spoke of the warm emotions still felt by alumni for "our friends, who are dead."

17a. Commas and Non-restrictive Elements

There is a significant difference of meaning between the following two sentences:

> The dancers who wore black looked very elegant.

> The dancers, who wore black, looked very elegant.

In the first sentence, the words *who wore black* restrict the meaning of the noun *dancers*; the implication is that also present were dancers not wearing black, and perhaps looking rather less elegant. In the second sentence the words *who wore black* are set off in commas. This signifies that they do not act to restrict the meaning of the noun *dancers*. Instead, they add information that must be assumed to apply to the entire group; we infer that all the dancers wore black.

One important use of commas, then, is to set off non-restrictive elements of sentences:

restrictive	A company that pays no attention to its customers is unlikely to survive.
non-restrictive	The local grocery, which is always attentive to its customers, has been a fixture for generations.
restrictive	The man with abdominal pains was treated before any of the others.
non-restrictive	Mr. Smith, who suffered from abdominal pains, was treated before the others.
restrictive	The film *Chinatown* is in many ways reminiscent of films of the 1950s.
non-restrictive	Polanski's seventh film in English, *Chinatown*, is regarded by many as the finest film ever made.

Notice that the commas here come in pairs. If a non-restrictive element is being set off in the middle of a sentence, it must be set off on both sides.

needs checking	My sister Caroline, has done very well this year in her studies.
revised	My sister, Caroline, has done very well this year in her studies.

needs checking	The snake which had been killed the day before, was already half-eaten by ants.
revised	The snake, which had been killed the day before, was already half-eaten by ants.

17b. That and Which

It is correct to use *that* in restrictive clauses and *which* in non-restrictive clauses.

needs checking	The only store which sells this brand is now closed.
revised	The only store that sells this brand is now closed.

needs checking	The position which Marx adopted owed much to the philosophy of Hegel.
revised	The position that Marx adopted owed much to the philosophy of Hegel.

Although the use of the word *which* in any restrictive clause provokes a violent reaction among some English instructors, there are some instances in which one is quite justified in using *which* in this way. Such is the case when the writer is already using at least one *that* in the sentence:

needs checking	He told me that the radio that he had bought was defective.
revised	He told me that the radio which he had bought was defective.

17c. Extra Comma

Commas should follow the grammatical structure of a sentence; you should not throw in a comma simply because a sentence is getting long.

needs checking	The ever increasing gravitational pull of the global economy, is drawing almost every area of the earth into its orbit.
revised	The ever increasing gravitational pull of the global economy is drawing almost every area of the earth into its orbit.

17d. Commas and Lists

An important use of commas is to separate the entries in lists. Some authorities feel that a comma need not appear between the last and second last entries in a list, since these are usually separated already by the word *and*. Omitting the last comma in a series, however, will occasionally lead to ambiguity. When in doubt, it is always best to include the serial comma.

needs checking	The book is dedicated to my parents, Ayn Rand and God.
revised	The book is dedicated to my parents, Ayn Rand, and God.

When a list includes items that have commas within them, use a semi-colon to separate the items in the list.

needs checking	The three firms involved were McCarthy and Walters, Harris, Jones, and Engelby, and Cassells and Wirtz.
revised	The three firms involved were McCarthy and Walters; Harris, Jones, and Engelby; and Cassells and Wirtz.

18. THE QUESTION MARK

Any direct question should be followed by a question mark.

needs checking	Would Britain benefit from closer ties with Europe. Close to forty years after the UK joined the EC, the question continues to bedevil British political life.

> revised   Would Britain benefit from closer ties with Europe? Close to forty years after the UK joined the EC, the question continues to bedevil British political life.

If a polite request is couched as a question, a question mark is appropriate.

> needs checking   Would you please make sure the pages are in proper order.
>
> revised   Would you please make sure the pages are in proper order?

19. THE EXCLAMATION MARK

This mark is used to give extremely strong emphasis to a statement or a command. It is often used in personal or business correspondence, but it should be used very sparingly, if at all, in formal written work.

20. THE SEMI-COLON

The chief use of the semi-colon is to separate independent clauses whose ideas are closely related to each other. In most such cases a period could be used instead; the semi-colon simply signals to the reader the close relationship between the two ideas.

> correct   The team is not as good as it used to be. It has lost four of its five last games.
>
> also correct   The team is not as good as it used to be; it has lost four of its five last games.

As discussed elsewhere in this book (pages 122–24) the semi-colon may often be used to correct a comma splice. The semi-colon is also used to divide items in a series that includes other punctuation:

The following were told to report to the coach after practice: Jackson, Form 2B; Marshall, Form 3A; Jones, Form 1B.

21. THE COLON

This mark is often believed to be virtually the same as the semicolon in the way it is used. In fact, there are some important differences. The most common uses of the colon are as follows:

- in headings or titles to announce that more is to follow, or that the writer is about to list a series of things
- after an independent clause to introduce a quotation
- after an independent clause to indicate that what follows provides an explanation[1]

Here are some examples:

Unquiet Union: A Study of the Federation of Rhodesia and Nyasaland.

In the last four weeks he has visited five different countries: Mexico, Venezuela, Panama, Haiti, and Belize.

The theory of the Communists may be summed up in the single phrase: abolition of private property.

Be sure to use a colon to introduce a list.

needs checking   The dealership has supplied Mr. Bomersbach with four luxury cars, two Cadillacs, a Mercedes, and a Jaguar.

revised   The dealership has supplied Mr. Bomersbach with four luxury cars: two Cadillacs, a Mercedes, and a Jaguar.

---

1   This use is very similar to the main use of the semi-colon. The subtle differences are that the semi-colon can be used in such situations when the ideas are not quite so closely related, and the colon asks the reader to pause for a slightly longer period.

22. THE HYPHEN

This mark may be used to separate two parts of a compound word (e.g., *tax-free*, *hand-operated*). Notice that many such combinations are only hyphenated when they are acting as an adjective:

No change is planned for the short term.

> [*Term* here acts as a noun, with the adjective *short* modifying it.]

This is only a short-term plan.

> [Here the compound *short-term* acts as a single adjective, modifying the noun *plan*.]

The course will cover the full range of nineteenth-century literature.

> [Here the compound *nineteenth-century* acts as a single adjective, modifying the noun *literature*.]

The course will cover the full scope of literature in the nineteenth century.

> [*Century* acts here as a noun, with the adjective *nineteenth* modifying it.]

Hyphens are also used to break up words at the end of a line. When they are used in this way, hyphens should always be placed between syllables. Proper nouns (i.e., nouns beginning with a capital letter) should not be broken up by hyphens.

23. THE DASH

Dashes are often used in much the same way as parentheses, to set off an idea within a sentence. Dashes, however, call attention to the set-off idea in a way that parentheses do not:

Taipei 101 (then the tallest building in the world) was completed in 2005.

Taipei 101—then the tallest building in the world—was completed in 2005.

A dash may also be used in place of a colon to set off a word or phrase at the end of a sentence:

> He fainted when he heard how much he had won: one million dollars.
> He fainted when he heard how much he had won—one million dollars.

When typing, you may use two hyphens (with no space before or after them) to form a dash.

24. PARENTHESES

Parentheses are used to set off an interruption in the middle of a sentence, or to make a point which is not part of the main flow of the sentence. They are frequently used to give examples, or to express something in other words. Example:

> Several world leaders of the 1980s (Deng in China, Reagan in the US, etc.) were very old men.

25. SQUARE BRACKETS

Square brackets are used for parentheses within parentheses, or to show that the words within the parentheses are added to a quotation by another person.

> Lentricchia claims that "in reading James' Preface [to *What Maisie Knew*] one is struck as much by what is omitted as by what is revealed."

26. THE APOSTROPHE

The two main uses of the apostrophe are to show possession (e.g., "Peter's book") and to shorten certain common word combinations (e.g., *can't, shouldn't, he's*).

26a. Contractions

Contractions should be avoided in formal written work. Use *cannot*, not *can't*; *did not*, not *didn't*; and so on.

informal	The experiment wasn't a success, because we'd heated the solution to too high a temperature.
more formal	The experiment was not a success, because we had heated the solution to too high a temperature.

26b. Possession
(See also **its/it's**, page 319.)

The correct placing of the apostrophe to show possession can be a tricky matter. When the noun is singular, the apostrophe must come before the s (e.g., *Peter's, George's, Canada's*), whereas when the noun is plural and ends in an *s* already, the apostrophe comes after the *s*.

worth checking	His parent's house is filled with antiques.
revised	His parents' house is filled with antiques.
	[Note that no apostrophe is needed when a plural is not possessive.]

needs checking	His parent's were away for the weekend.
revised	His parents were away for the weekend.

When a singular noun already ends in *s*, authorities differ as to whether or not a second s should be added after the apostrophe:

correct	Ray Charles' music has been very influential.
correct	Ray Charles's music has been very influential.

Whichever convention a writer chooses, he should be consistent. And be sure in such cases not to put the apostrophe before the first *s*.

needs checking	Shield's novel is finely, yet delicately constructed.
	[concerning novelist Carol Shields]
revised	Shields' novel is finely, yet delicately constructed.
	[or "Shields's novel"]

27. QUOTATION MARKS

The main use of quotation marks is to show that the exact words that a person has spoken or written are being repeated:

"I don't know anyone called Capone," she told the court.

"I will not make age an issue of this campaign," Ronald Reagan famously remarked when running for president at the age of 73. "I am not going to exploit, for political purposes, my opponent's youth and inexperience," he added.

While the principle of using quotation marks in these ways is straightforward, in practice it is often easy to go wrong. For a discussion of some of the details, see "Direct and Indirect Speech" below (pages 143–47); for a discussion of how to integrate quotations into written work, see the sections on MLA Style and APA Style (pages 179–89 and 244–54).

27a. Other Uses of Quotation Marks

According to different conventions, words that are being mentioned rather than used may be set off by quotation marks, single quotation marks, or italics:

The words "except" and "accept" are sometimes confused.

The words 'except' and 'accept' are sometimes confused.

The words *except* and *accept* are sometimes confused.

Quotation marks (or single quotation marks) are sometimes also used to indicate that the writer does not endorse the quoted statement, claim, or description. Quotation marks are usually used in this way only with a word or brief phrase. When so used they have the connotation of *supposed* or *so-called*; they suggest that the quoted word or phrase is either euphemistic or downright false:

After a workout the weightlifters would each consume a "snack" of a steak sandwich, half a dozen eggs, several pieces of bread and butter, and a quart of tomato juice.

In the following two versions of the same report the more sparing use of quotation marks in the second version signals clearly to the reader the writer's scepticism as to the honesty of the quoted claim.

> President Charez appeared to stagger as he left the plane. "The President is feeling tired and emotional," his Press Secretary later reported.

> A "tired and emotional" President Charez appeared to stagger as he left the plane.

27b. Misuse of Quotation Marks to Indicate Emphasis

Quotation marks (unlike italics, bold letters, capital letters, or underlining) should never be used to try to lend emphasis to a particular word or phrase. Because quotation marks may be used to convey the sense *supposed* or *so-called* (see above), the common misuse of quotation marks to try to lend emphasis often creates ludicrous effects.

needs checking   All our bagels are served "fresh" daily.
           [The unintended suggestion here is that the claim of freshness is a dubious one.]
revised   All our bagels are served fresh daily.
or   All our bagels are served **fresh** daily.
           [if emphasis is required in an advertisement]

27c. Single Quotation Marks

In North America the main use of single quotation marks is to mark quotations within quotations:

> According to the Press Secretary, "When the Minister said, 'I never inhaled,' he meant it."

Depending on convention, single quotation marks may also be used to show that a word or phrase is being mentioned rather than used (see above).

In the United Kingdom and some other countries, quotation marks and single quotation marks are used for direct speech in precisely the opposite way that North Americans use them; single quotation marks (or inverted commas, as they are sometimes called) are used for direct speech, and double marks are used for quotations within quotations. Here is the correct British version of the above sentence:

> According to the Press Secretary, 'When the Minister said, "I never inhaled", he meant it'.

Note here that UK usage also places closing punctuation marks outside closing quotation marks.

27d. Direct and Indirect Speech

i) Direct speech

The main rules for writing direct speech in English are as follows:

- The exact words spoken—and no other words—must be surrounded by quotation marks.
- A comma should precede a quotation, but according to North American convention other punctuation should be placed inside the quotation marks. Examples:
  - He said, "I think I can help you."
    (The period after *you* comes before the quotation marks.)
  - "Drive slowly," she said, "and be very careful."
    (The comma after *slowly* and period after *careful* both come inside the quotation marks.)

Additional Material Online
Exercises on direct and indirect speech may be found at
sites.broadviewpress.com/writing.
Click on **Exercises** and go to
"Punctuation."

With each change in speaker a new paragraph should begin. Example:

> "Let's go fishing this weekend," Mary suggested. "It should be nice and cool by the water."
>
> "Good idea," agreed Faith. "I'll meet you by the store early Saturday morning."

Canadian usage demands that all punctuation go inside the quotation marks in quotations that are stand-alone sentences:

- "An iron curtain is descending across Europe," declared Winston Churchill in 1946.

At the same time, Canadian usage allows writers either to follow the American convention or to make an exception when the punctuation clearly pertains only to the structure of the surrounding sentence and not to the quoted word or phrase:

- Was it Churchill who described the post-war divide between newly Communist Eastern Europe and the West as "an iron curtain"?

The most common difficulties experienced when recording direct speech are as follows:

omission of quotation marks: This happens particularly frequently at the end of a quotation.

needs checking   She said, "I will try to come to see you tomorrow. Then she left.

revised   She said, "I will try to come to see you tomorrow." Then she left.

placing punctuation outside the quotation marks:

needs checking   He shouted, "The house is on fire"!

revised   He shouted, "The house is on fire!"

including the word *that* before direct speech: *That* is used before passages of indirect speech, not before passages of direct speech.

needs checking	My brother said that, "I think I have acted stupidly."
revised	My brother said, "I think I have acted stupidly."
or	My brother said that he thought he had acted stupidly.
needs checking	The official indicated that, "we are not prepared to allow galloping inflation."
revised	The official said, "We are not prepared to allow galloping inflation."
or	The official indicated that his government was not prepared to allow galloping inflation.

when to indent: In a formal essay, any quotation longer than four lines[1] should normally be single-spaced and indented to set it off from the body of the text. Any quotation of more than three lines from a poem should also be single-spaced and indented. Quotations set off from the body of the text in this way should not be preceded or followed by quotation marks.

needs checking	Larkin's "Days" opens with childlike simplicity: "What are days for? / Days are where we live. / They come, they wake us / Time and time over." But with Larkin, the shadow of mortality is never far distant.

revised	Larkin's "Days" opens with childlike simplicity:
	    What are days for?
	    Days are where we live.
	    They come, they wake us
	    Time and time over.
	But with Larkin, the shadow of mortality is never far distant.

ii) Indirect speech

Indirect speech reports what was said without using the same words that were used by the speaker. The rules for writing indirect speech are as follows:

---

1   This is what the MLA recommends; the APA specifies up to forty words, and *The Chicago Manual of Style* up to 100 words.

- Do not use quotation marks.
- Introduce statements with the word *that*, and do not put a comma after *that*. Questions should be introduced with the appropriate question word (*what, why, whether, if, how, when*, etc.).
- First-person pronouns and adjectives (e.g., *I, me, we, us, my, our*) must often be changed to third person (*he, she, they, him, her, them*, etc.) if the subject of the main clause is in third person.

> *correct*   "I am not happy with our team's performance," said Paul.
>
> *also correct*   Paul said that he was not happy with his team's performance.
>
> *correct*   I said, "I want my money back."
>
> *also correct*   I said that I wanted my money back.
>   [Here the subject, *I*, is first person.]

- Second-person pronouns must also sometimes be changed.
- Change the tenses of the verbs to agree with the main verb of the sentence. Usually this involves moving the verbs one step back into the past from the tenses used by the speaker in direct speech. Notice in the first example above, for instance, that the present tense *am* has been changed to the past tense *was* in indirect speech. Here are other examples:

> *correct*   "We will do everything we can," he assured me.
>
> *correct*   He assured me that they would do everything they could.
>   [*Will* and *can* change to *would* and *could*.]
>
> *correct*   "You went to school near Brandon, didn't you?" he asked me.
>
> *correct*   He asked me if I had gone to school near Brandon.
>   [*Went* changes to *had gone*.]

- Change expressions having to do with time. This is made necessary by the changes in verbs discussed above. For example, *today* in direct speech normally becomes *on that day* in indirect speech, *yesterday* becomes *on the day before*, *tomorrow* becomes *the next day*, and so on.

The most common problems experienced when indirect speech is being used are as follows:

confusion of pronouns: Many writers do not remember to change all the necessary pronouns when shifting from direct to indirect speech.

- When I met him he said, "You have cheated me." (direct)

needs checking   When I met him he said that you had cheated me.
revised   When I met him he said that I had cheated him.

- He will probably say to you, "I am poor. I need money."

needs checking   He will probably tell you that he is poor and that I
                   need money.
revised   He will probably tell you that he is poor and that
            he needs money.

verb tenses: Remember to shift the tenses of the verbs one step back into the past when changing something into indirect speech.

- She said, "I will check my tires tomorrow."

needs checking   She said that she will check her tires the next day.
revised   She said that she would check her tires the next
            day.

- "Can I go with you later this afternoon?" he asked.

needs checking   He asked if he can go with us later that afternoon.
revised   He asked if he could go with us later that afternoon.

28. ELLIPSES

An ellipsis is made up of three spaced periods. In narrative writing an ellipsis may be used to indicate a pause or to show that a sentence or thought has not been completed:

> "I can't think why you…." Denise left the rest unsaid.

In academic writing ellipses are frequently used with quoted material: three dots are used to indicate the omission of one or more words needed to complete a sentence or other grammatical construction. Note that when used in a quotation an ellipsis comes inside the quotation marks, and that when an ellipsis precedes a period the sentence should end with four dots. If an ellipsis is used to indicate a deletion of more than a sentence of material in the middle of a passage, a period should appear before the three ellipsis dots—again, making a total of four dots.

As a general rule, an ellipsis is not necessary at the beginning or at the end of a quotation; it is understood that a passage of quoted text will have been preceded by other material, and be followed by other material. If, however, you are changing a letter from upper case to lower case at the beginning of a quotation, MLA and some other styles specify that this should be indicated with square brackets:

> Barrie conveys a vivid sense of the shadow as a physical presence:
>
>> [U]nfortunately Mrs. Darling could not leave it hanging out at the window. It looked so like the washing and lowered the whole tone of the house…. She decided to roll the shadow up and put it carefully away in a drawer….

In the passage quoted, the word "unfortunately" does not begin the sentence; hence the square brackets around the capital letter. In the passage quoted there is also material that follows "in a drawer" before the end of that sentence; hence the second ellipsis. (See pages 186–87 and 251 for more on MLA and APA styles and ellipses.)

It is of course vitally important that ellipses not be used to distort the meaning of a passage.

needs checking "I … believe that these people are either English or Jewish because they are endowed with certain innate qualities," Shapiro writes in his introduction to *Shakespeare and the Jews* (4).

revised "I do not believe that these people are either English or Jewish because they are endowed with certain innate qualities," Shapiro writes in his introduction to *Shakespeare and the Jews* (4).

FORMAT
AND SPELLING

29. CAPITALIZATION

Proper nouns (naming specific persons, places, or things) should always be capitalized. Common nouns are not normally capitalized. Here are a few examples:

PROPER	*COMMON*
June	summer
Parliament of Canada	in parliament
Mother (used as a name)	my mother
Remembrance Day	in remembrance
Memorial Day	as a memorial
National Gallery	a gallery
Director	a director
Professor	a professor
the Enlightenment	the eighteenth century
the Restoration (historical period in England)	the restoration (other uses of the word)
the Renaissance	a renaissance
God	a god
Catholic (belonging to that particular church)	catholic (meaning *wide-ranging* or *universal*)
a Liberal (belonging to the Liberal Party)	a liberal (holding liberal ideas)
a Democrat (belonging to the Democratic Party)	a democrat (believing in democratic ideals)

Names of academic subjects are not capitalized (unless they are names of languages).

Major words in the titles of books, articles, stories, poems, films, and so on should be capitalized; articles, short prepositions, and conjunctions are not normally capitalized unless they are the first word of a title or subtitle.

needs checking	She became a Director of the company in 2015.
revised	She became a director of the company in 2015.
or	She became a member of the Board of Directors in 2015.

needs checking	Robert Boardman discusses *The Bridge On The River Kwai* extensively in his book.
revised	Robert Boardman discusses *The Bridge on the River Kwai* extensively in his book.

30. ABBREVIATIONS

Abbreviations are a convenient way of presenting information in a smaller amount of space. This section discusses conventions for using abbreviations in formal writing.

30a. Titles

Titles are normally abbreviated when used immediately before or after a person's full name.

Mr. Isaiah Thomas
Sammy Davis Jr.
Dr. Jane Phelps
Marcia Gibbs, MD

When using a title together with the last name only, the full title should be written out.

Prof. Marc Ereshefsky	Professor Ereshefsky
Sen. Keith Davey	Senator Davey

30b. Academic and Business Terms

Common abbreviations are acceptable in formal writing so long as they are likely to be readily understood. Otherwise, the full name should be written out when first used and the abbreviation given in parentheses. Thereafter, the abbreviation may be used on its own.

The Atomic Energy Commission (AEC) has broad-ranging regulatory authority.
The American Philosophical Association (APA) holds three large regional meetings annually.

30c. Latin Abbreviations

Several abbreviations of Latin terms are common in formal academic writing:

cf.   compare (Latin *confer*)
e.g.   for example (Latin *exempli gratia*)
et al.   and others (Latin *et alia*)
etc.   and so on (Latin *et cetera*)
i.e.   that is (Latin *id est*)
NB   note well (Latin *nota bene*)

31. NUMBERS

Numbers of one or two words should be written out. Use figures for all other numbers.

needs checking   The building is 72 storeys tall.
revised   The building is seventy-two storeys tall.

The same principle applies for dollar figures (or figures in other currencies).

needs checking   She lent her brother 10 dollars.
revised   She lent her brother ten dollars.

It is acceptable to combine figures and words for very large numbers:

The government is projecting a $200 billion deficit.

In general, figures should be used in addresses, dates, percentages, and reports of scores or statistics.

needs checking   In the third game of the tournament, Canada and the Czech Republic tied three three.
revised   In the third game of the tournament, Canada and the Czech Republic tied 3–3.

32. ITALICS

Italics may be represented in handwritten or typed papers by underlining. Italics serve several different functions. While the titles of short stories, poems, and other short works are set off by quotation marks, titles of longer works and the names of newspapers, magazines, and so on should appear in italics:

"The Dead"	*Dubliners*
"Burnt Norton"	*Four Quartets*
"Budget Controversy Continues"	*The Economist*
"Smells like Teen Spirit"	*Nevermind*

Italics are also used for the names of paintings and sculptures, television series, and software.

Italics are also used for words or phrases from other languages in written English.

needs checking   The play ends with an appearance of a deus ex machina.

revised   The play ends with an appearance of a *deus ex machina*.

Either italics or quotation marks may be used to indicate that words are mentioned rather than used. (See above, under **quotation marks**.)

Finally, italics are often used to provide special emphasis that is not otherwise clear from the context or the structure of the sentence.

33. SPELLING

The wittiest example of the illogic of English spelling remains Bernard Shaw's famous spelling of *fish* as *ghoti*. The *gh* sounds like the *gh* in enough; the *o* sounds like the *o* in *women* (once spelled *wimmen*, incidentally); and the *ti* sounds like the *ti* in *nation* or *station*. Shaw passionately advocated a rationalization of English spelling; it still has not happened, and probably never will.

Perhaps the best way to learn correct spelling is to be tested by someone else, or to test yourself every week on a different group of words. For example, you might learn the words from the list below beginning with a and b one week, the words beginning with c and d the next week, and so on.

33a. Spell-Check

No computer can be a substitute for careful proofreading. Spell-check is wonderful, but it cannot tell if it is your friend or your fiend, or if you have signed off a letter with best wishes or beast wishes.

33b. Spelling and Sound

Many spelling mistakes result from similarities in the pronunciation of words with very different meanings. These are covered in the list below. Other words that cause spelling difficulties are listed separately.

absent (adjective)	absence (noun)
absorb	absorption
accept	except
access (entry)	excess (too much)
advice (noun)	advise (verb)
affect (to influence)	effect (result)
allowed (permitted)	aloud
alter (change)	altar (in a church)
appraise (value)	apprise (inform)
base (foundation)	bass (in music)
bath (noun)	bathe (verb)
berry (fruit)	bury (the dead)
beside (by the side of)	besides (as well as)
birth	berth (bed)
bitten	beaten
bizarre (strange)	bazaar (market)
bloc (political grouping)	block
breath (noun)	breathe (verb)

buoy (in the water)	boy
buy (purchase)	by
cash	cache (hiding place)
casual (informal)	causal (to do with causes)
cause	case
ceased (stopped)	seized (grabbed)
ceiling (above you)	sealing
chick	cheek
chose (past tense)	choose (present tense)
cite (make reference to)	sight/site
climatic	climactic
cloths (fabric)	clothes
coma (unconscious)	comma (punctuation)
compliment (praise)	complement (make complete)
conscious (aware)	conscience (sense of right)
contract	construct
conventional (usual)	convectional
conversation	conservation/concentration
convinced	convicted (of a crime)
cord (rope)	chord (music)
council (group)	counsel (advice)
course	coarse (rough)
credible (believable)	creditable (deserving credit)
critic (one who criticizes)	critique (piece of criticism)
defer (show respect)	differ
deference (respect)	difference
deprecate (criticize)	depreciate (reduce in value)
desert (dry place)	dessert (sweet)
device (thing)	devise (to plan)
died/had died	dead/was dead
dissent (protest)	descent (downward motion)
distant (adjective)	distance (noun)
edition (of a book etc.)	addition (something added)
emigrant	immigrant
envelop (verb)	envelope (noun)
except	expect
fear	fair/fare (payment)
feeling	filling

fell	feel/fill
flaunt (display)	flout
formally	formerly (previously)
forth (forward)	fourth (after third)
forward	foreword (in a book)
foul	fowl (birds)
future	feature
genus (biological type)	genius (creative intelligence)
greet	great/grate (scrape)
guerillas (fighters)	gorillas (apes)
guided (led)	guarded (protected)
had	heard/head
heat	heart/hate
heir (inheritor)	air
human	humane (kind)
illicit (not permitted)	elicit (bring forth)
illusion (unreal image)	allusion (reference)
immigrate	emigrate
independent (adjective)	independence (noun)
inhabit (live in)	inhibit (retard)
instance (occurrence)	instants (moments)
intense (concentrating)	intents
isle (island)	aisle (to walk in)
kernel	colonel
know	no/now
lack	lake
later	latter/letter
lath (piece of wood)	lathe (machine)
lead	led
leave	leaf
leave	live
leaving	living
lessen (reduce)	lesson
let	late
lightning (from clouds)	lightening (becoming lighter)
lose (be unable to find)	loose (not tight)
mad (insane)	maid (servant)
man	men

martial (to do with fighting)	marshal
mental	metal
merry	marry
met	meet/mate
minor (underage)	miner (underground)
mist (light fog)	missed
moral (ethical)	morale (spirit)
mourning (after death)	morning
new	knew
of	off
on	own
ones	once
pain	pane (of glass)
patients (sick people)	patience (ability to wait)
peer (look closely)	pier (wharf)
perpetrate (be guilty of)	perpetuate (cause to continue)
perquisite (privilege)	prerequisite (requirement)
personal (private)	personnel (employees)
perspective (vision)	prospective (anticipated)
poor	pour (liquid)/pore
precede (go before)	proceed (continue)
precedent	president
price (cost)	prize (reward)
prostate	prostrate
quay	key
(wharf—pronounced *key*)	
quite	quiet (not noisy)
rein (to control animals)	rain/reign
release (let go)	realize (discover)
relieve (verb)	relief (noun)
response (noun)	responds (verb)
rid	ride
ridden	written
rise	rice
rite (ritual)	right/write
rod	rode/reared
rote (repetition)	wrote
saved	served

saw	seen
saw	so/sew
scene (location)	seen
seam (in clothes etc.)	seem (appear)
secret	sacred (holy)
sell (verb)	sail (boat)
senses	census (population count)
shed	shade
shone	shown
shot	short
sit	sat/set
smell	smile
snake	snack (small meal)
soar	sore (hurt)
sole (single)	soul (spirit)
sort (type or kind)	sought (looked for)
steal (present tense)	stole (past tense)
straight (not crooked)	strait (of water)
striped (e.g., a zebra)	stripped (uncovered)
suite (rooms or music)	suit/sweet
super	supper (meal)
suppose	supposed to
sympathies (noun)	sympathize (verb)
tale (story)	tail
talk	took
tap	tape
than	then
they	there/their
thing	think
this	these
throw	threw (past tense)
tied	tired
urban (in cities)	urbane (sophisticated)
vanish (disappear)	varnish
vein (to carry blood)	vain
waist (your middle)	waste
wait	weight (heaviness)
waive (give up)	wave

wants	once
weak (not strong)	week
weather (sunny, wet, etc.)	whether (or not)
wedding	weeding
were	where
wholly (completely)	holy (sacred)/holly
woman	women
won	worn
yoke (for animals)	yolk (of an egg)

33c. American Spelling, British Spelling, Canadian Spelling

A number of words that cause spelling difficulties are spelled differently in different countries. In the following list the British spelling is on the right, the American on the left. Either is correct in Canada, so long as the writer is consistent.

behavior	behaviour
center	centre
cigaret	cigarette
color	colour
defense	defence
favor	favour
favorite	favourite
fulfill	fulfil
humor	humour
likable	likeable
maneuver	manoeuvre
marvelous	marvellous
neighbor	neighbour
omelet	omelette
program	programme
Shakespearian	Shakespearean
skeptical	sceptical
skillful	skilful
theater	theatre
traveling	travelling

33d. Other Spelling Mistakes

Following is a list of some other commonly misspelled words.

abbreviation
absence
accelerator
accident
accidentally
accommodation
achieve
acknowledge
acquire
acquisition
acquit
acre
across
address
adjacent
advertisement
affidavit
ambulance
ammonia
amoeba
among
amortize
amount
anachronism
analogous
analysis
anchor
androgynous
annihilate
antecedent
anti-Semitic
anxious
apocalypse

apparatus
apparently
appreciate
approach
architect
arguable
argument
arsonist
arteriosclerosis
artillery
asinine
author
auxiliary
bacteria
basically
battery
beautiful
beginning
believe
boast
boastful
breakfast
bulletin
burglar
burial
buried
business
candidate
capillary
cappuccino
Caribbean
carpentry
cautious

ceiling
changeable
character
chlorophyll
choir
cholesterol
chrome
chromosome
chronological
chrysalis
chrysanthemum
coincidence
colleague
colonel
colossal
column
commitment
committee
comparative
competition
competitor
complexion
conceive
condemn
conjunction
connoisseur
consensus
consistent
controller
convenience
cooperation
cooperative
courteous

courtesy
creator
creature
criticism
cyst
decisive
definite
delicious
description
desirable
despair
despise
destroy
develop
diesel
different
dilemma
dining
disappear
disappoint
disastrous
discrimination
disease
disintegrate
dissatisfied
dominate
dormitory
double
doubtful
drunkard
drunkenness
duchess
due
dying
eclipse
effective
efficient
eighth

embarrass
employee
encourage
enemy
enmity
enormous
entertain
enthusiasm
entitle
entrepreneur
environment
enzyme
epidermis
epididymis
erroneous
esophagus
especially
espresso
essential
exaggerate
excessive
excite
exercise
exhilaration
existence
existent
experience
extraordinary
Fahrenheit
faithful
faithfully
farinaceous
fault
financial
foreigner
foretell
forty
fourth

gamete
gauge
germination
government
grammar
grateful
gruesome
guarantee
guerrillas
guilty
happened
happiest
hatred
hectare
helpful
hyena
hypothesis
ichthyology
idiosyncratic
imaginary
imagine
immersible
immigration
impeccable
importance
impresario
inchoate
incomprehensible
independent
indestructible
indigenous
indispensable
ineffable
infinitesimal
inoculate
insufferable
intention
intentional

interrupt
irrelevant
irresponsible
isosceles
isthmus
itinerary
jealous
jeopardy
journalist
jump
junction
kneel
knowledge
knowledgeable
laboratories
laboratory
language
lazy, laziness
ledger
leisure
liaise, liaison
liberation
library
licence
lieutenant
liquid, liquefy
literature
lying
medicine
medieval
membrane
merciful
mermaid
millennia
millennium
millionaire
minuscule
mischief

mischievous
naked
naughty
necessary
necessity
noticeable
nuclear
nucleus
obscene
obsolescent
obsolete
occasion
occasional
occupy
occur
occurred
occurrence
omit
ourselves
paid
parallel
parliament
parliamentary
party
permissible
permission
perpendicular
perseverance
photosynthesis
playful
possess
possession
poultry
predictable
pregnancy
pregnant
prerogative
prescription

privilege
properly
psychiatric
psychological
punctuation
pursue
questionnaire
really
receipt
recommend
referee
reference
regret
repeat
repetition
replies
reply
residence (place)
residents (people)
restaurant
revolutionary
rheumatism
rhododendron
rhombus
rhubarb
rhyme
rhythm
saddest
sandals
scene
schedule
schizophrenic
science
scintillate
scissors
scream
scrumptious
search

seize
sense
separate
shining
shotgun
sigh
significant
simultaneous
sincerely
slippery
slogan
smart
solemn
spaghetti
speech
spongy
sponsor
stale
stingy
stomach
stubborn
studious
studying

stupefy
stupid
subordinate
subpoena
substitute
subtle, subtlety
suburbs
succeed
success, successful
sue, suing
summary
surprised
surreptitious
surrounded
survive
symbol
talkative
tarred
television
temperature
tendency
theoretical
theory

title
tough
tragedy
trophy
truly
unique
until
vacancy
vacillate
valuable
vegetable
vehicle
vicious
visitor
volume
voluntary
Wednesday
welcome
whisper
writer
writing
written
yield

RESEARCH AND
DOCUMENTATION

34. APPROACHES TO RESEARCH

How does an industrious student locate voices that she can be confident are responsible ones, regardless of whether or not she may in the end agree with their conclusions? Search engines such as Google will turn up vast amounts of material on almost any topic—more than could possibly be taken account of in a single essay, perhaps more than could be read in an entire academic year. How do you choose? And how do you judge what is likely to be reliable, and what isn't?

One important research principle is to give consideration to material that has been refereed. The term "refereed journal" (or "refereed monograph," where a book-length academic study is concerned) refers to the publishers' practice of sending all submissions to respected academic authorities to be vetted before the material is published. (Another term often used for the same process is "peer-review"—the research of one scholar is reviewed by his or her peers before it is accepted for publication.) The process of refereeing or peer review is far from foolproof, and it's often the case that refereed journal articles or monographs will come to very different conclusions. But it is one important filtering device that can help separate responsible sources from irresponsible ones.

You should be aware that most refereed journals (and the electronic copies of most academic monographs) are not accessible to anyone who goes online. It is often the case that the article will be listed by your search engine but protected by a paywall, such that only a brief abstract (or the first page of the article) will be publicly accessible, and nothing more. It is also often the case that outstanding academic material will be given such a low score by the search engine's algorithm that you are never likely to find it in an ordinary Google search; like other search engines, Google tends to put frequently consulted material at the head of lists—a practice that may place pieces by popular astrologers or political cranks far ahead of the less flamboyant but more reliable work of reputable scholars. For academic research, Google Scholar (scholar.google.

com) is often a far better choice than the main Google search engine. But like Google, Google Scholar will give you no more than an abstract or the first page of a scholarly article—just as Google Books (or Amazon's "Look Inside" feature) will typically provide only selected pages of monographs. It's worth making a note of anything that looks interesting from your initial search process on Google and Google Scholar—but to fully explore many of the articles and books that look to be interesting and relevant to your research, you'll need to be inside the paywall that protects them.

Getting inside that paywall, then, is a vitally important first step in academic research. The way to do that, of course, is through your institution's library. If you are a college or university student in good standing, you will have been given an identification number and passcode to access the library's collection. Almost all university libraries today include a vast array of electronic material: newspapers, magazines, scholarly journals, and academic monographs that cannot be accessed by anyone without a passcode. It's never a good idea to give up easily if the first indication from the university library search engine is that the library doesn't provide access to a particular scholarly journal or academic monograph. (This is one area where libraries vary quite significantly; some university libraries seem to have search engines just as good as those of Google Scholar, whereas others are clunky and unpredictable.)

Whatever combination of search engines you are using, chances are high that you will find far more material than you can easily deal with. How can you avoid spending a large amount of time merely amassing a large quantity of material, much of which may be unreliable or not relevant for your purposes?

There is no one easy answer to this question. Part of the answer is often psychological; it can be important for many writers to start actually writing even before they are sure they have all the information they will want; the very process of writing often helps them to realize what sorts of information they still need. But much of the answer is also in what priority you give to different sorts of material. Whether or not material has been reviewed is one criterion. Another is how often you find it cited. Many good researchers like to start by making a very brief list of materials to consult, working purely on the basis of what seems most relevant to the topic they are tackling. Then, as they are scanning those, they will pay attention to which other books or articles are referred to most often by the authors. If a work is frequently cited by others, it will be one that you should take into account.

Where articles are concerned, the researcher should pay attention to the journal or newspaper in which the piece was originally published. Often she will be able to pick up on clues as to whether or not it is a publication with a good reputation. So far as newspapers are concerned, *The New York Times*, *The Washington Post*, *Los Angeles Times*, and *The Wall Street Journal* are all American newspapers with strong reputations; in Canada the equivalents are *The Globe and Mail* and *National Post*; in the UK *The Times*, *The Telegraph*, *The Independent*, *The Guardian*, and *The Economist* (the latter now published weekly in a magazine format, but still resolutely styling itself as a "newspaper"). Though all these are reputable publications, it is also helpful to know that some (e.g., *The Wall Street Journal*, *National Post*, *The Telegraph*) tend to be ideologically very conservative, while others (e.g., *The Washington Post*, *The Guardian*) tend to be ideologically somewhat to the left.

If you are uncertain about how reputable a source may be, it is a good idea to consult your instructor. She will be able to tell you, for example, that *The American Historical Review* and *The Journal of American History* are both highly reputable, that *The Journal of Philosophy* is a much more reputable publication than is *Animus: A Philosophical Journal for Our Time*, and so on. That should not lead you to agree with everything you find in *The Journal of Philosophy*, of course—but it should save you some time.

It's also worth thinking of the credentials of the publisher. Whether in bound or electronic form, a book or journal published by one of the world's most prestigious university presses (among them Oxford and Cambridge in Britain; California, Chicago, Duke, Harvard, Princeton, Stanford, and Yale in the

US; Toronto and McGill-Queen's in Canada) is more likely to provide reliable information than one from Pelican Publishing (a non-scholarly Louisiana publisher of books on politics, cooking, and various other topics) or from Sentinel Press (an imprint within the Penguin Group that dedicates itself to the promotion of right-wing causes). The experienced researcher will thus take account of the publisher of any book or article. But at the same time, one should never take a book's reliability for granted based on the reputation of the publisher. The university presses of Oxford and Harvard may be highly reputable, but even the most prestigious presses have published some real duds in their time. And, because librarians often have standing orders for all books from such prestigious presses as these, the chances of a real dud from such a press finding its way onto the library's shelves or databases are far greater than the chances of an inferior book from a lesser known publisher being included in the library's offerings.

With the growth of the Open Access movement in recent years, it is becoming more and more common for leading scholars and other reputable writers to bypass the traditional "gatekeepers" and post material online without it having been vetted beforehand by any process of peer review or assessment by publishers. There may often be significant advantages to this approach for both authors and readers; open access publishing makes up-to-date research available more quickly; makes available not only a larger volume of material, but also a wider range of viewpoints; and reduces the undue influence that a handful of academic journal publishers have for many years exerted over the dissemination of research. But when you are checking out material published through an open-access publisher, you should be aware that not every publisher is alike. Open access publishers such as PLOS and SSRN were founded by academics and are highly reputable. Even where there may be no formal process of peer review for self-archived pieces, basic vetting has been carried out with material published on these sites, such that articles by cranks and crackpots are few and far between. Some other open access publishers, on the other hand, operate primarily through unsupervised self-archiving, where authors of any sort post their own work. Outstanding work may certainly sometimes be found on such a site, but it is likely to constitute a much smaller percentage of the total than it does on PLOS or SSRN. Outstanding work may also be found on websites or blogs unaffiliated with any institution or aggregating site—but as a general principle, material on a site with the domain name of an accredited university is likely to be more reliable. (In some countries accredited institutions may be identified by the style of their domain names; in the US, for example, accredited universities and colleges have .edu domain names, whereas in Britain they have .ac.uk domain names.)

Think too of the credentials of the author. Is he or she an academic at a respected institution, and has he or she published widely on the topic? And think of how recent the material is; for certain sorts of research there is an obvious

Searching through Old Newspapers

Here's one small example of how difficult it can be for a novice to navigate the world of electronic research. Imagine you are doing an essay on some aspect of nineteenth-century British history or literature and you would like to check out what the newspapers of that era had to say about a particular figure—the poet Augusta Webster, say, or the activist and inventor Lewis Gompertz. So far as newspapers go, you might well think of *The Times* of London, and no doubt you would try to google their archives. You would quickly find that, as with most newspaper archives nowadays, they are protected by a paywall.

Luckily for you, almost every university library has a subscription to the *Times* archive. If you check your university library's website you are likely to find "The Times of London Digital Archive" quite readily—listed under "newspapers," as one would expect. It's protected by a paywall, but so long as you have your university ID and passcode you'll be able to access it easily—and utilize its very good search engine to quickly find electronic facsimiles of all articles mentioning Webster or Gompertz.

But what about other British newspapers of the nineteenth century? Chances are you won't find nineteenth-century archives for any other British newspapers listed in the same section of your library's website. Don't give up! If you root about a bit using Google or another search engine outside the library site, you are likely to find pointers to what you're looking for. Googling "Victorian newspapers" or "British Newspapers 1800–1900" will likely bring up "19th Century British Library Newspapers"—a database that brings together four dozen different British newspapers covering the years 1800 to 1913. Back on your university's library site you'll find it under "databases," not "newspapers." Like the *Times* site, it has an excellent search engine; once you are on the site you will quickly and easily be able to search those 48 newspapers and check out all the articles in any of them that mentioned Webster or Gompertz at any time during the nineteenth century.

If Google fails you in such situations, you still need not give up; you can always ask your instructor, or your university librarian. Chances are they will either be able to point you in the direction of what you want—or, at the very least, save you from hours of fruitless searching by letting you know that there is no convenient way to find what you'd like to find!

premium to be placed on more recent material. But the most recent is not always the best, of course. Ask too if the work provides sources to back up the arguments made. And is it possible readily to check the accuracy of those sources?

Another important criterion for certain sorts of research is point of view. If you are conducting research on a controversial topic, it's important to make sure that you consult a range of different viewpoints. You should not feel obligated, though, to give equal weight to all points of view. Particularly where material on the Web is concerned, it will sometimes be the case that implausible or downright irresponsible points of view will be more widely represented than views that deserve greater respect. Such is obviously the case with websites promulgating racist, homophobic, or otherwise bigoted views, but it may also be the case with certain scientific matters. By the late 1990s, for example, the vast majority of reputable scientific opinion was in broad agreement as to the dangers of global climate change. Dissenting scientific voices comprised only a small minority among the community of reputable scientists—but for years their views received disproportionate space on the Web, where numerous sites were largely devoted to casting doubt on the consensus scientific view on climate change (and, not by coincidence, to preserving the status quo for the coal industry, the oil and gas industry, and so on). Where such ideologically charged issues as these are concerned, it is worth paying particularly close attention to accounts that run counter to the normal ideological stance of the publication. When the right-wing magazine *The Economist* accepted several years ago that the weight of evidence overwhelmingly supported the argument that global warming posed a real danger, or when the left-of-centre British newspaper *The Guardian* concluded that despite its socialist rhetoric the Mugabe government in Zimbabwe was denying its people both economic justice and basic human rights, such views deserve special respect.

Finally, the experienced researcher is willing to trust her own judgement: to glance at the table of contents and skim quickly through two or three dozen works on a subject and in each case make a snap decision as to its likely usefulness. These decisions are not, of course, irreversible; she may well find that one of the books initially set aside with barely a moment's notice is generally regarded as among the most important works in the field (in which case she will, of course, return to it with more care). But she must in the first instance have some way of making the mass of material manageable.

What of the opposite problem? What if there seems to be little or nothing published on the subject? Perhaps it's an area on the border with one or more other territories; in that case, surveying those territories may be necessary. Perhaps it's a relatively new subject; in that case—as indeed for any research—it's always helpful to check the relevant indices of journal articles. Some of the most important of these for work in the arts and social sciences are as follows:

- *Humanities Index:* covers articles published from 1974 onwards in such disciplines as English, history, and philosophy.
- *MLA Bibliography:* offers articles on the English language and literature as well as on French, German, Italian, Spanish, and so on.
- *Philosopher's Index:* the most comprehensive listing of articles on philosophy.
- *Social Sciences Index:* covers articles published from 1974 onwards in such areas as anthropology, economics, political science, psychology, and sociology.

These days, virtually all indices appear in electronic form; keyword searches are indispensable for researchers. The idea is to use a single word—or a combination of words—that you consider to be the "key" or main focus of your topic. The computer system will look through every author, title, and subject heading that includes the keywords (in any order). Queen's University provides its students with the following "Basic Search Tips":

Title or journal article
- Omit initial article (*a*, *the*, *le*)
- Type just the first few words
- Use journal title for magazines, journals, newspapers

Research

Author
- Type last name first: *einstein, a*
- Add first initial if known
- For organizations use normal word order

Keyword
- Results can include any of your words
- Must use + to indicate essential terms
- Use ? to truncate; use quotes for phrases: "*meech lake*"

Call number
- Include punctuation and spaces

One further note about academic research in the second decade of the twenty-first century: it's worth remembering that your academic library doesn't exist only in electronic form. It still has a physical location, where you will be sure to find a number of helpful librarians. Their job is to help you understand how to do research and do it well; they really can help. And the library also provides a great deal of material that you can touch and turn the pages of. It's worth doing that for at least two reasons. One is the process of browsing in the stacks of the library can lead you to make connections and generate ideas in ways that don't always happen when you are searching and reading online. The second may surprise you: some important material is simply not available electronically. That's not only true of certain books and articles from decades or centuries ago; it's also true of some very recent material. The respected academic journal *Studies in Canadian Literature*, for example, is available only in bound volumes for the first three years after publication; you can access an article that's three years old electronically, but for a recent article you'll need to check out your library in person—unless you subscribe to the journal yourself.

Whether the information comes from bound volumes of printed material or articles in an electronic database, when it comes time to use research in an essay it is essential to strike an appropriate balance between one's own ideas and those of others.

35. AVOIDING PLAGIARISM

When incorporating research into their essays, good writers are careful to document their sources accurately and completely. This is, first of all, a service to readers who would like to embark on a fuller investigation into the topic of a paper by looking up its sources themselves; every academic citation system gives readers all the information they need to access original source material. But it is also critical that there be complete clarity about which parts of an essay are the author's and which parts come from elsewhere. To allow any blurriness on this question is to be dishonest, to engage in a kind of cheating, in fact—known as plagiarism.

Most people understand that taking someone else's writing and passing it off as one's own is intellectual thievery. But it is important to be aware that you may commit plagiarism even if you do not use precisely the same words another person wrote in precisely the same order. For instance, here is an actual example of plagiarism. *Globe and Mail* newspaper columnist Margaret Wente borrowed material for one of her columns from a number of works, including an article by Dan Gardner that had appeared the previous year in another newspaper (the *Ottawa Citizen*) and a book by Robert Paarlberg called *Starved for Science* (which was the subject of Gardner's article). The similarities were brought to light by media commentator Carol Wainio, who presented a series of parallel passages, including the following, on her blog *Media Culpa* (the fonts are Wainio's—simple bold is for direct copying; the bold + italics is for "near copying"):

> Gardner: ***Many NGOs working in Africa in the area of development and the environment have been advocating against the modernization of traditional farming practices***, Paarlberg says. "**They believe that traditional farming in Africa incorporates indigenous knowledge that shouldn't be replaced by science-based knowledge introduced from the outside.** They encourage Africa to stay away from fertilizers, and be certified as organic

instead. And in the case of genetic engineering, they warn African governments against making these technologies available to farmers."

Wente: ***Yet, many NGOs working in Africa have tenaciously fought the modernization of traditional farming practices.*** **They believe traditional farming in Africa incorporates indigenous knowledge that shouldn't be replaced by science-based knowledge introduced from the outside.** As Prof. Paarlberg writes, "They encourage African farmers to stay away from fertilizers and be certified organic instead. And they warn African governments to stay away from genetic engineering."

Wente does not always use exactly the same words as her sources, but no one reading the passages can doubt that one writer is appropriating the phrasings of the others. Additionally, where Wente *does* quote Paarlberg directly, the quotation is lifted from Gardner's article and should be identified as such.

The penalties for such practices are not trivial; Wente was publicly reprimanded by her employer, and the CBC radio program *Q* removed her from its media panel. Other reporters have been, justifiably, fired under similar circumstances. At most colleges and universities, students are likely to receive a zero if they are caught plagiarizing—and they may be expelled from the institution. It's important to be aware, too, that penalties for plagiarism make no allowance for intent; it is no defense that a writer took someone else's words "by mistake" rather than intentionally.

How, then, can you be sure to avoid plagiarism? First of all, be extremely careful in your note-taking, so as to make it impossible to imagine, a few days later, that words you have jotted down from somewhere else are your own. This is why notes need to be in a separate file or book from your own ideas. (In her *Globe and Mail* column responding to the plagiarism charges, Wente, in fact, claimed that she had accidentally mixed a quotation into her own ideas.) If your note-taking is reliable, then you will know which words need to be credited. One way to rewrite the passage above would simply be to remove the material taken from Gardner and to credit Paarlberg by quoting him directly, if you were able to access his book and could do so: "As Robert Paarlberg has argued in his book *Starved for Science*, many NGOs 'believe that traditional farming in Africa incorporates indigenous knowledge that shouldn't be replaced by science-based knowledge introduced from the outside.'" You would, of course, look up and provide the page number as well.

You may notice that the quoted material is a statement of opinion rather than fact—controversial views are being given, but without any evidence provided to back them up—so a careful reader would wonder whether NGOs are really as anti-science as the quotation suggests, or whether the writer hasn't done enough research on the debate. If you were to make an assertion like this in a paper of your own it would not be enough just to quote Paarlberg; you would need to do much more research and find information to support or deny your claim. If you are including quotations in an essay, the best sources to quote are not necessarily those which express opinions that mirror the ones you are putting forward. In a case such as this, for example, the argument would have been much more persuasive if Wente had quoted an official statement from one of the NGOs she was attacking. If her article had quoted a source making this specific case against "science-based knowledge" and then argued directly against that source's argument, Wente's own position would have been strengthened. Quoting many such sources would provide proof that the article's characterization of the position of NGOs was factually accurate.

Whenever you do quote someone else, it's important to cite the source. But do you need a citation for everything that did not come from your own knowledge? Not necessarily. Citations are usually unnecessary when you are touching on common knowledge (provided it is, in fact, common knowledge, and provided your instructor has not asked you to do otherwise). If you refer to the chemical composition of water, or the date when penicillin was discovered, you are unlikely to need to provide any citation, even if you used a source to find the information, since such facts are generally available and uncontroversial. (Make sure, however, to check any "common knowledge" with several reputable sources; if your information is incorrect, it reflects poorly on you, especially if you have not cited your source.) If you have any doubts about whether something is common knowledge or not, cite it; over-cautiousness is not a serious problem, but plagiarism always is.

36. CITATION AND DOCUMENTATION

Citing sources is fundamental to writing a good research paper, but no matter how diligent you are in making your acknowledgements, your paper will not be taken seriously unless its documentation is formatted according to an appropriate and accepted referencing style. For the sake of consistency, each academic discipline has adopted a particular system of referencing as its standard, which those writing in that discipline are expected to follow. *The Broadview Pocket Guide to Citation and Documentation* outlines the four most common of these systems. Almost all of the humanities use the documentation guidelines developed by the Modern Language Association (MLA), a notable exception being history, which tends to prefer those of the *Chicago Manual of Style* (Chicago Style). The social and some health sciences typically follow the style rules of the American Psychological Association (APA), while the basic sciences most commonly use the referencing systems of the Council of Science Editors (CSE). Each of these styles is exacting and comprehensive in its formatting rules; following with precision the one recommended for a given paper's discipline is one of a responsible research writer's duties. Details of these systems are in the pages that follow.

As important as documentation is to a well-written paper, by itself it is not always enough. Writers must also be attentive to the ways in which they integrate borrowed material into their essays.

36a. Incorporating Sources

There are three main ways of working source material into a paper: summarizing, paraphrasing, and quoting directly. In order to avoid plagiarism, care must be taken with all three kinds of borrowing, both in the way they are handled and in their referencing. In what follows, a passage from page 102 of a book by Terrence W. Deacon (*The Symbolic Species: The Co-Evolution of Language and the Brain*, New York: Norton, 1997) serves as the source for a sample summary, paraphrase, and quotation. The examples feature the MLA style of in-text parenthetical citations, but the requirements for presenting the source material are the same for all academic referencing systems. For a similar discussion with a focus on APA style, see Incorporating Sources in APA Style (starting on page 244).

original source Over the last few decades language researchers seem to have reached a consensus that language is an innate ability, and that only a significant contribution from innate knowledge can explain our ability to learn such a complex communication system. Without question, children enter the world predisposed to learn human languages. All normal children, raised in normal social environments, inevitably learn their local language, whereas other species, even when raised and taught in this same environment, do not. This demonstrates that human brains come into the world specially equipped for this function.

● Summarizing

An honest and competent summary, whether of a passage or an entire book, must not only represent the source accurately but also use original wording and include a citation. It is a common misconception that only quotations need to be acknowledged as borrowings in the body of an essay. In fact, without a citation, even a fairly worded summary or paraphrase is an act of plagiarism. The first example below is faulty on two counts:

it borrows wording (underlined) from the source, and it has no parenthetical reference.

needs checking <u>Researchers</u> agree that language learning is <u>innate, and that only innate knowledge can explain</u> how we are able <u>to learn</u> a <u>system</u> of <u>communication</u> that is so <u>complex</u>. <u>Normal children raised in normal</u> ways will always <u>learn their local language</u>, <u>whereas other species do not, even when taught</u> human language and exposed to the <u>same environment</u>.

The next example correctly avoids the wording of the source passage, and a signal phrase and parenthetical citation note the author and page number.

revised As Terrence W. Deacon notes, there is now wide agreement among linguists that the ease with which human children acquire their native tongues, under the conditions of a normal childhood, demonstrates an inborn capacity for language that is not shared by any other animals, not even those who are reared in comparable ways and given human language training (102).

● Paraphrasing

Whereas a summary is a shorter version of its original, a paraphrase tends to be about the same length. However, paraphrases, just like summaries, must reflect their sources accurately, must use original wording, and must include a citation. Even though it is properly cited, the paraphrase of the first sentence of the Deacon passage, below, falls short by being too close to the wording of the original (underlined).

needs checking <u>Researchers</u> in <u>language</u> have come to <u>a consensus</u> in the past <u>few decades</u> that the acquisition of language is <u>innate</u>; such <u>contributions</u> <u>from knowledge</u> <u>contribute significantly</u> to <u>our ability</u> to master <u>such a complex system</u> of <u>communication</u> (Deacon 102).

Simply substituting synonyms for the words and phrases of the source, however, is not enough to avoid plagiarism. Despite its original wording, the next example also fails but for a very different reason: it follows the original's sentence structure too closely, as illustrated in the interpolated copy below it.

needs checking   Recently, linguists appear to have come to an agreement that speaking is an inborn skill, and that nothing but a substantial input from inborn cognition can account for the human capacity to acquire such a complicated means of expression (Deacon 102).

Recently (*over the last few decades*), linguists (*language researchers*) appear to have come to an agreement (*seem to have reached a consensus*) that speaking is an inborn skill (*that language is an innate ability*), and that nothing but a substantial input (*and that only a significant contribution*) from inborn cognition (*from innate knowledge*) can account for the human capacity (*can explain our ability*) to acquire such a complicated means of expression (*to learn such a complex communication system*) (Deacon 102).

What follows is a good paraphrase of the passage's opening sentence; this paraphrase captures the sense of the original without echoing the details and shape of its language.

revised   Linguists now broadly agree that children are born with the ability to learn language; in fact, the human capacity to acquire such a difficult skill cannot easily be accounted for in any other way (Deacon 102).

● Quoting Directly

Unlike paraphrases and summaries, direct quotations must use the exact wording of the original. Because they involve importing outside words, quotations pose unique challenges.

Quote too frequently, and you risk making your readers wonder why they are not reading your sources instead of your paper. Your essay should present something you want to say—informed and supported by properly documented sources, but forming a contribution that is yours alone. To that end, use secondary material to help you build a strong framework for your work, not to replace it. Quote sparingly, therefore; use your sources' exact wording only when it is important or particularly memorable.

To avoid misrepresenting your sources, be sure to quote accurately, and to avoid plagiarism, take care to indicate quotations as quotations, and cite them properly. Below are two problematic quotations. The first does not show which words come directly from the source.

needs checking   Terrence W. Deacon maintains that children enter the world predisposed to learn human languages (102).

The second quotation fails to identify the source at all.

needs checking   Linguists believe that "children enter the world predisposed to learn human languages."

The next example corrects both problems by naming the source and indicating clearly which words come directly from it.

revised   Terrence W. Deacon maintains that "children enter the world predisposed to learn human languages" (102).

● Formatting Quotations

There are two ways to signal an exact borrowing: by enclosing it in double quotation marks and by indenting it as a block of text. Which you should choose depends on the length and genre of the quotation and the style guide you are following.

Short prose quotations

What counts as a short prose quotation differs among the various reference guides. In MLA style, "short" means up to four lines; in APA, up to forty words; and in Chicago Style, up to one hundred words. All the guides agree, however, that short quotations must be enclosed in double quotation marks, as in the examples below.

Short quotation, full sentence:
According to Terrence W. Deacon, linguists agree that a human child's capacity to acquire language is inborn: "Without question, children enter the world predisposed to learn human languages" (102).

Short quotation, partial sentence:
According to Terrence W. Deacon, linguists agree that human "children enter the world predisposed to learn human languages" (102).

Long prose quotations

Longer prose quotations should be double-spaced and indented, as a block, one tab space from the left margin. Do not include quotation marks; the indentation indicates that the words come exactly from the source. Note that indented quotations are often introduced with a full sentence followed by a colon.

Terrence W. Deacon, like most other linguists, believes that human beings are born with a unique cognitive capacity:

Without question, children enter the world predisposed to learn human languages. All normal children, raised in normal social environments, inevitably learn their local language, whereas other species, even when raised and taught in this same environment, do not. This demonstrates that human brains come into the world specially equipped for this function. (102)

Verse quotations

Quoting from verse is a special case. Poetry quotations of three or fewer lines (MLA) may be integrated into your paragraph and enclosed in double quotation marks, with lines separated by a forward slash with a space on either side of it, as in the example below.

> Pope's "Epistle II. To a Lady," in its vivid portrayal of wasted lives, sharply criticizes the social values that render older women superfluous objects of contempt: "Still round and round the Ghosts of Beauty glide, / And haunt the places where their Honor dy'd" (lines 241–42).

If your quotation of three or fewer lines includes a stanza break, MLA style requires you to mark the break by inserting two forward slashes (//), with spaces on either side of them.

> The speaker in "Ode to a Nightingale" seeks, in various ways, to free himself from human consciousness, leaving suffering behind. Keats uses alliteration and repetition to mimic the gradual dissolution of self, the process of intoxication or death: "That I might drink, and leave the world unseen, / And with thee fade away into the forest dim: // Fade far away, dissolve, and quite forget" (lines 19–21).

Poetry quotations of more than three lines in MLA, or two or more lines in Chicago Style, should be, like long prose quotations, indented and set off in a block from your main text. Arrange the lines just as they appear in the original.

> The ending of Margaret Avison's "September Street" moves from the decaying, discordant city toward a glimpse of an outer/inner infinitude:
>
> >   On the yellow porch
> >   one sits, not reading headlines; the old eyes
> >   read far out into the mild
> >   air, runes.
> >   See. There: a stray sea-gull. (lines 20–24)

Quotations within quotations

You may sometimes find, within the original passage you wish to quote, words already enclosed in double quotation marks. If your quotation is short, enclose it all in double quotation marks, and use single quotation marks for the embedded quotation.

> Terrence W. Deacon is firm in maintaining that human language differs from other communication systems in kind rather than degree: "Of no other natural form of communication is it legitimate to say that 'language is a more complicated version of that'" (44).

If your quotation is long, keep the double quotation marks of the original.

> Terrence W. Deacon is firm in maintaining that human language differs from other communication systems in kind rather than degree:
>
> > Of no other natural form of communication is it legitimate to say that "language is a more complicated version of that." It is just as misleading to call other species' communication systems *simple* languages as it is to call them languages. In addition to asserting that a Procrustean mapping of one to the other is possible, the analogy ignores the sophistication and power of animals' non-linguistic communication, whose capabilities may also be without language parallels. (44)

● Adding to or Deleting from a Quotation

While it is important to use the original's exact wording in a quotation, it is allowable to modify a quotation somewhat, as long as the changes are clearly indicated and do not distort the meaning of the original.

Using square brackets to add to a quotation

You may want to add to a quotation in order to clarify what would otherwise be puzzling or ambiguous to someone who does not know its context; in that case, put whatever you add in square brackets.

> Terrence W. Deacon writes that children are born "specially equipped for this [language] function" (102).

Using an ellipsis to delete from a quotation

If you would like to streamline a quotation by omitting anything unnecessary to your point, insert an ellipsis (three spaced dots) to show that you've left material out.

When the quotation looks like a complete sentence but is actually part of a longer sentence, you should provide an ellipsis to show that there is more to the original than you are using.

> Terrence W. Deacon says that ". . . children enter the world predisposed to learn human languages" (102).

Note that if the quotation is clearly a partial sentence, ellipses aren't necessary.

> Terrence W. Deacon writes that children are born "specially equipped" to learn human language (102).

When the omitted material runs over a sentence boundary or constitutes a whole sentence or more, insert a period plus an ellipsis.

> Terrence W. Deacon, like most other linguists, believes that human children are born with a unique ability to acquire their native language: "Without question, children enter the world predisposed to learn human languages. . . . [H]uman brains come into the world specially equipped for this function" (102).

Be sparing in modifying quotations; it is all right to have one or two altered quotations in a paper, but if you find yourself changing quotations often, or adding to and omitting from one quotation more than once, reconsider quoting at all. A paraphrase or summary is very often a more effective choice.

Integrating quotations

Quotations must be worked smoothly and grammatically into your sentences and paragraphs. Always, of course, mark quotations as such, but for the purpose of integrating them into your writing, treat them as if they were your own words. The boundary between what you say and what your source says should be grammatically seamless.

needs checking   Terrence W. Deacon points out, "whereas other species, even when raised and taught in this same environment, do not" (102).

revised   According to Terrence W. Deacon, while human children brought up under normal conditions acquire the language they are exposed to, "other species, even when raised and taught in this same environment, do not" (102).

Avoiding "dumped" quotations

Integrating quotations well also means providing a context for them. Don't merely drop them into your paper or string them together like beads on a necklace; make sure to introduce them by noting where the material comes from and how it connects to whatever point you are making.

needs checking   For many years, linguists have studied how human children acquire language. "Without question, children enter the world predisposed to learn human language" (Deacon 102).

revised   Most linguists studying how human children acquire language have come to share the conclusion articulated here by Terrence W. Deacon: "Without question, children enter the world predisposed to learn human language" (102).

needs checking   "Without question, children enter the world predisposed to learn human language" (Deacon 102). "There is . . . something special about human brains that enables us to do with ease what no other species can do even minimally without intense effort and remarkably insightful training" (Deacon 103).

revised   Terrence W. Deacon bases his claim that we "enter the world predisposed to learn human language" on the fact that very young humans can "do with ease what no other species can do even minimally without intense effort and remarkably insightful training" (102–03).

● Signal Phrases

To leave no doubt in your readers' minds about which parts of your essay are yours and which come from elsewhere, identify the sources of your summaries, paraphrases, and quotations with signal phrases, as in the following examples.

- As Carter and Rosenthal have demonstrated, . . .
- In the words of one researcher, . . .
- In his most recent book McGann advances the view that, as he puts it, . . .
- As Nussbaum observes, . . .
- Kendal suggests that . . .
- Freschi and other scholars have rejected these claims, arguing that . . .
- Morgan has emphasized this point in her recent research: . . .
- As Sacks puts it, . . .
- To be sure, Mtele allows that . . .
- In his later novels Hardy takes a bleaker view, frequently suggesting that . . .

In order to help establish your paper's credibility, you may also find it useful at times to include in a signal phrase information that shows why readers should take the source seriously, as in the following example:

In her landmark work, biologist and conservationist Rachel Carson warns that . . .

Here, the signal phrase mentions the author's professional credentials; it also points out the importance of her book, which is appropriate to do in the case of a work as famous as Carson's *Silent Spring*.

Below is a fuller list of words and expressions that may be useful in the crafting of signal phrases:

according to _____,	endorses
acknowledges	finds
adds	grants
admits	illustrates
advances	implies
agrees	in the view of _____,
allows	in the words of _____,
argues	insists
asserts	intimates
attests	notes
believes	observes
claims	points out
comments	puts it
compares	reasons
concludes	refutes
confirms	rejects
contends	reports
declares	responds
demonstrates	suggests
denies	takes issue with
disputes	thinks
emphasizes	writes

Additional Material
The discussion above of
"Your Arguments, Others' Arguments" (pages 42–44)
may also be helpful.

CONTENTS

37. MLA STYLE

"MLA style" refers to the referencing guidelines of the Modern Language Association, which are favoured by many disciplines in the humanities. The main components of the MLA system are in-text author-page number citations, which appear in the body of an essay, and a bibliography giving publication details—the list of "Works Cited"—at the end of the essay.

This section outlines the key points of MLA style. Sample essay pages appear at the end of this section, and additional sample essays can be found on the Broadview website; go to sites.broadviewpress.com/writing. Consult the *MLA Handbook* (8th edition, 2016) if you have questions not answered here; you may also find answers at the website of the MLA, www.mla.org, where updates and answers to frequently asked questions are posted.

37a. About In-text Citations

1. in-text citations: Under the MLA system a quotation or specific reference to another work is followed by a parenthetical page reference:

- Bonnycastle refers to "the true and lively spirit of opposition" with which Marxist literary criticism invigorates the discipline (204).

    The work is then listed under "Works Cited" at the end of the essay:

- Bonnycastle, Stephen. *In Search of Authority: An Introductory Guide to Literary Theory*. 3rd ed., Broadview Press, 2007.

    (See below for information about the "Works Cited" list.)

2. no signal phrase (or author not named in signal phrase): If the context does not make it clear who the author is, that information must be added to the in-text citation. Note that no comma separates the name of the author from the page number.

- Even in recent years some have continued to believe that Marxist literary criticism invigorates the discipline with a "true and lively spirit of opposition" (Bonnycastle 204).

3. placing of in-text citations: Place in-text citations at the ends of clauses or sentences in order to keep disruption of your writing to a minimum. The citation comes before the period or comma in the surrounding sentence. (If the quotation ends with punctuation other than a period or comma, then this should precede the end of the quotation, and a period or comma should still follow the in-text citation.)

- Ricks refuted this point early on (16), but the claim has continued to be made in recent years.
- In "The Windhover," on the other hand, Hopkins bubbles over; "the mastery of the thing!" (8), he enthuses when he thinks of a bird, exclaiming shortly thereafter, "O my chevalier!" (10).

When a cited quotation is set off from the text, however, the in-text citation should be placed after the concluding punctuation.

- Muriel Jaeger draws on the following anecdote in discussing the resistance of many wealthy Victorians to the idea of widespread education for the poor:

  > In a mischievous mood, Henry Brougham once told [some well-off acquaintances who were] showing perturbation about the likely results of educating the "lower orders" that they could maintain their superiority by working harder themselves. (105)

4. in-text citation when text is in parentheses: If an in-text citation occurs within text in parentheses, square brackets are used for the reference.

- The development of a mass literary culture (or a "print culture," to use Williams's expression [88]) took several hundred years in Britain.

5. page number unavailable: Many Web sources lack page numbers. If your source has no page or section numbers, no number should be given in your citation. Do not count paragraphs yourself, as the version you are using may differ from others.

- In a recent Web posting a leading critic has clearly implied that he finds such an approach objectionable (Bhabha).

If the source gives explicit paragraph or section numbers, as many Websites do, cite the appropriate abbreviation, followed by the number.

- Early in the novel, Austen makes clear that the "business" of Mrs. Bennet's life is "to get her daughters married" (ch. 1).

- In "The American Scholar" Emerson asserts that America's "long apprenticeship to the learning of other lands" is drawing to a close (par. 7).

Note that (as is not the case with page numbers), MLA style requires a comma between author and paragraph or section numbers in a citation.

- Early in the novel, Mrs. Bennet makes it clear that her sole business in life is "to get her daughters married" (Austen, ch. 1).

6. one page or less: If a source is one page long or less, it is advisable to still provide the page number (though MLA does not require this).

- In his *Chicago Tribune* review, Bosley calls the novel's prose "excruciating" (1).

7. multiple authors: If there are two authors, both authors should be named either in the signal phrase or in the in-text citation, connected by *and*.

- Chambliss and Best argue that the importance of this novel is primarily historical (233).

- Two distinguished scholars have recently argued that the importance of this novel is primarily historical (Chambliss and Best 233).

If there are three or more authors, include only the first author's name in the in-text citation, followed by *et al.*, short for the Latin *et alia*, meaning *and others*.

- Meaning is not simply there in the text, but in the complex relationships between the text, the reader, and the Medieval world (Black et al. xxxvi).

8. corporate author: The relevant organization or the title of the piece should be included in the in-text citation if neither is included in the body of your text; make sure enough information is provided for readers to find the correct entry in your Works Cited list. Shorten a long title to avoid awkwardness, but take care that the shortened version begins with the same word as the corresponding entry in "Works Cited" so that readers can move easily from the citation to the bibliographic information. For example, *Comparative Indo-European Linguistics: An Introduction* should be shortened to *Comparative Indo-European* rather than *Indo-European Linguistics*. The first two examples below cite unsigned newspaper or encyclopedia articles; the last is a corporate author in-text citation.

- As *The New York Times* reported in one of its several December 2 articles on the Florida recount, Vice-President Gore looked tired and strained as he answered questions ("Gore Press Conference" A16).

- In the 1990s Sao Paulo began to rapidly overtake Mexico City as the world's most polluted city ("Air Pollution" 21).

- There are a number of organizations mandated "to foster the production and enjoyment of the arts in Canada" (Canada Council for the Arts 2).

9. more than one work by the same author cited: If you include more than one work by the same author in your list of Works Cited, you must make clear which work is being cited each time. This may be done either by mentioning the work in a signal phrase or by including in the citation a short version of the title.

- In *The House of Mirth*, for example, Wharton writes of love as keeping Lily and Selden "from atrophy and extinction" (282).

- Wharton sees love as possessing the power to keep humans "from atrophy and extinction" (*House of Mirth* 282).

- Love, as we learn from the experience of Lily and Selden, possesses the power to keep humans "from atrophy and extinction" (Wharton, *House of Mirth* 282).

10. multi-volume works: Note, by number, the volume you are referring to, followed by a colon and a space, before noting the page number. Use the abbreviation "vol." when citing an entire volume.

- Towards the end of *In Darkest Africa* Stanley refers to the Victoria Falls (2: 387).

- In contrast with those of the medieval period, Renaissance artworks show an increasing concern with depicting the material world and less and less of an interest in metaphysical symbolism (Hauser, vol. 2).

11. two or more authors with the same last name: If the Works Cited list includes two or more authors with the same last name, the in-text citation should supply both first initials and last names, or, if the first initials are also the same, the full first and last names:

- One of the leading economists of the time advocated wage and price controls (Harry Johnston 197).

- One of the leading economists of the time advocated wage and price controls (H. Johnston 197).

12. indirect quotations: When an original source is not available but is referred to by another source, the in-text citation includes *qtd. in* (an abbreviation of *quoted in*) and a reference to the second source. In the example below, Casewell is quoted by Bouvier; the in-text citation directs readers to an entry in Works Cited for the Bouvier work.

- Casewell considers Lambert's position to be "outrageously arrogant" (qtd. in Bouvier 59).

13. short poems: For short poems, cite line numbers rather than page numbers.

- In "Dover Beach" Arnold hears the pebbles in the waves bring the "eternal note of sadness in" (14).

If you are citing the same poem repeatedly, use just the numbers for subsequent references.

- The world, in Arnold's view, has "really neither joy, nor love, nor light" (33).

14. longer poems: For longer poems with parts, cite the part (or section, or "book") as well as the line (where available). Use Arabic numerals, and use a period for separation.

- In "Ode: Intimations of Immortality" Wordsworth calls human birth "but a sleep and a forgetting" (5.1).

15. novels or short stories: When a work of prose fiction has chapters or numbered divisions the citation should include first the page number, and then book, chapter, and section numbers as applicable. (These can be very useful in helping readers of a different edition to locate the passage you are citing.) Arabic numerals should be used. A semicolon should be used to separate the page number from the other information.

- When Joseph and Fanny are by themselves, they immediately express their affection for each other, or, as Fielding puts it, "solace themselves" with "amorous discourse" (151; ch. 26).

- In *Tender Is the Night* Dick's ambition does not quite crowd out the desire for love: "He wanted to be loved too, if he could fit it in" (133; bk. 2, ch. 4).

16. plays: Almost all plays are divided into acts and/or scenes. For plays that do not include line numbering throughout, cite the page number in the edition you have been using, followed by act and/or scene numbers as applicable:

- As Angie and Joyce begin drinking together Angie pronounces the occasion "better than Christmas" (72; act 3).

- Near the conclusion of Inchbald's *Wives as They Were* Bronzely declares that he has been "made to think with reverence on the matrimonial compact" (62; act 5, sc. 4).

For plays written entirely or largely in verse, where line numbers are typically provided throughout, you should omit the reference to page number in the citation. Instead, cite the act, scene, and line numbers, using Arabic numerals. For a Shakespeare play, if the title isn't clear from the introduction to a quotation, an abbreviation of the title may also be used. The in-text citation below is for Shakespeare's *The Merchant of Venice*, Act 2, Scene 3, lines 2–4:

- Jessica clearly has some fondness for Launcelot: "Our house is hell, and thou, a merry devil, / Dost rob it of some taste of tediousness. / But fare thee well; there is a ducat for thee" (*MV* 2.3.2–4).

17. works without page numbers: If you are citing literary texts where you have consulted editions from other sources (on the Web or in an ebook, for instance), the principles are exactly the same, except that you need not cite page numbers. For example, if the online Gutenberg edition of Fielding's *Joseph Andrews* were being cited, the citation would be as follows:

- When Joseph and Fanny are by themselves, they immediately express their affection for each other, or, as Fielding puts it, "solace themselves" with "amorous discourse" (ch. 26).

Students should be cautioned that online editions of literary texts are often unreliable. Typically there are far more typos and other errors in online versions of literary texts than there are in print versions, and such things as the layout of poems are also frequently incorrect. It is often possible to exercise judgement about such matters, however. If, for example, you are not required to base your essay on a particular copy of a Thomas Hardy poem but may find your own, you will be far better off using the text you will find on the Representative Poetry Online site run out of the University of Toronto than you will using a text you might find on a "World's Finest Love Poems" site.

18. sacred texts: The Bible and other sacred texts that are available in many editions should be cited in a way that enables the reader to check the reference in any edition. For the Bible, book, chapter, and verse should all be cited, using periods for separation. The reference below is to Genesis, chapter 2, verse 1.

- According to the Judeo-Christian story of creation, at the end of the sixth day "the heavens and the earth were finished" (Gen. 2.1).

19. works in an anthology or book of readings: In the in-text citation for a work in an anthology, use the name of the author of the work, not that of the editor of the anthology. The page number, however, should be that found in the anthology. The following citation refers to an article by Frederic W. Gleach in an anthology edited by Jennifer Brown and Elizabeth Vibert.

- One of the essays in Brown and Vibert's collection argues that we should rethink the Pocahontas myth (Gleach 48).

In your list of Works Cited, this work should be alphabetized under Gleach, the author of the piece you have consulted, not under Brown. If you cite another work by a different author from the same anthology or book of readings, that should appear as a separate entry in your list of Works Cited—again, alphabetized under the author's name.

20. tweets: Cite tweets by giving the author's name in your text rather than in an in-text citation.

- Jack Welch quickly lost credibility when he tweeted that the US Bureau of Labor had manipulated monthly unemployment rate statistics in order to boost the post-debate Obama campaign: "Unbelievable job numbers..these Chicago guys will do anything..can't debate so change numbers."

37b. About Works Cited: MLA Core Elements

The Works Cited list in MLA style is an alphabetized list at the end of the essay (or article or book). The entire list, like the main part of the essay, should be double-spaced throughout, and each entry should be given a hanging indent: the first line is flush with the left-hand margin, and each subsequent line is indented one tab space.

The Works Cited list should include information about all the sources you have cited. Do not include works that you consulted but did not cite in the body of your text.

MLA style provides a set of citation guidelines that the writer follows and adapts, regardless of whether the source being cited is print, digital, audio, visual, or any other form of media. All sources share what the MLA call "Core Elements," and these, listed in order, create the citation for all your entries: Author, Title of Source, Title of Container (larger whole), Other Contributors, Version, Number, Publisher, Publication Date, and Location. Each element is followed by the punctuation marks shown in the table below, unless it is the last element, which should always close with a period. (There are a few exceptions to this rule, which are outlined below.) Most sources don't have all the elements (some don't have an author, for example, or a version, or a location); if you find that this is the case, omit the element and move on to the next.

1. Author.
2. Title of source.
3. Title of container,
4. Other contributors,
5. Version,
6. Number,
7. Publisher,
8. Publication Date,
9. Location.

The table can function as a guide when creating citations. Once you have found all the publication details for your source, place them in order and punctuate according to the table, leaving out any elements for which you don't have information.

In the sections below, you will discover how to identify the core elements of MLA style and how to use them across media. For a list of examples, please see pages 219 to 231.

Author

This element begins your citation. For a **single author**, list the author's last name first, followed by a comma, and then the author's first name or initials (use whatever appears on the work's title page or copyright page), followed by a period.

Graham, Jorie. *From the New World.* Ecco, 2015.

McKerlie, Dennis. *Justice between the Young and the Old.* Oxford UP, 2013.

If a source has **two authors**, the first author's name should appear with the last name first, followed by a comma and *and*. Note also that the authors' names should appear in the order they are listed; sometimes this is not alphabetical.

Rectenwald, Michael, and Lisa Carl. *Academic Writing, Real World Topics.* Broadview Press, 2015.

If there are **three or more authors**, include only the first author's name, reversed, followed by a comma and *et al.* (the abbreviation of the Latin *et alia*, meaning *and others*).

Blais, Andre, et al. *Anatomy of a Liberal Victory.* Broadview Press, 2002.

Sources that are **edited** rather than authored are usually cited in a similar way; add "editor" or "editors" after the name(s) and before the title.

Renker, Elizabeth, editor. *Poems: A Concise Anthology.* Broadview Press, 2016.

When referring to an edited version of a work written by another author or authors, list the editor(s) after the title, in the Other Contributors element.

Trollope, Anthony. *The Eustace Diamonds.* 1873. Edited by Stephen Gill and John Sutherland, Penguin, 1986.

Authors can be organizations, institutions, associations, or government agencies ("corporate authors"). If a work has been issued by a **corporate author** and no author is identified, the entry should be listed by the name of the organization that produced it.

Ontario, Ministry of Natural Resources. *Achieving Balance: Ontario's Long-Term Energy Plan.* Queen's Printer for Ontario, 2016, www.energy.gov.on.ca/en/ltep/achieving-balance-ontarios-long-term-energy-plan. Accessed 10 May 2016.

If the work is published by the same organization that is the corporate author, skip the author element and list only the publisher. The citation will begin with the source title.

2014 Annual Report. Broadview Press, 2015.

"History of the Arms and Great Seal of the Commonwealth of Massachusetts." Commonwealth of Massachusetts, www.sec.state.ma.us/pre/presea/sealhis/htm. Accessed 9 May 2016.

"Our Mandate." Art Gallery of Ontario, www.ago.net/mandate. Accessed 10 May 2016.

Works with an **anonymous author** should be alphabetized by title, omitting the author element.

Sir Gawain and the Green Knight. Edited by Paul Battles, Broadview Press, 2012.

Works under a **pseudonym** should appear with the pseudonym in place of the author's name. Online usernames are copied out exactly as they appear on the screen.

@newyorker. "With the resignation of Turkey's Prime Minister, the country's President now stands alone and unchallenged." *Twitter*, 6 May 2016, twitter.com/NewYorker/status/ 728676985254379520.

Note that the author element is flexible. If you are discussing the work of a film director, for example, the director's name should be placed in the author element, with a descriptor.

Hitchcock, Alfred, director. *The Lady Vanishes*. United Artists, 1938.

If, on the other hand, you are discussing film editing, you would place the film editor in the author element. In this case, you might also include Hitchcock's name in the "Other Contributors" element.

Dearing, R.E., film editor. *The Lady Vanishes*, directed by Alfred Hitchcock, United Artists, 1938.

If no single contributor's work is of particular importance in your discussion of a film or television source, omit the author element altogether.

"The Buys." *The Wire*, created by David Simon and Ed Burns, directed by Peter Medak, season 1, episode 3, HBO, 16 June 2002, disc 1.

If you are citing a **translated source** and the translation itself is the focus of your work, the translator or translators can be placed in the author element.

Lodge, Kirsten, translator. *Notes from the Underground*. By Fyodor Dostoevsky, edited by Kirsten Lodge, Broadview Press, 2014.

When the work itself is the focus, as is usually the case, the author should remain in the author element, and the translator moved to the "other contributors" element:

Dostoevsky, Fyodor. *Notes from the Underground*. Translated and edited by Kirsten Lodge, Broadview Press, 2014.

This principle holds true across media and elements. Adapt the MLA structure to create citations that are clear, most relevant to your work, and most useful to your reader.

Title of Source

The title of your source follows the author element. Copy the title as you find it in the source, but with MLA-standard capitalization and punctuation. Capitalize the first word, the last word, and all key words, but not articles, prepositions, coordinating conjunctions, or the *to* in infinitives.

Carson, Anne. *The Albertine Workout*. New Directions, 2014.

If there is a **subtitle**, include it after the main title, following a colon.

Bök, Christian. *The Xenotext: Book 1*. Coach House Books, 2015.

Your title gives the reader information about the source. Italicized titles indicate that the source is a complete, independent whole. A title enclosed in quotation marks tells the reader that the source is part of a larger work.

A **book** is an independent whole, so the title is italicized.

Wordsworth, William. *Poems, in Two Volumes*. Edited by Richard Matlak, Broadview Press, 2016.

Other examples include **long poems** (*In Memoriam*), **magazines** (*The New Yorker*), **newspapers** (*The Guardian*), **journals** (*The American Poetry Review*), **websites** (*The Camelot Project*), **films** (*Memento*), **television shows** (*The X-Files*), and **compact discs** or **record albums** (*Dark Side of the Moon*).

A **poem**, **short story**, or **essay** within a larger collection is placed in quotation marks.

Wordsworth, William. "The Solitary Reaper." *Poems, in Two Volumes*, edited by Richard Matlak, Broadview Press, 2016, p. 153.

Other examples include **chapters in books** ("The Autist Artist" in *The Man Who Mistook His Wife for a Hat and Other Clinical Tales*), **encyclopedia articles** ("Existentialism"), **essays in books or journals** ("Salvation in the Garden: Daoism and Ecology" in *Daoism and Ecology: Ways within a Cosmic Landscape*), **short stories** ("Young Goodman Brown"), **short**

poems ("Daddy"), **pages on websites** ("The Fisher King" from *The Camelot Project*), **episodes of television shows** ("Small Potatoes" from *The X-Files*), and **songs** ("Eclipse" from *Dark Side of the Moon*). Put the titles of **public lectures** in double quotation marks as well ("Walls in *The Epic of Gilgamesh*").

These formatting rules apply across media forms. A website is placed in italics; a posting on the website is placed in quotation marks.

Stein, Sadie. "Casting the Runes." *The Daily: The Paris Review Blog*, 9 Oct. 2015, www.theparisreview.org/blog/2015/10/09/ casting-the-runes/.

If the title of a stand-alone work contains the title of a work that is not independent, the latter is put in double quotation marks, and the entire title is put in italics (*"Self-Reliance" and Other Essays*). If the title of a stand-alone work appears within the title of another independent work, MLA recommends that the latter be put in italics and the former not (*Chaucer's* House of Fame*: The Poetics of Skeptical Fideism*). If the title of a non-independent work is embedded in another title of the same kind, put the inner title into single quotation marks and the outer title in double quotation marks ("The Drama of Donne's 'The Indifferent'").

When a stand-alone work appears in a **collection**, the work's title remains in italics.

James, Henry. *The American. Henry James: Novels 1871-1880*, edited by William T. Stafford, Library of America, 1983.

Title of Container

Very often your source is found within a larger context, such as an **anthology**, **periodical**, **newspaper**, **digital platform**, or **website**. When this is the case, the larger whole is called the "container." For an article in a newspaper, for example, the article is the "source" and the newspaper is the "container." For a song in an **album**, the song is the "source" and the album is the "container."

The title of the container is usually italicized and followed by a comma.

Gladwell, Malcolm. "The Art of Failure: Why Some People Choke and Others Panic." *The New Yorker,* 21 Aug. 2000, www.newyorker.com/magazine/2000/08/21/the-art-of-failure. Accessed 18 Feb. 2013.

The container can be a website; a book that is a collection of stories, poems, plays, or essays; a magazine; a journal; an album; or a database.

When doing research, particularly online, one often comes across nested containers, in which, for example, an article is found in a collection of essays, which is itself found on a database. All containers are recorded in the citation, so your reader knows exactly how to find your source. Add more Container elements as needed. Additional containers should follow the period at the end of the information given for the preceding container (usually after the date or location element).

It can be helpful to see this process charted out. Notice that the publication information for the container follows that of the source.

Here is an example of an **article from a periodical**, accessed from an online database.

1. Author.	Sohmer, Steve.
2. Title of source.	"12 June 1599: Opening Day at Shakespeare's Globe."
CONTAINER 1:	
3. Title of container,	*Early Modern Literary Studies: A Journal of Sixteenth- and Seventeenth-Century English Literature,*
4. Other contributors,	
5. Version,	
6. Number,	vol. 3, no.1,
7. Publisher,	
8. Publication Date,	1997.
9. Location.	
CONTAINER 2:	
3. Title of container,	*ProQuest,*
4. Other contributors,	
5. Version,	
6. Number,	
7. Publisher,	
8. Publication Date,	
9. Location.	www.extra.shu.ac.uk/emls/emlshome.html.

Citation as It Would Appear in Works Cited List:

Sohmer, Steve. "12 June 1599: Opening Day at Shakespeare's Globe." *Early Modern Literary Studies: A Journal of Sixteenth- and Seventeenth-Century English Literature,* vol. 3, no.1, 1997. *ProQuest,* www.extra.shu.ac.uk/emls/emlshome.html.

The next example is an **e-book version** of Jane Austen's *Emma*, accessed from a publisher's website. The novel is self-contained, so no title of a container is given until the digital platform information is recorded in the second container.

1. Author.	Austen, Jane.
2. Title of source.	*Emma.*
CONTAINER 1:	
3. Title of container,	
4. Other contributors,	Edited by Kristen Flieger Samuelian,
5. Version,	
6. Number,	
7. Publisher,	
8. Publication Date,	2004.
9. Location.	
CONTAINER 2:	
3. Title of container,	*Broadview Press,*
4. Other contributors,	
5. Version,	
6. Number,	
7. Publisher,	
8. Publication Date,	
9. Location.	www.broadviewpress.com/ product/emma/#tab-description.

Citation as It Would Appear in Works Cited List:

Austen, Jane. *Emma.* Edited by Kristen Flieger Samuelian, 2004. *Broadview Press,* www.broadviewpress.com/product/emma/#tab-description. Accessed 5 Feb. 2016.

The elements are recorded sequentially to create your citation. Notice that any elements that don't apply to this source are left out. Any element that is the same for both containers (in this case, the publisher) is recorded in the last (here the second) container; however, the location of this e-book (the website) contains the name of the publisher, so in this case the publisher field is left empty. This removes the need to repeat information in the citation.

Here is an example citation of a **performance in a television series**, accessed on Netflix.

1. Author.	Spacey, Kevin, performer.
2. Title of source.	"Chapter 5."
CONTAINER 1:	
3. Title of container,	*House of Cards*,
4. Other contributors,	directed by Joel Schumacher,
5. Version,	
6. Number,	season 1, episode 5,
7. Publisher,	
8. Publication Date,	2013.
9. Location.	
CONTAINER 2:	
3. Title of container,	Netflix,
4. Other contributors,	
5. Version,	
6. Number,	
7. Publisher,	
8. Publication Date,	
9. Location.	www.netflix.com/search/house? jbv=70178217&jbp=0&jbr=021.

Citation as It Would Appear in Works Cited List:

Spacey, Kevin, performer. "Chapter 5." *House of Cards*, directed by Joel
  Schumacher, season 1, episode 5, 2013. *Netflix*, www.netflix.com/
  search/house?jbv=70178217&jbp=0&jbr=021.

Notice that in this case Netflix produced the show, so the publisher field is left empty in both containers. If the source had
been an episode from a series produced by, for example, the
BBC, you would include the BBC as publisher.

Tennant, David, performer. "Gridlock." *Dr. Who*, directed by Richard
  Clark, series 3, episode 3, BBC, 2007. *Netflix*, www.netflix.com/
  search/dr%20who?jbv=70142441&jbp=0&jbr=0.

Other Contributors

There may be other key people who should be credited in
your citation as contributors. This element follows the title
of the source and the container (if there is one). The MLA
recommends that you include the names of contributors who
are important to your research, or if they help your reader to
identify the source. Before each name, place a description of
the role (do not abbreviate):

adapted by	introduction by
directed by	narrated by
edited by	performance by
illustrated by	translated by

If your listing of a contributor follows the source title, it is
capitalized (following a period). If the contributor follows a
container, it will be lower-case (following a comma).

Lao Tzu. *Tao Te Ching: A Book about the Way and the Power of the
  Way*. Translated by Ursula K. Le Guin. Shambhala, 1997.

James, Henry. *The American. Henry James: Novels 1871-1880*, edited
  by William T. Stafford, Library of America, 1983.

In the Other Contributors element, include the most relevant
contributors not already mentioned in the author element. If

you are writing about a television episode and a certain performance is one of the elements you discuss, for example, include the performer's name in the Other Contributors element, along with any other contributors you wish to include.

Medak, Peter, director. "The Buys." *The Wire*, created by David Simon and Ed Burns, performance by Dominic West, season 1, episode 3, HBO, 16 June 2002.

Note that the MLA guidelines are flexible; for this part of the citation especially, consider what your readers most need to know about your source and include that information. Note also that there is some flexibility in the author element; if a particular performance or other contribution is the major focus in your discussion of source, it can be cited in the author element instead.

Version

If your source is **one of several editions**, or if it is a **revised version**, record those details in this element of your citation, followed by a comma. The word "edition" is abbreviated in your citation (ed.).

Fowles, John. *The Magus*. Rev. ed., Jonathan Cape, 1977.

Shelley, Mary. *Frankenstein*. Edited by D.L. Macdonald and Kathleen Sherf, 3rd ed., Broadview Press, 2012.

You may also come across **expanded editions**, **revised editions**, and **updated editions**, all of which can be noted in this element of your citation. Different media might use different terminology. For example in film you may find a **director's cut**, or in music an **abridged version** of a concerto: use the same principles as above, providing the relevant information in the Version element of your citation.

Coen, Ethan, and Joel Coen, directors. *Blood Simple*. Director's cut, Universal, 2001.

Number

If your source is part of a **multi-volumed work**, or if it is part of a journal that is issued in numbers and/or volumes, include the volume information in this Number element of your citation.

If you are citing **two or more volumes** of a multi-volume work, the entry should note the total number of volumes. If you cite only one of the volumes, list it after the title.

Jeeves, Julie, editor. *A Reference Guide to Spanish Architecture.* 3 vols, Hackett, 2005.

Mercer, Bobby, editor. *A Reference Guide to French Architecture.* Vol. 1, Hackett, 2002.

Include the **volume and issue numbers** for journals. Use the abbreviations *vol.* for volume and *no.* for issue number.

Gregory, Elizabeth. "Marianne Moore's 'Blue Bug': A Dialogic Ode on Celebrity, Race, Gender, and Age." *Modernism/Modernity*, vol. 22, no. 4, 2015, pp. 759–86.

Some journals do not use volume numbers and give only an issue number.

Sanger, Richard. "Goodbye, Seamus." *Brick*, no. 93, Summer 2014, pp. 153–57.

The Number element is also where you record issue numbers for comic books, or the season and episode numbers for a television series.

Spacey, Kevin, performer. "Chapter 5." *House of Cards*, directed by Joel Schumacher, season 1, episode 5, 2013. *Netflix*, www.netflix.com/search/house?jbv=70178217&jbp=0&jbr=021.

Publisher

In this element of your citation, record the organization that produced the source, whether it be publisher of a book, the organization running a website, or the studio producing a film.

(In the case of a secondary container, include the organization that produced the container.) Do not abbreviate, except in the case of university presses, which may be abbreviated as *UP*.

To find the publisher of a **book**, look on the title page or on the copyright page.

Dickens, Charles. *The Uncommercial Traveller*. Edited by Daniel Tyler, Oxford UP, 2015.

Rush, Rebecca. *Kelroy*. Edited by Betsy Klimasmith, Broadview Press, 2016.

For a **film** or **television series**, the studio or company that produced the show is recorded in the information on the back of a DVD or in the opening and closing credits.

Simon, David, creator. *The Wire*. HBO, 2002–2008.

For **websites**, the publisher's information can often be found in the copyright notice at the bottom of the page.

Bogan, Louise. "Women." 1922. *Representative Poetry Online*, edited by Ian Lancashire, University of Toronto, 2000.

A **blog network** may be cited as the publisher of the blogs it hosts.

Cairney, Paul, and Kathryn Oliver. "If scientists want to influence policymaking, they need to understand it." *Political Science*, The Guardian Science Blog Network, 27 Apr. 2016.

You may omit a publisher's name in the following kinds of publications:

- A periodical (journal, magazine, newspaper).
- A work published by its author or editor.
- A website whose title is essentially the same as the name of the publisher.
- A website not involved in producing the works it is making available (YouTube, JSTOR, ProQuest). These are listed as containers, but not as publishers.

If **two or more publishers** are listed for your source, cite them both and separate them with a forward slash (/).

Banting, Keith G., editor. *Thinking Outside the Box: Innovation in Policy Ideas*. School of Policy Studies, Queen's University / McGill–Queen's University Press, 2015.

Publication Date

In this element of your citation, record the date of publication for your source. For **books**, this date is found on the copyright page (and sometimes on the title page). If several editions are listed, use the date for the edition you have consulted.

Stevenson, Robert Louis. *Strange Case of Dr. Jekyll and Mr. Hyde*. Edited by Martin A. Danahay, 3rd ed., Broadview Press, 2015.

Online sources almost always have a date posted, and this is the date you should record in this element.

Heller, Nathan. "The Big Uneasy: What's Roiling the Liberal-Arts Campus?" *The New Yorker*, 30 May 2016, www.newyorker.com/magazine/2016/05/30/the-new-activism-of-liberal-arts-colleges.

A source may be associated with **more than one publication date**. An article online may have been previously published in print, or an article printed in a book may have been published previously in a periodical. In this case, the MLA recommends that you record the date that is most relevant to your use of the source. If you consulted the online version of an article, for example, ignore the date of print publication and cite the online publication date.

For books, we record the year of publication. For other sources, whether to include a year, month, and day depends on your source and the context in which you are using it. If you are citing an **episode from a television series**, for example, it is usually enough to record the year it aired.

Medak, Peter, director. "The Buys." *The Wire*, created by David Simon and Ed Burns, season 1, episode 3, HBO, 2002.

If, however, the context surrounding the episode is being discussed in your work, you should be more specific about the date:

Medak, Peter, director. "The Buys." *The Wire*, created by David Simon and Ed Burns, season 1, episode 3, HBO, 16 June 2002.

For a **video posted on a website**, include the date on which the video was posted. In the example below, the posting date should be included in the second container, which records the details for the digital platform. The date the video was released is included in the publication details for the source.

Gleeson, Thomas, director. *Home*. Screen Innovation Production, 2012. *Vimeo*, uploaded by Thomas Gleeson, 31 Jan. 2013, www.vimeo.com/58630796.

If you are citing a **comment posted on a Web page**, and the time the content was posted is indicated, include the time in your entry.

Evan. Comment on "Another Impasse on Gun Bills, Another Win for Hyperpolitics." *The New York Times*, 21 June 2016, 9:02 a.m., www.nytimes.com/2016/06/22/us/politics/washington-congress-gun-control.html.

Larger projects are created over a longer span of time. If you are documenting a Web project as a whole, include the full range of years during which it was developed.

Secord, James A., et al., editors. *Darwin Correspondence Project*. 1974–2016, www.darwinproject.ac.uk/.

The dates of publication for **periodicals** vary. Include in full the information provided by the copyright page, whether it be indicated by season, year, month, week, or day.

Sanger, Richard. "Goodbye, Seamus." *Brick*, no. 93, Summer 2014, pp. 153–57.

Trousdale, Rachel. "'Humor Saves Steps': Laughter and Humanity in Marianne Moore." *Journal of Modern Literature,* vol. 35, no. 3, 2012, pp.121–38. *JSTOR*, www.jstor.org/stable/10.2979/jmodelite.35.3.121.

Location

The content of the Location element varies considerably between print, digital, and other sources.

For **print sources** within a periodical or anthology, record a page number (preceded by p.) or a range of page numbers (preceded by pp.).

Gregory, Elizabeth. "Marianne Moore's 'Blue Bug': A Dialogic Ode on Celebrity, Race, Gender, and Age." *Modernism/Modernity*, vol. 22, no. 4, 2015, pp. 759–86.

Walcott, Derek. "The Sea Is History." *The Broadview Anthology of Poetry*, edited by Herbert Rosengarten and Amanda Goldrick Jones, Broadview Press, 1992, p. 757.

Wills, Garry. "A Masterpiece on the Rise of Christianity." Review of *Through the Eye of a Needle: Wealth, the Fall of Rome, and the Making of Christianity in the West, 350–550 AD*, by Peter Brown. *New York Review of Books*, 11 Oct. 2012, pp. 43–45.

An **online work** is located by its URL, or Web address. When copying the URL into your citation, remove the *http://*; this means that usually the URL will begin with *www*. If you need to break a URL over two or more lines, do not insert any hyphens at the break point; instead, when possible, break after a colon or slash or before other marks of punctuation.

Trousdale, Rachel. "'Humor Saves Steps': Laughter and Humanity in Marianne Moore." *Journal of Modern Literature* vol. 35, no. 3, 2012, pp. 121–38. *JSTOR*, www.jstor.org/stable/10.2979/jmodelite.35.3.121.

Some publishers assign DOIs (Digital Object Identifiers) to their online publications, and these, when available, are preferable to URLs, as they do not change when the source moves (whereas URLs do). If your source has no DOI but offers a "stable" URL, choose that one to include in your citation. The publisher in this case has agreed not to change the URL.

Yearling, R. "*Hamlet* and the Limits of Narrative." *Essays in Criticism: A Quarterly Journal of Literary Criticism,* vol. 65, no. 4, 2015, pp. 368–82. *Proquest,* doi:dx.doi.org/10.1093/escrit/cgv022.

We find a **television episode** on a DVD by its disc number. Place the disc number in the Location element.

"The Buys." *The Wire,* created by David Simon and Ed Burns, directed by Peter Medak, season 1, episode 3, HBO, 2002, disc 1.

For a **work of art** that you have seen in person, cite the name of the institution and city where you saw it in the Location element. Leave out the name of the city if the city name is part of the institution name (e.g., The Art Institute of Chicago).

Sargent, John Singer. *Henry James.* 1913, National Portrait Gallery, London.

Some **archived sources** have a different system for locating objects in the archive. Where this is the case, include the code or number in the Location element.

Blake, William. *The Marriage of Heaven and Hell.* 1790–1793. The Fitzwilliam Museum, Cambridge, 123-1950. Illuminated printed book.

If you are citing a **live performance** or **lecture**, name the location and the city. Omit the city name if it is part of the location name.

Royal Winnipeg Ballet. *The Princess and the Goblin.* Directed and choreographed by Twyla Tharp, performances by Paloma Herrera and Dmitri Dovgoselets, 17 Oct. 2012, Centennial Concert Hall, Winnipeg.

Optional Elements

You may include any of the following elements in your citation if you think they are helpful to your reader.

Date of Original Publication

If your source has been republished, it may give your reader some important context if you include the date of original publication. If you do so, place the date immediately after the source title and close with a period.

Trollope, Anthony. *The Eustace Diamonds*. 1873. Edited by Stephen Gill and John Sutherland, Penguin, 1986.

City of Publication

Including the city of publication is not very useful these days, so the MLA has decided to remove this element from citations. There are two situations, however, where you may wish to include the city. If the book was published before 1900, the city of publication is associated more closely with the source than the publisher. For these books, you may substitute the city of publication for the publisher.

Dickens, Charles. *Our Mutual Friend*. Vol. 1, New York, 1800.

Some publishers release more than one version of a text in different countries (a British and an American edition, for example). In you are reading an unexpected version of a text, or the version you are reading has historical significance, place the name of the city in front of the publisher.

Lawrence, D.H. *Lady Chatterley's Lover*. London, Penguin, 1960.

Books in a Series

If your source is a book in a series, you may add the series name in roman (i.e., without italics) at the end of your citation, preceded by a period.

Shakespeare, William. *As You Like It*. Edited by David Bevington, Broadview Press, 2012. Broadview Internet Shakespeare Editions.

Unexpected Type of Work

If your source needs further explanation, place a descriptive term (e-mail, transcript, broadcast, street performance, talk, address) at the end of the citation, preceded by a period.

Rosenheim, Jeff. "Diane Arbus." Art Gallery of Ontario, 6 May 2016, Toronto. Lecture.

Date of Access

It is optional to include a date of access for your online citations, but it can be a good idea, particularly if the source does not have a date of publication.

Crawford, Isabella Valancy. "The Canoe." *Representative Poetry Online*, edited by Ian Lancashire, Web Development Group, Information Technology Services, University of Toronto Libraries, www.tspace.library.utoronto.ca/html/1807/4350/poem596.html. Accessed 24 Nov. 2015.

37c. Examples

The following are examples of MLA-style citations for sources across various media. While these examples can offer useful guidance, remember that the MLA guidelines may be adapted to suit the details of the sources you are documenting, as well as the context in which you are using them.

21. single author:

Graham, Jorie. *From the New World*. Ecco, 2015.

Malory, Thomas. *Le Morte D'Arthur: Selections*. Edited by Maureen Okun, Broadview Press, 2014.

22. two authors:

Auden, W.H., and Louis MacNiece. *Letters from Iceland*. Faber & Faber, 2002.

Rectenwald, Michael, and Lisa Carl. *Academic Writing, Real World Topics*. Broadview Press, 2015.

23. three or more authors:

Blais, Andre, et al. *Anatomy of a Liberal Victory*. Broadview Press, 2002.

Fromkin, Victoria, et al. *An Introduction to Language*. 4th Canadian ed., Nelson, 2010.

24. corporate author:

2014 Annual Report. Broadview Press, 2015.

"History of the Arms and Great Seal of the Commonwealth of Massachusetts." Commonwealth of Massachusetts, www.sec .state.ma.us/pre/presea/sealhis/htm. Accessed 9 May 2016.

Ontario, Ministry of Natural Resources. *Achieving Balance: Ontario's Long-Term Energy Plan.* Queen's Printer for Ontario, 2016, www.energy.gov.on.ca/en/ltep/achieving-balance-ontarios-long-term-energy-plan. Accessed 10 May 2016.

25. works with an anonymous author: Works with an anonymous author should be alphabetized by title.

Beowulf. Edited and translated by R. M. Liuzza. 2nd ed., Broadview Press, 2012.

26. two or more works by the same author: The author's name should appear for the first entry only; for subsequent entries substitute three hyphens for the name of the author.

Menand, Louis. "Bad Comma: Lynne Truss's Strange Grammar." Review of *Eats, Shoots and Leaves*, by Lynne Truss. *The New Yorker,* 28 June 2004, www.newyorker.com/magazine/2004/06/28/bad-comma. Accessed 18 Feb. 2013.

---. *The Metaphysical Club: A Story of Ideas in America.* Farrar, Straus and Giroux, 2001.

27. works under a pseudonym: These are given using the same formatting as author's names. Online usernames are given as they appear.

@newyorker. "With the resignation of Turkey's Prime Minister, the country's President now stands alone and unchallenged." *Twitter,* 6 May 2016, twitter.com/NewYorker/status/728676985254379520.

28. edited works:

Renker, Elizabeth, editor. *Poems: A Concise Anthology.* Broadview Press, 2016.

When referring to an edited version of a work written by another author or authors, list the editor(s) after the title.

Trollope, Anthony. *The Eustace Diamonds*. 1873. Edited by Stephen Gill and John Sutherland, Penguin, 1986.

29. works in translation:
The translator is normally listed in the Other Contributors element of the citation.

Bolaño, Roberto. *By Night in Chile*. Translated by Chris Andrews, New Directions, 2003.

If your work focuses on the translation itself, you may list the translator in the author element, moving the author to the Other Contributors element.

Andrews, Chris, translator. *By Night in Chile*. By Roberto Bolaño, New Directions, 2003.

30. selections from anthologies or collections of readings: A selection from a collection of readings or an anthology should begin with the name of the author of the selection. If they are available, be sure to add the selection's inclusive page numbers after the anthology's publication date.

Crawford, Isabella Valancy. "The Canoe." *Representative Poetry Online*, edited by Ian Lancashire, U of Toronto, 1997, www.rpo .library.utoronto.ca/poems/canoe. Accessed 20 Apr. 2015.

Gleach, Frederic W. "Controlled Speculation: Interpreting the Saga of Pocahontas and Captain John Smith." *Reading Beyond Words: Contexts for Native History*, edited by Jennifer S. H. Brown and Elizabeth Vibert, Broadview Press, 1996, pp. 21–42.

Mahfouz, Naguib. "Half a Day." *The Picador Book of African Stories*, edited by Stephen Gray, Picador, 2001, pp. 3–6.

31. cross-references for works from the same collection or anthology: It can be more efficient to create a full entry for the collection or anthology, and then to list each cited item in its own entry. Position the entries in the Works Cited list alphabetically, as you normally would, and use a short form for the collection or anthology, as in the following example:

Brown, Jennifer S. H., and Elizabeth Vibert, editors. *Reading Beyond Words: Contexts for Native History*. Broadview Press, 1996.

Cruikshank, Julie. "Discovery of Gold on the Klondike: Perspectives from Oral Tradition." Brown and Vibert, pp. 433–59.

Gleach, Frederic W. "Controlled Speculation: Interpreting the Saga of Pocahontas and Captain John Smith." Brown and Vibert, pp. 21–42.

32. multi-volume works: If you are citing one or more of the volumes, list them after the title. The entry may note the total number of volumes at the end of the citation (this is optional).

Mercer, Bobby, editor. *A Reference Guide to French Architecture*. Vol. 1, Hackett, 2002. 3 vols.

Jeeves, Julie, editor. *A Reference Guide to Spanish Architecture*. 3 vols., Hackett, 2005.

33. different editions: The edition should be specified whenever it is not the first edition. Include whatever the title page indicates about the particular edition, and use abbreviations (e.g., *rev. ed.* for *revised edition*, *2nd ed.* for *second edition*, and so on).

Fowles, John. *The Magus*. Rev. ed. by Jonathan Cape, 1977.

Shelley, Mary. *Frankenstein*. 1818. Edited by Lorne Macdonald and Kathleen Scherf, 2nd ed., Broadview Press, 1999.

The Bible. Authorized King James Version, Oxford UP, 2008.

34. republished sources: When a source was previously published in a different form, you may include information about the prior publication. This is an optional element; include this information at your discretion, if you feel it would give your reader important context for the source.

MacMillan, Margaret. "Hubris." *History's People: Personalities and the Past, Massey Lectures*, CBC Radio, 3 Nov. 2015, www.cbc.ca/radio/ideas/history-s-people-personalities-the-past-lecture-2-1.3301571. Podcast. Originally delivered at the Arts and Culture Centre, St. John's, NL, 25 Sept. 2015, 7:00 p.m. Lecture.

35. reference work entries: List by the author of the entry, if known; otherwise, list by the entry itself. The citation of a well-known reference work (because such works are frequently updated) should not have full publication details; provide the edition number, date, and location only. Don't include page numbers for works that arrange their entries alphabetically.

"Artificial." *Oxford English Dictionary.* 2nd ed., 1989.

Fowler, H.W. "Unique." *The King's English*, 2nd ed., 1908. *Bartleby. com*, bartleby.com/116/108.html#2. Accessed 5 Mar. 2016.

Marsh, James. "Canoe, Birchbark." *The Canadian Encyclopedia*, 2000 ed., McClelland & Stewart, 1999.

36. works with a title in the title: A title that is usually italicized should remain italicized when it appears within quotation marks:

Yearling, R. "*Hamlet* and the Limits of Narrative." *Essays in Criticism: A Quarterly Journal of Literary Criticism,* vol. 65, no. 4, 2015, pp. 368–82. *Proquest*, doi:dx.doi.org/10.1093/escrit/cgv022.

Titles that are in quotation marks that appear within other titles in quotation marks are enclosed by single quotation marks:

Bettelheim, Bruno. "'The Goose Girl': Achieving Autonomy." *The Uses of Enchantment: The Meaning and Importance of Fairy Tales*, Vintage-Random House, 1989, pp. 136–43.

An italicized title that is included within another italicized title is neither italicized nor placed in quotation marks. It appears in roman:

Morelli, Stefan. *Stoppard's* Arcadia *and Modern Drama*. Ashgate, 2004.

If a title normally enclosed in quotation marks appears in an italicized title, keep the quotation marks:

Wimsatt, C.W. *"Fern Hill" and British Poetry in the 1950s*. ECW, 2004.

37. material from prefaces, introductions, etc.: If you refer to something from a work's preface, introduction, or foreword, the reference under Works Cited should begin with the name of the author of that preface, introduction, or foreword. Add inclusive page numbers after the date of publication.

Warkentin, Germaine. Introduction. *Set in Authority*, by Sara Jeannette Duncan, Broadview Press, 1996, pp. 9–51.

38. magazine articles: The title of the article should appear in quotation marks, the title of the magazine in italics. If no author is identified, the title of the article should appear first. If the magazine is published monthly or every two months, give the date as month and year. For magazines published weekly or every two weeks, give the date as day, month, and year. Abbreviate the names of months (except for *May*, *June*, and *July*).

MacRitchie, Lynn. "Ofili's Glittering Icons." *Art in America,* Jan. 2000, pp. 44–56.

"Greens in Pinstriped Suits." *The Economist.* 21 May 2016, www.economist.com/news/business/21699141-climate-conscious-shareholders-are-putting-big-oil-spot-greens-pinstriped-suits.

If you accessed the article online yourself, you may include the date of access, though it is an optional element. If the website is hosted by a body other than the magazine itself, include it as a second container with its accompanying publication details.

Gladwell, Malcolm. "The Art of Failure: Why Some People Choke and Others Panic." *The New Yorker,* 21 Aug. 2000, www.newyorker.com/magazine/2000/08/21/the-art-of-failure. Accessed 18 Feb. 2013.

Kreimer, Julian. "Mernet Larsen." *Art in America*, vol. 104, no. 4, 2016, pp. 115–16. *Academic Search Complete*, www.search.ebscohost.com/login.aspx?direct=true&db=a9hAN=114088897&site=eh ost-live. Accessed 4 Nov. 2015.

39. newspaper articles: The basic principles to follow with newspaper articles or editorials are the same as with magazine articles (see above). Note, however, that when the newspaper's sections are paginated separately, section as well as page numbers are often required. If an article is not printed on consecutive pages, include only the first page number followed by a plus sign. In the following reference the article begins on page 3 of the first section:

Yakabuski, Konrad. "Many Looking for Meaning in Vice-Presidential Debate." *The Globe and Mail,* 12 Oct. 2012, p. A3+.

If you are citing an online version of a newspaper article you should include the date you accessed the site. The site name, if it is different from the container title, should also be included.

Kaplan, Thomas. "Bernie Sanders Wins Oregon; Hillary Clinton Declares Victory in Kentucky." *The New York Times,* 17 May 2016, www.nytimes.com/2016/05/18/us/politics/bernie-sanders-oregon-results.html. Accessed 17 May 2016.

40. journal articles: The basic principles are the same as with magazine articles, but entries for journal articles include the volume and issue numbers.

Roy, Indrani. "Irony and Derision in Congreve's *The Way of the World.*" *PMLA,* vol. 120, no.6, 2005, pp. 60–72.

If you are citing an online version of a journal article you should include the date you accessed the site, as well as any additional containers and their publication details (databases, for example).

Sohmer, Steve. "12 June 1599: Opening Day at Shakespeare's Globe." *Early Modern Literary Studies: A Journal of Sixteenth- and Seventeenth-Century English Literature,* vol. 3, no.1, 1997. *Pro-Quest,* www.extra.shu.ac.uk/emls/emlshome.html. Accessed 18 May 2016.

41. book reviews: The name of the reviewer (if it has been provided) should come first, followed by the title of the review (if there is one), and the information on the book itself.

Leiter, Brian, and Michael Weisberg. "Do You Only Have a Brain? On Thomas Nagel." Review of *Why the Materialist Neo-Darwinian Conception of Nature Is Almost Certainly False*, by Thomas Nagel, *The Nation,* 22 Oct. 2012, www.thenation.com/article/do-you-only-have-brain-thomas-nagel/. Accessed 22 Oct. 2012.

Wills, Garry. "A Masterpiece on the Rise of Christianity." Review of *Through the Eye of a Needle: Wealth, The Fall of Rome, and the Making of Christianity in the West, 350–550 AD*, by Peter Brown, *New York Review of Books,* 11 Oct. 2012, pp. 43–45.

42. periodical publications in online databases:

Hill, Katherine C. "Virginia Woolf and Leslie Stephen: History and Literary Revolution." *PMLA*, vol. 96, no.3, 1981, pp. 351–62. *JSTOR*, www.jstor.org/stable/461911. Accessed 6 Oct. 2012.

43. illustrated books: Include the illustrator's name as well as the author's name.

Juster, Norman. *The Phantom Tollbooth*. Illustrated by Jules Feiffer, Yearling-Random House, 1961.

44. graphic narratives: In many graphic narratives, both the illustrations and the text are created by one person; these kinds of works should be documented as in the first example below. Use the second example's format for works whose text is by one person and illustrations by another.

Leavitt, Sarah. *Tangles: A Story about Alzheimer's, My Mother, and Me*. Freehand Books, 2010.

Pekar, Harvey. *Ego and Hubris: The Michael Malice Story*. Art by Gary Dumm, Ballantine-Random House, 2006.

45. films or television episodes: These entries may be tailored to the context in which you are citing the work. If you are discussing the work of a director, for example, place the director's name in the Author element:

Zeitlin, Behn, director. *Beasts of the Southern Wild*. Performances by Quvenzhané Wallis and Dwight Henry, Fox Searchlight, 2012.

Medak, Peter, director. "The Buys." *The Wire*, created by David Simon and Ed Burns, season 1, episode 3, HBO, 16 June 2002.

If you are discussing a particular performance, place the actor's name in the Author element.

Moss, Elizabeth, performer. "A Little Kiss." *Mad Men*, directed by Jennifer Getzinger, AMC, 25 Mar. 2012.

Spacey, Kevin, performer. "Chapter 5." *House of Cards*, directed by Joel Schumacher, season 1, episode 5. *Netflix*, www.netflix.com/search/house?jbv=70178217&jbp=0&jbr=021.

46. online videos: If your source is a video on a website, cite, if you can, who uploaded the video, and the date on which the video was posted.

Gleeson, Thomas, director. "Home." Screen Innovation Production Fund, 2012. *Vimeo*, uploaded by Thomas Gleeson, 31 Jan. 2013, www.vimeo.com/58630796.

47. radio broadcasts:

"Glenn Gould Special." *The Sunday Edition*, narrated by Robert Harris and Michael Enright, CBC Radio One, 23 Sept. 2012.

48. podcasts:

"Too Old to Be Governable Too Young to Die Edition." *Slate's Culture Gabfest*, narrated by Stephen Metcalf, Julia Turner, and Laura Miller, 18 May 2016, www.slate.com/articles/podcasts/culture-gabfest/2016/05/. Accessed 18 May 2016.

49. recorded music:

Williams, Lucinda. "Real Love." *Little Honey*, Lost Highway, 2008.

50. live performances: If you are citing a live performance or lecture, include the physical location and the city where the performance or lecture was delivered, as well as the date. Omit the city name if it is part of the location name. Include other information about the performance—the names of the director, the conductor, and/or lead performers, for instance—where such information is relevant. If your work focuses on the contribution of a performance's director, for example, cite that person in the Author element. Other important contributors follow the title in the Other Contributors element.

Bedford, Brian, director. *The Importance of Being Earnest*, by Oscar Wilde. Performances by Brian Bedford, Santino Fontana, David Furr, Charlotte Parry, and Sarah Topham, Roundabout Theatre Company, American Airlines Theatre, New York. 3 July 2011.

MacMillan, Margaret. "Hubris." *History's People: Personalities and the Past*, Arts and Culture Centre, St. John's NL, 25 Sept. 2015, 7:00 p.m. Massey Lecture.

51. works of visual art: When citing a physical object you have experienced, such as a work of art, provide in the Location element the name of the institution and city where you experienced it. Leave out the name of the city if the city name is part of the institution name (e.g. Art Institute of Chicago).

Housser, Yvonne McKague. *Cobalt*. 1931. National Gallery of Canada, Ottawa.

Sargent, John Singer. *Henry James*. 1913. National Portrait Gallery, London.

If you access a work of art online or in a book, you should include full information about the website or volume you consulted.

Colquhoun, Ithell. *Scylla*. 1938. Tate Gallery, London. *Tate Women Artists*, by Alicia Foster, Tate, 2004, p. 85.

Giotto di Bondone. *Lamentation*. 1304–06. Capella Scrovegni, Padua, *Web Gallery of Art*, www.wga.hu/frames-e.html?/html/g/giotto/. Accessed 29 Jan. 2013.

52. interviews: Begin all entries for interviews with the name of the person being interviewed, and if there is a title for the interview, include it (in quotation marks if it is part of another work, or in italics if it has been published by itself). If there is no title, or if the title does not make clear that the work is an interview, write *Interview*, and give the name of the interviewer, if known. Finish with whatever publication information is appropriate. If you conducted the interview yourself, give the name of the person you interviewed, the medium (*Personal interview*, *Telephone interview*), and the date.

Erdrich, Louise. Interview by Bill Moyers, *Bill Moyers Journal*, PBS, 9 Apr. 2010, www.pbs.org/moyers/journal/04092010/watch2.html. Accessed 16 Jan. 2013.

Nelson, Willie. "The Silver-Headed Stranger." Interview by Andrew Goldman, *New York Times Magazine,* 16 Dec. 2012, p. 12.

Rosengarten, Herbert. Personal interview, 21 Jan. 2013.

53. online projects: In the case of large projects, cite the full range of years during which the project has been developed:

Secord, James A., et al., editors. *Darwin Correspondence Project.* 1974–2016, www.darwinproject.ac.uk/.

Willett, Perry, editor. *Victorian Women Writers Project.* Indiana University Digital Library Program, 1995–2016, webapp1.dlib.indiana.edu/vwwp/welcome.do. Accessed 26 Nov. 2012.

54. e-books: E-books should be documented according to the same principles as other digital media. Make sure to add a Container element citing the digital platform from which the e-book has been accessed or downloaded.

Austen, Jane. *Pride and Prejudice.* 1813. *Project Gutenberg,* 2008, www.gutenberg.org/files/1342/1342-h/1342-h.htm. Accessed 20 Feb. 2016.

Emerson, Ralph Waldo. *The American Scholar.* 1837. *American Transcendentalism Web,* ed. Ann Woodlief, Virginia Commonwealth U, 1999, www.transcendentalism-legacy.tamu.edu/authors/emerson/essays/amscholar.html. Accessed 16 Mar. 2013.

Herman, Jonathan R. *I and Tao: Martin Buber's Encounter with Chuang Tzu.* State U of New York P, 1996. *Google Books*, google.ca/books?id=l1U10Ei80b0C. Downloaded 30 May 2015.

Shakespeare, William. *As You Like It.* Edited by David Bevington, Broadview Press, 2012. *Broadview Press,* www.broadviewpress.com/product/as-you-like-it/#tab-description. Downloaded 3 Mar. 2016.

55. information databases:

Gaston, Craig. "Consumption-related greenhouse gas emissions in Canada, the United States and China." *Statistics Canada*, 8 Dec. 2011, www.statcan.gc.ca/pub/16-002-x/2011004/part-partie4-eng.htm. Accessed 17 Apr. 2016.

56. entry in a wiki: Wikis are online sites that can be added to and edited by any site user; as such, they may be subject to frequent changes made by any number of authors and editors. Do not, therefore, provide any authors' names. Start with the entry's title; then give the name of the wiki, the site publisher, the date of the entry's last update, the medium, and the date you accessed the site.

"William Caxton." *Wikipedia*. Wikimedia Foundation, 20 Oct. 2012, www.en.wikipedia.org/wiki/William_Caxton. Accessed 26 Oct. 2012.

57. blog post: Include the title of the posting as your source title, the blog title as the first container, and the name of the blog host as a publisher.

LePan, Don. "Reading and Writing and Work." *Animals, Rising Stories, Etc.*, Blogspot, 21 May 2016, www.donlepan.blogspot.ca. Accessed 24 May 2016.

58. e-mail message: Use the subject as the title and place it within quotation marks.

Milton, Frank. "Thoughts on Animal Rights." Received by the author, 15 Jan. 2013.

If it is not clear from the context of your work that the source being cited is an e-mail, you may wish to add an optional element to the end of your citation that indicates the type of work.

Stuart, Jennifer. "My Experience of the Attack." Received by the author, 17 May 2016. E-mail.

59. tweet: Copy the full, unchanged text of the tweet in the title element and enclose it in quotation marks. The username is included as the Author element.

@newyorker. "With the resignation of Turkey's Prime Minister, the
    country's President now stands alone and unchallenged." *Twitter*, 6
    May 2016, twitter.com/NewYorker/status/728676985254379520.

60. comment posted on a web page: Usernames are given in full, unchanged. If the comment is anonymous, skip the author element. If the comment does not have its own title, provide instead a description of the comment that includes the title of the work being commented on (e.g. Comment on "Clinton Aims for Decisive Victory"). If it is available, include the exact time of posting in the Publication Date element.

Evan. Comment on "Another Impasse on Gun Bills, Another Win
    for Hyperpolitics." *The New York Times*, 21 June 2016, 9:02 a.m.,
    www.nytimes.com/2016/06/22/us/politics/washington-congress-
    gun-control.html.

37d. MLA Style Sample Essay Pages

Following are sample pages from an essay written in MLA style. Note that the complete essay, as well as further sample essays, some of which also employ MLA style, are available on the companion website associated with this book.

Among the details to notice in this referencing system:

- MLA style focuses on the process of documentation, not the prescriptive following of specific guidelines (though consistent formatting according to MLA principles is still vital to communicate clearly with your reader).

- To create a citation, list the relevant elements in the order prescribed by MLA (see the table on page 200). Any elements that don't apply to a given source are left out (placeholders for unknown information like *n.d.* ("no date") are not required).

- Follow the punctuation guidelines in the table on page 200. Any elements recorded after a period should be capitalized; elements following a comma should be lower-case.

- Your citation should give your reader a map to your exact source. If you are documenting an article found in a periodical, for example, which was itself found on a database, you should include the publication details of both "containers" (periodical and database) as part of your citation. See the "Title of Container" section above for details.

- Terms such as *editor*, *edited by*, *translator*, *translated by*, and *review* are not abbreviated.

- If there are three or more authors or editors, only the first name is given, reversed, followed by *et al.*

- Citations for journals include abbreviations for volume and issue ("vol. 40, no. 3").

- Give the publisher's name in full, but drop business words such as "Company." For University presses, use the abbreviations *U*, *P*, and *UP*.

- City names are not required as part of the publication details.

- The date of access for an online source is optional.

- Page numbers are preceded by *p.* for a single page reference, or *pp.* for a range of pages.

- Include the URL (with *http:* removed) or the DOI in the location element for digital sources. Do not surround the address with angle brackets and do conclude with a period.

- You do not have to identify the media type of your source, unless it is required for clarity.

cover page (not required in MLA style, but may be required by some instructors)

What Limits to Freedom?

Freedom of Expression and the Brooklyn Museum's

"Sensation" Exhibit

by Melissa Davis

Prof. K. D. Smith

Humanities 205

16 June 2015

all text centred

Melissa Davis   Davis 1
Professor Smith
Humanities 205
16 June 2015

name
and page
number in
top right
corner

What Limits to Freedom?

Freedom of Expression and the Brooklyn Museum's

"Sensation" Exhibit

first line
of all
paragraphs
indented

text left-
justified
and
ragged
right

text
double-
spaced
through-
out

For over a century public galleries in Western democracies
have been forums not only for displaying works by "old
Masters" but also for presenting art that is new, as well as
ideas that are sometimes radical and controversial. In the
United States that tradition has been under wide attack in
the past generation. Various political and religious leaders
have criticized exhibits of works of art that they claim offend
against notions of public decency, and have crusaded against
providing public funding for the creation or display of such
works. The largest such controversy of the past generation
was sparked by the display of a painting entitled "The Holy
Virgin Mary," by the British artist Chris Ofili at the Brooklyn
Museum in 1999. Though the image appears inoffensive at
a distance, the artist has affixed to the painting cutouts of
body parts from magazines, and has incorporated clumps
of elephant dung into the piece, both below the main body
of the work as if supporting it and as part of the collage. The

Davis 2

uproar that surrounded the painting's exhibition led both to a widely publicized court case and to an ongoing campaign to support "decency" in artistic expression. Should such art be banned? Should it be exhibited at public expense? In the course of the Ofili controversy cultural conservatives raised legitimate concerns about the obligation of any society to provide funding for activities of which it disapproves. This essay will argue, however, that the greater concern is in the other direction; a free society must continue to provide opportunities for the free expression both of artistic vision and of controversial thought.

The Ofili piece was part of a much-hyped exhibit entitled "Sensation: Young British Artists from the Saatchi Collection." As the title indicated, the show was made up entirely of works from one collection, that of the wealthy British advertising executive Charles Saatchi.[1] The exhibition had been shown first at the Royal Academy of Arts in London and then at a major gallery in Berlin. (In London what sparked controversy was not Ofili's work but rather a realistic painting by Marcus Harvey of child-murderer Myra Hindley that incorporated hundreds of children's handprints into the image.) Bringing the show to Brooklyn cost one million dollars—a cost covered in part by Christie's, a London auctioneer—and from the outset it could be argued

first paragraph ends with a statement of the essay's thesis

numbered note for additional information provided as an aside

MLA Style

Davis 3

paren-
thetical
reference;
Internet
source
has no
page
number

that the museum was courting controversy. It claimed in its advertising that the exhibition "may cause shock, vomiting, confusion, panic, euphoria, and anxiety. If you suffer from high blood pressure, a nervous disorder, or palpitations, you should consult your doctor" (qtd. in Barry and Vogel).

No doubt that warning was tongue-in-cheek, but there was nothing ironic about the angry reactions provoked by the show in general and directed toward the Ofili piece in particular. On one side art critics and civil libertarians were full of praise; in *The New York Times* the work was praised as "colourful and glowing" (Kimmelman). On the other side John Cardinal O'Connor called it "an attack on religion," and the president of the Catholic League for Religious and Civil Rights called on citizens to picket the exhibition (Vogel). The United States Senate and the House of Representatives both passed resolutions condemning the exhibit. Even more vehement was the response of New York Mayor Rudy Giuliani; he declared himself "offended" and the work itself "disgusting" (Barry and Vogel). As Peter Cramer has detailed, Giuliani's comments received widespread attention in the press—especially the informal remark "I mean, this is like, sick stuff," from which the phrase "sick stuff" was extracted for repeated circulation. But Giuliani and Deputy Mayor Joseph J. Lhota, the city administration's "enforcer in the case" (Barbaro 2), did much

italics
used for
titles of
books,
news-
papers,
journals,
etc.

paren-
thetical
references
at end
of short
quotations
followed
by punctu-
ation

Davis 4

more than comment. They ordered that ongoing city funding of the museum be withheld until the offensive work was removed, and launched eviction proceedings against the museum. Other conservative politicians—then-Texas Governor George W. Bush prominent among them—spoke out in support of Giuliani's stand ("Bush Backs Giuliani").

What was the substance of Mayor Giuliani's case? Here is how he explained his stance to the press:

> You don't have a right to a government subsidy to desecrate someone else's religion. And therefore we will do everything that we can to remove funding from the [museum] until the director comes to his senses and realizes that if you are a government subsidized enterprise then you can't do things that desecrate the most personal and deeply held views of people in society. (Brooklyn Institute of Arts and Sciences v. City of New York 7)

In Giuliani's view, the constitution's guarantee of freedom of speech was not the central issue:

> "If somebody wants to do that privately and pay for that privately . . . that's what the First Amendment is all about," he said. "You can be offended by it and upset by it, and you don't have to go see it, if somebody else is paying for it. But to have the government subsidize something like that is outrageous." (qtd. in Vogel)

long quotations indented— no quotation marks used except for quotation within a quotation

Davis 5

The issue for Guiliani, then, is not one of censorship per se. He is not arguing that works of art should be banned for causing offense to a significant segment of the public; it is merely the provision of any government funding for such activity that he finds "outrageous."

But is it in fact outrageous? Let us examine the implications of Giuliani's argument. According to him, government should never provide funding for activities that some people may find deeply offensive. But governments have long funded much artistic and intellectual activity in advance on the grounds that such activity in general represents a social good, without knowing precisely what sort of artistic work will be created or exhibited, what results academic research may come up with, and so on. If such funding were to be always contingent on no one ever being deeply offended by the results of the artistic or intellectual activity, the effect would be to severely damage freedom of speech and expression. (Here it is important to note that the actions Giuliani took were retroactive; the annual funding for the museum had not been provided with strings attached.[2])

Social conservatives are often characterized as favouring censorship of any material they find offensive; to be fair, that is clearly not the position Giuliani takes here. Nor is the issue whether or not the material is offensive; Hillary Clinton, for

Davis 17

Notes

1. Saatchi contributed $100,000 to mounting the show, the economics of which became another subject for controversy when it was shown in Brooklyn. As well as complaining about the content of the works in the exhibit, Mayor Rudy Giuliani and others suggested that the show had been intended in large part to raise the value of works in the Saatchi collection, and on those grounds, too, argued that the exhibit should not be receiving a subsidy from taxpayers.

2. Because its content was recognized as controversial, city officials had been provided in advance of the "Sensation" show with photographs and full descriptions of all pieces to be included in the exhibit, including the information that Ofili's works incorporated elephant dung into the images they portrayed. The mayor insisted that he personally had not been alerted to the content of the show beforehand, however.

3. Animal rights activists have protested against works by the renowned British artist Damien Hirst, which present, among other things, a sectioned cow and a bisected pig in formaldehyde cases. (Several such works by Hirst were included in the "Sensation" show.) In Toronto, art student Jesse Power and two friends pleaded guilty in 2001 to charges of animal cruelty and public mischief after making what they called an

Davis 23

Works Cited

Associated Press. "Bush Backs Giuliani on Museum Flap."

Washington Post, 4 Oct. 1999, www.washingtonpost.com/

wp-srv/aponline/19991004/aponline163720_000.htm.

Accessed 20 May 2015.

Baker, Kenneth. "Show's Cancellation a Rare Case of Artists

Advocating Censorship." *San Francisco Chronicle,* 1 Apr.

2008, p. E1.

Barbaro, Michael. "For Mayoral Hopeful Who Lost Fight to

Remove Art, No Regrets." *New York Times,* 27 March

2013, www.nytimes.com/2013/03/28/nyregion/for-lhota-

mayoral-hopeful-who-lost-fight-to-remove-art-no-regrets.

html?_r=0. Accessed 14 May 2015.

Barry, Dan, and Carol Vogel. "Giuliani Vows to Cut Subsidy

over Art He Calls Offensive." *New York Times,* 23 Sept.

1999, partners.nytimes.com/library/arts/092399brooklyn-

museum-funds.html. Accessed 20 May 2015.

Blatchford, Christie. "Face to Face with Cruelty." *Globe and

Mail,* 4 Sept. 2004, p. A13.

Brooklyn Institute of Arts and Sciences v. City of New York

99CV 6071. *National Coalition Against Censorship,* 1 Nov.

1999, ncac.org/resource/brooklyn-institute-of-arts-and-

sciences-v-city-of-new-york. Accessed 2 May 2015.

each
entry
begins at
left margin;
subsequent
lines are
indented

works
cited are
listed
alphabeti-
cally

Davis 24

Brooks, Katherine. "Russia's Hermitage Museum Under
Investigation For 'Blasphemous' Jake and Dinos
Chapman Exhibit." *Huffington Post*, 11 Dec. 2012,
www.huffingtonpost.com/2012/12/11/hermitage-
museum-blasphemy-investigation-jake-and-dinos-
chapman_n_2272987.html. Accessed 3 May 2015.

Bruce, Tammy. *The Death of Right and Wrong.* Three Rivers
Press, 2003.

Catholic League. "Piss-Christ Coming to New York." *Catholic
League for Civil and Religious Rights*, 21 Sept. 2012,
www.catholicleague.org/piss-christ-coming-to-nyc/.
Accessed 19 May 2015.

Cramer, Peter. "Sick Stuff: A Case Study of Controversy in a
Constitutive Attitude." *Rhetoric Society Quarterly*, vol. 43,
no. 2, 2013, pp. 177–201. Taylor & Francis Online, DOI:
10.1080/02773945.2013.768352. Accessed 21 May 2015.

Danto, Arthur C. "'Sensation' in Brooklyn." *The Nation,* 1 Nov.
1999, www.thenation.com/article/sensation-brooklyn/.
Accessed 4 May 2015.

Darts, David. "The Art of Culture War: (Un)Popular Culture,
Freedom of Expression, and Art Education." *Studies in
Art Education,* vol. 49, no. 2, Winter 2008, pp. 103–21.
JSTOR, www.jstor.org/stable/25475862. Accessed 3 May
2015.

double
spacing
used
throughout

italics used
for titles
of books,
journals,
magazines,
etc.

CONTENTS

38. APA STYLE

The American Psychological Association (APA) style is used in many behavioural and social sciences. Like MLA style, APA style calls for parenthetical references in the body of a paper, although the main components in these are author and date rather than author and page number. APA also requires that full bibliographical information about the sources be provided in a list called "References" at the end of the essay.

This section outlines the key features of APA style and includes, at the end, a sample excerpt using APA citation. Additional full sample essays in APA style are available on the Broadview website; go to <http://sites.broadviewpress.com/writing/>. If you have more detailed questions, consult *Concise Rules of APA Style* (6th edition, 2010). You may also find answers at www.apastyle.org.

38a. Incorporating Sources in APA Style

The following material should be read in conjunction with the introductory discussion of citation, documentation, and plagiarism (see pages 166-78).

There are three main ways of working source material into a paper: summaries, paraphrases, and direct quotations. In order to avoid plagiarism, care must be taken with all three kinds of borrowing, both in the way they are handled and in their referencing. In what follows, a passage from page 102 of a book by Terrence W. Deacon (*The Symbolic Species: The Co-Evolution of Language and the Brain*, published in New York City by Norton in 1997) serves as the source for a sample summary, paraphrase, and quotation. The examples feature the APA style of in-text parenthetical citations, but the requirements for presenting the source material are the same for all academic referencing systems.

original source   Over the last few decades language researchers seem to have reached a consensus that language is an innate ability, and that only a significant contribution from innate knowledge can explain our ability to learn such a complex communication system. Without question, children enter the world predisposed to learn human languages. All normal children, raised in normal social environments, inevitably learn their local language, whereas other species, even when raised and taught in this same environment, do not. This demonstrates that human brains come into the world specially equipped for this function.

• Summarizing

An honest and competent summary, whether of a passage or an entire book, must not only represent the source accurately but also use original wording and include a citation. It is a common misconception that only quotations need to be acknowledged as borrowings in the body of an essay, but without a citation, even a fairly worded summary or paraphrase is an act of plagiarism. The first example below is faulty on two counts: it borrows wording (underlined) from the source, and it has no parenthetical reference.

needs checking   Researchers agree that language learning is innate, and that only innate knowledge can explain how we are able to learn a system of communication that is so complex. Normal children raised in normal ways will always learn their local language, whereas other species do not, even when taught human language and exposed to the same environment.

The next example avoids the wording of the source passage, and a parenthetical citation notes the author and date (but note that no page number is provided, as APA does not require these in citations of summarized material).

revised   There is now wide agreement among linguists that the ease with which human children acquire their native tongues, under the conditions of a normal childhood, demonstrates an inborn capacity for language that is not shared by any other animals, not even those who are reared in comparable ways and given human language training (Deacon, 1997).

● Paraphrasing

Whereas a summary is a shorter version of its original, a paraphrase tends to be about the same length. However, paraphrases, like summaries, must reflect their sources accurately while using original wording, and must include a citation. The original material's page number (or paragraph number for a nonpaginated online source) is not absolutely essential for a paraphrase, but APA suggests it be added as an aid to any reader who would like to refer to the original text. What follows is a paraphrase of the first sentence of the Deacon passage, which despite having a proper citation, falls short by being too close to the wording of the original (underlined).

needs checking   Researchers in language have come to a consensus in the past few decades that the acquisition of language is innate; such contributions from knowledge contribute significantly to our ability to master such a complex system of communication (Deacon, 1997, p. 102).

Simply substituting synonyms for the words and phrases of the source, however, is not enough to avoid plagiarism. Even with its original wording, the next example also fails but for a very different reason: it follows the original's sentence structure, as illustrated in the interpolated copy below it.

needs checking   Recently, linguists appear to have come to an agreement that speaking is an in-born skill, and that nothing but a substantial input from in-born cognition can account for the human capacity to acquire such a complicated means of expression (Deacon, 1997, p. 102).

Recently (*over the last few decades*), linguists (*language researchers*) appear to have come to an agreement (*seem to have reached a consensus*) that speaking is an in-born skill (*that language is an innate ability*), and that nothing but a substantial input (*and that only a significant contribution*) from in-born cognition (*from innate knowledge*) can account for the human capacity (*can explain our ability*) to acquire such a complicated means of expression (*to learn such a complex communication system*) (Deacon, 1997, p. 102).

What follows is a good paraphrase of the passage's opening sentence; this paraphrase captures the sense of the original without echoing the details and shape of its language.

revised Linguists now broadly agree that children are born with the ability to learn language; in fact, the human capacity to acquire such a difficult skill cannot easily be accounted for in any other way (Deacon, 1997, p. 102).

● Quoting Directly

Unlike paraphrases and summaries, direct quotations must use the exact wording of the original. Because they involve importing outside words, quotations pose unique challenges. Quote too frequently, and you risk making your readers wonder why they are not reading your sources instead of your paper. Your essay should present something you want to say—informed and supported by properly documented sources, but forming a contribution that is yours alone. To that end, use secondary material to help you build a strong framework for your work, not to replace it. Quote sparingly, therefore; use your sources' exact wording only when it is important or particularly memorable.

To avoid misrepresenting your sources, be sure to quote accurately, and to avoid plagiarism, take care to indicate quotations as quotations, and cite them properly. If you use the author's name in a signal phrase, follow it with the date in parentheses, and be sure the verb of the phrase is in the past tense (*demonstrated*) or present perfect tense (*has demonstrated*). For all direct quotations, you must also include the page number (or paragraph number for a nonpaginated online source) of the original in your citation, as in the following examples.

Below are two problematic quotations. The first does not show which words come directly from the source.

needs checking Deacon (1997) maintained that children enter the world predisposed to learn human languages (p. 102).

The second quotation fails to identify the source at all.

needs checking Many linguists have argued that "children enter the world predisposed to learn human languages."

The next example corrects both problems by naming the source and indicating clearly which words come directly from it.

revised Deacon (1997) maintained that "children enter the world predisposed to learn human languages" (p. 102).

● Formatting Quotations

There are two ways to signal an exact borrowing: by enclosing it in double quotation marks and by indenting it as a block of text. Which you should choose depends on the length and genre of the quotation and the style guide you are following.

Short Quotations

What counts as a short quotation differs among the various reference guides. In MLA style, "short" means up to four lines; in APA, up to forty words; and in Chicago Style, up to one hundred words. All the guides agree, however, that short quotations must be enclosed in double quotation marks, as in the examples below.

Short quotation, full sentence:	According to Deacon (1997), linguists agree that a human child's capacity to acquire language is inborn: "Without question, children enter the world predisposed to learn human languages" (p. 102).
Short quotation, partial sentence:	According to Deacon (1997), linguists agree that human "… children enter the world predisposed to learn human languages" (p. 102).

Long Quotations

In APA style, longer quotations of forty words or more should be double-spaced and indented, as a block, about one-half inch from the left margin. Do not include quotation marks; the indentation indicates that the words come exactly from the source. Note that indented quotations are often introduced with a full sentence followed by a colon.

> Deacon (1997) maintained that human beings are born with a unique cognitive capacity:
>
> > Without question, children enter the world predisposed to learn human languages. All normal children, raised in normal social environments, inevitably learn their local language, whereas other species, even when raised and taught in this same environment, do not. This demonstrates that human brains come into the world specially equipped for this function. (p. 102)

Quotations within Quotations

You may sometimes find, within the original passage you wish to quote, words already enclosed in double quotation marks. If your quotation is short, enclose it all in double quotation marks, and use single quotation marks for the embedded quotation.

> Deacon (1997) was firm in maintaining that human language differs from other communication systems in kind

> rather than degree: "Of no other natural form of communication is it legitimate to say that 'language is a more complicated version of that'" (p. 44).

If your quotation is long, keep the double quotation marks of the original. Note as well that in the example below, the source's use of italics (*simple*) is also faithfully reproduced.

> Deacon (1997) was firm in maintaining that human language differs from other communication systems in kind rather than degree:

>> Of no other natural form of communication is it legitimate to say that "language is a more complicated version of that." It is just as misleading to call other species' communication systems *simple* languages as it is to call them languages. In addition to asserting that a Procrustean mapping of one to the other is possible, the analogy ignores the sophistication and power of animals' non-linguistic communication, whose capabilities may also be without language parallels. (p. 44)

● *Adding to or Deleting from a Quotation*

While it is important to use the original's exact wording in a quotation, it is allowable to modify a quotation somewhat, as long as the changes are clearly indicated and do not distort the meaning of the original. You may want to add to a quotation in order to clarify what would otherwise be puzzling or ambiguous to someone who does not know its context; put whatever you add in square brackets.

Using Square Brackets to Add to a Quotation

> Deacon (1997) concluded that children are born "specially equipped for this [language] function" (p. 102).

If you would like to streamline a quotation by omitting anything unnecessary to your point, insert an ellipsis (three spaced dots) to show that you've left material out.

Using an Ellipsis to Delete from a Quotation

When the quotation looks like a complete sentence but is actually part of a longer sentence, you should provide an ellipsis to show that there is more to the original than you are using.

> Deacon (1997) concluded that "… children enter the world predisposed to learn human languages" (p. 102).

Note the square brackets example above; if the quotation is clearly a partial sentence, ellipses aren't necessary.

When the omitted material runs over a sentence boundary or constitutes a whole sentence or more, insert a period plus an ellipsis.

> Deacon (1997) claimed that human children are born with a unique ability to acquire their native language: "Without question, children enter the world predisposed to learn human languages.… [H]uman brains come into the world specially equipped for this function" (p. 102).

Be sparing in modifying quotations; it is all right to have one or two altered quotations in a paper, but if you find yourself changing quotations often, or adding to and omitting from one quotation more than once, reconsider quoting at all. A paraphrase or summary is very often a more effective choice.

Integrating Quotations

Quotations must be worked smoothly and grammatically into your sentences and paragraphs. Always, of course, mark quotations as such, but for the purpose of integrating them into your writing, treat them otherwise as if they were your own words. The boundary between what you say and what your source says should be grammatically seamless.

needs checking   Deacon (1997) pointed out, "whereas other species, even when raised and taught in this same environment, do not" (p. 102).

> *revised* According to Deacon (1997), while human children brought up under normal conditions acquire the language they are exposed to, "other species, even when raised and taught in this same environment, do not" (p. 102).

Avoiding "Dumped" Quotations

Integrating quotations well also means providing a context for them. Don't merely drop them into your paper or string them together like beads on a necklace; make sure to introduce them by noting where the material comes from and how it connects to whatever point you are making.

> *needs checking* For many years, linguists have studied how human children acquire language. "Without question, children enter the world predisposed to learn human language" (Deacon, 1997, p. 102).

> *revised* Most linguists studying how human children acquire language have come to share the conclusion articulated by Deacon (1997): "Without question, children enter the world predisposed to learn human language" (p. 102).

> *needs checking* "Without question, children enter the world predisposed to learn human language" (Deacon, 1997, p. 102). "There is ... something special about human brains that enables us to do with ease what no other species can do even minimally without intense effort and remarkably insightful training" (Deacon, 1997, p. 103).

> *revised* Deacon (1997) based his claim that we "enter the world predisposed to learn human language" on the fact that very young humans can "do with ease what no other species can do even minimally without intense effort and remarkably insightful training" (pp. 102–103).

● Signal Phrases

To leave no doubt in your readers' minds about which parts of your essay are yours and which come from elsewhere, identify the sources of your summaries, paraphrases, and quotations with signal phrases, as in the following examples.

- As Carter and Rosenthal (2011) demonstrated, …
- According to Ming, Bartlett, and Koch (2014), …
- In his latest article McGann (2015) advanced the view that, …
- As Beyerstein (2000) observed, …
- Kendal and Ahmadi (1998) have suggested that …
- Freschi (2004) was not alone in rejecting these claims, arguing that …
- Cabral, Chernovsky, and Morgan (2015) emphasized this point in their recent research: …
- Sayeed (2003) has maintained that …
- In a landmark study, Mtele (1992) concluded that …
- In her later work, however, Hardy (2005) overturned previous results, suggesting that …

In order to help establish your paper's credibility, you may also find it useful at times to include in a signal phrase information that shows why readers should take the source seriously, as in the following example:

> In this insightful and compassionate work, clinical neurologist Oliver Sacks (1985) described …

Here, the signal phrase mentions the author's professional credentials; it also points out the importance of his book, which is appropriate to do in the case of a work as famous as Sacks' *The Man Who Mistook His Wife for a Hat.*

Below is a fuller list of words and expressions that may be useful in the crafting of signal phrases:

according to _____	endorsed
acknowledged	found
added	granted
admitted	illustrated
advanced	implied
agreed	in the view of _____,
allowed	in the words of _____,
argued	insisted
asserted	intimated
attested	noted
believed	observed
claimed	pointed out
commented	put it
compared	reasoned
concluded	refuted
confirmed	rejected
contended	reported
declared	responded
demonstrated	suggested
denied	thought
disputed	took issue with
emphasized	wrote

38b. About In-text Citations

1. **in-text citation:** The APA system emphasizes the date of publication, which must appear within an in-text citation. Whenever a quotation is given, the page number, preceded by the abbreviation *p.*, must also be provided:

- Bonnycastle (2007) refers to "the true and lively spirit of opposition" (p. 204) with which Marxist literary criticism invigorates the discipline.

It is common to mention in the body of your text the surnames of authors that you are citing, as is done in the example above. If author names are not mentioned in the body of the text, however, they must be provided within the in-text citation. In the example below, note the comma between the name and date of publication.

- One overview of literary theory (Bonnycastle, 2007) has praised "the true and lively spirit of opposition" (p. 204) with which Marxist literary criticism invigorates the discipline.

If the reference does not involve a quotation (as it commonly does not in social science papers), only the date need be given as an in-text citation, provided that the author's name appears in the signal phrase. For paraphrases, APA encourages, though does not require, a page number reference as well. The in-text citation in this case must immediately follow the author's name:

- Bonnycastle (2007) argues that the oppositional tone of Marxist literary criticism invigorates the discipline.

A citation such as this connects to a list of references at the end of the paper. In this case the entry under "References" at the end of the paper would be as follows:

- Bonnycastle, S. (2007). *In search of authority: A guide to literary theory* (3rd ed.). Peterborough, ON: Broadview Press.

Notice here that the date of publication is again foregrounded, appearing immediately after the author's name. Notice too that the formatting of titles differs from that of MLA style; the details are in the section below.

2 no signal phrase (or author not named in signal phrase). If the context does not make it clear who the author is, that information must be added to the in-text citation. Note that commas separate the name of the author, the date, and the page number (where this is given):

- Even in recent years some have continued to believe that Marxist literary criticism invigorates the discipline with a "true and lively spirit of opposition" (Bonnycastle, 2007, p. 4).

3. **titles of stand-alone works:** Stand-alone works are those that are published on their own rather than as part of another work. The titles of stand-alone works (e.g., journals, magazines, newspapers, books, and reports) should be in italics. Writers in the social and behavioural sciences do not normally put the titles of works in the bodies of their papers, but if you do include the title of a stand-alone work, all major words and all words of four letters or more should be capitalized. For book and report titles in the References list, however, capitalize only the first word of the title and subtitle (if any), plus any proper nouns. Journal, magazine, and newspaper titles in the list of References are exceptions; for these, capitalize all major words.

4. **titles of articles and chapters of books:** The titles of these works, and anything else that is published as part of another work, are also not usually mentioned in the body of an essay, though if they are, they should be put in quotation marks, with all major words capitalized. In the References, however, titles of these works should *not* be put in quotation marks or italicized, and no words should be capitalized, with the exception of any proper nouns, and the first word in the title and the first in the subtitle, if any.

5. **placing of in-text citations:** When the author's name appears in a signal phrase, the in-text citation comes directly after the name. Otherwise, the citation follows the paraphrased or quoted material. If a quotation ends with punctuation other than a period or comma, then this should precede the end of the quotation, and a period or comma should still follow the parenthetical reference, if this is grammatically appropriate.

- The claim has been convincingly refuted by Ricks (2010), but it nevertheless continues to be put forward (Dendel, 2015).
- One of Berra's favourite coaching tips was that "ninety per cent of the game is half mental" (Adelman, 2007, p. 98).
- Berra at one point said to his players, "You can observe a lot by watching!" (Adelman, 2007, p. 98).
- Garner (2011) associates statistics and pleasure.

6. **citations when text is in parentheses:** If a parenthetical reference occurs within text in parentheses, commas are used to set off elements of the reference.

- (See Figure 6.1 of Harrison, 2014, for data on transplant waiting lists.)

7. **electronic source—page number unavailable:** If a Web document cited is in PDF format, the page numbers are stable and may be cited as one would the pages of a printed source. The page numbers of many Web sources are unstable, however, and many more lack page numbers altogether. In such cases you should provide a section or paragraph number if a reference is needed. For paragraphs, use the abbreviation "para."

- In a recent Web posting a leading theorist has clearly stated that he finds such an approach "thoroughly objectionable" (Bhabha, 2012, para. 7).
- Bhabha (2012) has clearly stated his opposition to this approach.
- Carter and Zhaba (2009) describe this approach as "more reliable than that adopted by Perkins" (Method section, para. 2).

If you are citing longer texts from electronic versions, chapter references may be more appropriate. For example, if the online Gutenberg edition of Darwin's *On the Origin of Species* were being cited, the citation would be as follows:

- Darwin refers to the core of his theory as an "ineluctable principle" (1856, Chapter 26).

Notice that *chapter* is capitalized and not abbreviated.

Students should be cautioned that online editions of older or classic works are often unreliable; typically there are far more typos and other errors in such versions than there are in print versions. It is often possible to exercise judgement about such matters, however. If, for example, you are not required to base your essay on a particular edition of Darwin's *Origin of Species* but may find your own, you will be far better off using the text you will find on the reputable Project Gutenberg site than you will using a text you might find on a site such as "Manybooks.com."

8. **two or more dates for a work:** If you have consulted a re-issue of a work (whether in printed or electronic form), you should provide both the original date of publication and the date of the re-issue (the date of the version you are using).

- Emerson (1837/1909) asserted that America's "long apprenticeship to the learning of other lands" was "drawing to a close" (para. 1).

The relevant entry in the list of references would look like this:

- Emerson, R. W. (1909). *Essays and English traits*. New York, NY: P. F. Collier & Son. (Original work published 1837)

If you are citing work in a form that has been revised by the author, however, you should cite the date of the revised publication, not the original.

- In a preface to the latest edition of his classic work (2004), Watson discusses its genesis.

9. **multiple authors:** If there are two or three authors, all authors should be named either in the signal phrase or in the in-text citation. Use *and* in the signal phrase but *&* in parentheses.

- Chambliss and Best (2013) have argued that the nature of this research is practical as well as theoretical.
- Two distinguished scholars have argued that the nature of this research is practical as well as theoretical (Chambliss & Best, 2013).

three to five authors: In the body of the text list the names of all authors the first time the work is referred to; for subsequent references use only the first author's name, followed by *et al.* (short for the Latin *et alia*: *and others*).

- Chambliss, Best, Didby, and Jones (2015) have argued that the nature of this research is practical as well as theoretical.
- Four distinguished scholars have argued that the nature of this research is practical as well as theoretical (Chambliss, Best, Didby, & Jones, 2015).

more than five authors: Use only the first author's name, followed by *et al.* (short for the Latin *et alia*: *and others*).

- Chambliss et al. (2015) have argued that the nature of this research is practical as well as theoretical.
- Six distinguished scholars have argued that the nature of this research is practical as well as theoretical (Chambliss et al., 2015).

10. **corporate author:** As you would with an individual human author, provide the name of a corporate author either in the body of your text or in a parenthetical citation. Recommended practice is to provide the full name of an organization on the first occasion, followed by an abbreviation, and then to use the abbreviation for subsequent references:

- Blindness has decreased markedly but at an uneven pace since the late 1800s (National Institute for the Blind [NIB], 2013).

11. **author not given:** If the author of the source is not given, it may be identified in the parenthetical reference by a short form of the title.

- Confusion over voting reform is widespread ("Results of National Study," 2012).

12. **date not given:** Some sources, particularly electronic ones, do not provide a date of publication. Where this is the case, use the abbreviation *n.d.* for *no date*.

- Some still claim that evidence of global climate change is difficult to come by (Sanders, n.d.; Zimmerman, 2012).

13. **two or more works in the same citation:** In this case, the works should appear in in-text citations in the same order they do in the list of references. If the works are by different authors, arrange the sources alphabetically by author's last name and separate the citations with a semi-colon. If the works are by the same authors, arrange the sources by publication date. Add *a*, *b*, *c*, etc. after the year to distinguish works written by the same authors in the same year.

- Various studies have established a psychological link between fear and sexual arousal (Aikens, Cox, & Bartlett, 1998; Looby & Cairns, 2011).

- Various studies appear to have established a psychological link between fear and sexual arousal (Looby & Cairns, 1999, 2002, 2011).
- Looby and Cairns (1999a, 1999b, 2007, 2011a, 2011b) have investigated extensively the link between fear and sexual arousal.

14. **two or more authors with the same last name:** If the References list includes two or more authors with the same last name, the in-text citation should supply an initial:

- One of the leading economists of the time advocated wage and price controls (H. Johnston, 1977).

15. **works in a collection of readings or anthology:** In the in-text citation for a work in an anthology or collection of readings, use the name of the author of the work, not that of the editor of the anthology. If the work was first published in the collection you have consulted, there is only the one date to cite. But if the work is reprinted in that collection after having first been published elsewhere, cite the date of the original publication and the date of the collection you have consulted, separating these dates with a slash. The following citation refers to an article by Frederic W. Gleach that was first published in a collection of readings edited by Jennifer Brown and Elizabeth Vibert.

- One of the essays in Brown and Vibert's collection argues that we should rethink the Pocahontas myth (Gleach, 1996).

In your list of references, this work should be alphabetized under Gleach, the author of the piece you have consulted, not under Brown.

The next example is a lecture by Georg Simmel first published in 1903, which a student consulted in an edited collection by Roberta Garner that was published in 2001.

- Simmel (1903/2001) argues that the "deepest problems of modern life derive from the claim of the individual to preserve the autonomy and individuality of his existence" (p. 141).

The reference list entry would look like this:

Simmel, G. (2001). The metropolis and mental life. In R. Garner
(Ed.), *Social theory—Continuity and confrontation: A reader* (pp.
141–153). Peterborough, ON: Broadview Press. (Original work
published in 1903)

As you can see, in your reference list these works are listed
under the authors of the pieces (Gleach or Simmel), not under
the compilers, editors, or translators of the collection (Brown
& Vibert or Garner). If you cite another work by a different author from the same anthology or book of readings, that
should appear as a separate entry in your list of references—
again, alphabetized under the author's name.

16. **indirect source:** If you are citing a source from a reference
other than the source itself, you should use the phrase "as cited
in" in your in-text citation.

- In de Beauvoir's famous phrase, "one is not born a woman, one
becomes one" (as cited in Levey, 2015, para. 3).

In this case, the entry in your reference list would be for Levey,
not de Beauvoir.

17. **private and personal communications:** Since the list of
references should include only sources that your readers can
access themselves, it should not include personal, private, and
undocumented or unarchived communications, whether these
are by telephone, written letter, e-mail, or other means. Cite
these communications only in your text. Provide the initials
and surname of the person you communicated with as well as
the date of communication.

- K. Montegna (personal communication, January 21, 2015) has
expressed skepticism over this method's usefulness.

38c. About References

The list of references in APA style is an alphabetized listing of
sources that appears at the end of an essay, article, or book.
Usually, it includes all the information necessary to identify
and retrieve each of the sources you have cited, and only the

works you have cited. In this case the list is entitled *References*. If the list includes all works you have consulted, regardless of whether or not you have cited them, it should be entitled *Bibliography*. The list of references should include only sources that can be accessed by your readers, and so it should not include private communication, such as private letters, memos, e-mail messages, and telephone or personal conversations. Those should be cited only in your text (see the section above).

Entries should be ordered alphabetically by author surname, or, if there is no known author, by title. The first line of each entry should be flush with the left-hand margin, with all subsequent lines indented about one half inch. Double-space throughout the list of references.

The basic format for all entries is author (if available), date (give *n.d.* if there is no date), title, and publication information. Remember that one function of the list of references is to provide the information your readers need if they wish to locate your sources for themselves; APA allows any "non-routine" information that could assist in identifying the sources to be added in square brackets to any entry (e.g., [Sunday business section], [Motion picture], [Interview with O. Sacks]).

In the References examples that follow, information about entries for electronic sources has been presented in an integrated fashion alongside information about referencing sources in other media, such as print, film, and so on. Whenever you are required to give a website URL that does not all fit on one line, do not insert a hyphen; break the URL before a slash or period (with the exception of the slashes in *http://*).

18. **book with single author:** For a work with one author the entry should begin with the last name, followed by a comma, and then the author's initials as applicable, followed by the date of publication in parentheses. Note that initials are generally used rather than first names, even when authors are identified by first name in the work itself. For publishers in North America, give the city and an abbreviation of the state or province of publication; give the city and country for works

published elsewhere. Leave out abbreviations such as *Inc.* and *Co.* in publisher's names but keep *Press* and *Books*.

> Gee, J. P. (2012). *Social linguistics and literacies: Ideology in discourses* (4th ed.). London, England: Routledge.

19. **two to seven authors:** Last names should in all cases come first, followed by initials. Use commas to separate the authors' names, and use an ampersand rather than *and* before the last author. Note that the authors' names should appear in the order they are listed; sometimes this is not alphabetical.

> Eagles, M., Bickerton, J. P., & Gagnon, A. (1991). *The almanac of Canadian politics*. Peterborough, ON: Broadview Press.

20. **more than seven authors:** List the names of the first six authors, add an ellipsis, and then give the last author's name.

> Newsome, M. R., Scheibel, R. S., Hanten, G., Chu, Z., Steinberg, J. L., Hunter, J. V. … Levin, H. S. (2010). Brain activation while thinking about the self from another person's perspective after traumatic brain injury in adolescents. *Neuropsychology, 24*(2), 139–147.

21. **corporate author:** If a work has been issued by a government body, a corporation, or some other organization and no author is identified, the entry should be listed by the name of the group. If this group is also the work's publisher, write *Author* where the publisher's name would normally go.

> Broadview Press. (2007). *Annual report*. Calgary, AB: Author.
> Broadview Press. (n.d.). Questions and answers about book pricing. *Broadview Press Web Site*. Retrieved from www .broadviewpress.com/bookpricing.asp?inc=bookpricing
> City of Toronto, City Planning Division. (2000, June). *Toronto at the crossroads: Shaping our future*. Toronto, ON: Author.

22. **works with unknown author:** Works with an unknown author should be alphabetized by title.

> *Columbia encyclopedia* (6th ed.). (2001). New York, NY: Columbia University Press.

If you have referred to only one entry in an encyclopedia or dictionary, however, the entry in your list of references should be by the title of that entry (see below).

23. **two or more works by the same author:** The author's name should appear for all entries. Entries should be ordered by year of publication.

> Menand, L. (2002). *The metaphysical club: A story of ideas in America.* New York, NY: Knopf.
>
> Menand, L. (2004, June 28). Bad comma: Lynne Truss's strange grammar [Review of the book *Eats, shoots & leaves*]. *The New Yorker.* Retrieved from http://www.newyorker.com

If two or more cited works by the same author have been published in the same year, arrange these alphabetically and use letters to distinguish among them: (2011a), (2011b), and so on.

24. **edited works:** Entries for edited works include the abbreviation *Ed.* or *Eds.* The second example below is for a book with both an author and an editor; since the original work in this entry was published earlier than the present edition, that information is given in parentheses at the end.

> Gross, B., Field, D., & Pinker, L. (Eds.). (2002). *New approaches to the history of psychoanalysis.* New York, NY: Duckworth.
>
> Sapir, E. (1981). *Selected writings in language, culture, and personality.* D. G. Mandelbaum (Ed.). Berkeley, CA: University of California Press. (Original work published 1949)

25. **works with an author and a translator:** The translator's name, along with the designation *Trans.*, is included in parentheses after the title; the original publication date is given in parentheses following the present edition's publication information.

> Jung, C. G. (2006). *The undiscovered self* (R. F. C. Hull, Trans.). New York, NY: Signet. (Original work published 1959)

26. **selections from anthologies or collections of readings:** A selection from a collection of readings or an anthology should be listed as follows:

APA Style

Gleach, F. W. (1996). Controlled speculation: Interpreting the saga of Pocahontas and Captain John Smith. In J. Brown & E. Vibert (Eds.), *Reading beyond words: Contexts for Native history* (pp. 21–42). Peterborough, ON: Broadview.

Rosengarten, H. (2012). Fleiss's nose and Freud's mind: A new perspective. In B. Gross, D. Field, & L. Pinker (Eds.), *New approaches to the history of psychoanalysis* (pp. 232–243). New York, NY: Duckworth.

Taylor, E. (1992). Biological consciousness and the experience of the transcendent: William James and American functional psychology. In R. H. Wozniak (Ed.), *Mind and body: René Descartes to William James*. Retrieved from http://serendip.brynmawr.edu/Mind/James.html

27. electronic version of a print book: Give the site's URL in the place where publication information would normally go.

Bailey, K. D. (1994). *Sociology and the new systems theory: Toward a theoretical synthesis*. Retrieved from https://play.google.com/

28. journal articles: Notice that article titles are not enclosed in quotation marks, and that both the journal title and the volume number are in italics. If all issues of a given volume of a journal begin with page 1, include the issue number as well, directly after the volume number, in parentheses and not italicized. For online journal articles, you should also include the digital object identifier (DOI): a string of numbers, letters, and punctuation, beginning with *10*, usually located on the first or copyright page. If no DOI is available, you should include the URL for the journal's homepage.

Barker, P. (2004). The impact of class size on the classroom behaviour of special needs students: A longitudinal study. *Educational Quarterly, 25*(4), 87–99.

Best, R. K. (2012). Disease politics and medical research funding: Three ways advocacy shapes policy. *American Sociological Review, 77*, 780–803. Retrieved from http://asr.sagepub.com/

Laughlin, C. D., & Tiberia, V. A. (2012). Archetypes: Toward a Jungian anthropology of consciousness. *Anthropology of Consciousness, 23*, 127–157. doi:10.1111/j.1556-3537.2012.01063.x

Surtees, P. (2008). The psychology of the children's crusade of 1212. *Studies in Medieval History and Society, 3*(4), 279–325. doi:10.1008/smhs.2008.0581

29. abstract of a journal article: Cite as you would the journal article itself, adding *Abstract* in square brackets.

Laughlin, C. D., & Tiberia, V. A. (2012). Archetypes: Toward a Jungian anthropology of consciousness [Abstract]. *Anthropology of Consciousness, 23*, 127–157. doi:10.1111/j.1556-3537.2012.01063.x

30. magazine articles: The basic principles are the same as for journal articles. Note that neither quotation marks nor italics are used for the titles of articles. If no author is identified, the title of the article should appear first. For monthly magazines, provide the month as well as the year; for magazines issued more frequently, give the day, month, and year. Include the homepage URL for magazine articles online.

Dyer, A. (2012, November/December). The end of the world … again. *SkyNews, 18*(4), 38–39.

The rise of the yuan: Turning from green to red. (2012, October 20). *The Economist, 405*(42), 67–68.

Steavenson, W. (2012, November 12). Two revolutions: Women in the new Egypt. *The New Yorker, 88*(35), 32–38. Retrieved from http://www.newyorker.com

31. newspaper articles: The basic principles to follow with newspaper articles or editorials are the same as with magazine articles (see above), but volume and issue numbers are not included, and page numbers are preceded by *p.* or *pp.* APA requires that all page numbers for print versions be provided when articles do not continue on consecutive pages. Notice that if there is no letter assigned to a newspaper section, you should give the section's title in square brackets.

Bennett, J. (2012, December 16). How to attack the gender pay gap? *The New York Times* [Sunday business section], pp. 1, 6.

Gray, J. (2012, December 20). Stepping into the proxy frays. *The Globe and Mail*, p. B6.

If you are citing an online version of a newspaper article you have retrieved through a search of its website, you should provide the URL for the site, not for the exact location of the article. Since the online version of the article in the example below does not have page numbers, none are included in the References entry.

Gray, J. (2012, December 20). Stepping into the proxy frays. *The Globe and Mail*. Retrieved from http://www.globeandmail .com

32. **book reviews:** The name of the reviewer (if it has been provided) should come first, followed by the date and title of the review, and the information on the book itself, as follows:

Tavris, C. (2012, April 25). Psychology and its discontents. [Review of the book *Psychology's ghosts: The crisis in the profession and the way back*, by J. Kagan]. *Wall Street Journal*. Retrieved from http://online.wsj.com/article/SB10001424 05270230453790457727776026027614 8.html

33. **reference work entries:** List by the author of the entry, if known; otherwise, list by the entry itself.

Lister, M. (1999). Consumers' Association of Canada. *The Canadian encyclopedia* (Year 2000 ed.). Toronto, ON: McClelland & Stewart.

Saint Lawrence Seaway. (2001). *The Columbia encyclopedia* (6th ed.). Retrieved from http://www.bartleby.com/65/st /STLawrSwy.html

34. **films and video recordings:** Begin entries for motion pictures with the names of the producers and director, followed by the date of release, the film's title, the medium in square brackets, the location of origin, and the name of the studio.

Ball, C. J., Ryder, A., Tyrer, W., Dysinger, E., Todd, J., Todd, S., Thomas, E. (Producers), & Nolan, C. (Director). (2000). *Memento* [Blu-ray disc]. United States: Newmarket Films.

Egoyan, A., Weiss, J., Vroll, S., Iron, D. (Producers), & Polley, S. (Director). (2006). *Away from her* [Motion picture]. Canada: Lionsgate Films.

35. episodes from television series: Entries for television show episodes should begin with the names of the writer and director, followed by the date, episode title, medium, producer's name, series title, location, and production company's name. Identify the role, in parentheses, of each person listed.

Weiner, M. (Writer), & Getzinger, J. (Director). (2012). A little kiss [Television series episode]. In M. Weiner (Executive producer), *Mad men*. Santa Monica, CA: Lionsgate Television.

36. podcasts: Use the entry for a television series episode as a model, giving the type of podcast as the medium, and adding the website's URL. Give the full date of the original broadcast.

Eisen, J. (Writer). (2010, May 17–31). Have your meat and eat it too! Parts 1–3. [Audio podcast]. In L. Noth (Producer), *CBCideas*. Retrieved from http://www.cbc.ca/ideas/episodes/2010/05/17/have-your-meat-and-eat-it-too-part-1-2-listen/

37. music recordings: Arrange an entry for a music recording as follows: give the writer's name, the copyright date of the piece of music, its title, the album title, the medium in square brackets, the place of origin, and the label name. If the piece is recorded by someone other than the writer, note that in square brackets after the piece's title. Add the recording date at the end of the entry if it differs from the copyright date.

Berlin, I. (1935). Cheek to cheek [Recorded by J. Pass]. On *Blues for Fred* [CD]. Berkeley, CA: Pablo Records. (1988, February 3).

Waits, T. (1999). Eyeball kid. On *Mule Variations* [CD]. Los Angeles, CA: Anti.

38. **interviews:** How you format an entry for an interview will depend on where it is located. If you watched or listened to a recording of the interview, use the format appropriate to the medium. The second example below is for an interview of Jane Goodall on the television program *Bill Moyers Journal*, which was accessed online as a video webcast. Notice that the interviewee's name comes first, and that the entry is formatted in the same way as an entry for a television series episode that is available online. The first example is for an interview with Willie Nelson printed in a periodical. Here, the entry follows the format for a newspaper article, with the interviewer in the author position, and information about the interviewee in square brackets. Notice as well that, although the periodical is called a magazine, this publication goes by date only, not volume and issue number, and so the newspaper article format is the appropriate choice. These guidelines apply only to published interviews; unpublished interviews you have conducted yourself are considered private correspondence and should not be included in your References list.

> Goldman, A. (2012, December 16). The silver-headed stranger [Interview with W. Nelson]. *New York Times Magazine*, p. 12.
>
> Goodall, J. (2009, November 27). Interview by B. Moyers. In G. Ablow, W. Brangham, P. Meryash, B. Rate, & C. White (Producers), *Bill Moyers journal* [Video webcast]. Retrieved from http://www.pbs.org/moyers/journal/11272009/watch1.html

39. **documents on a website:** Give the author's name and date, if available (use *n.d.* for no date), the work's title, and the retrieval information.

> LePan, D. (n.d.) The psychology of skyscrapers. Retrieved from http://donlepan.com

40. **blog posts:** Start with the writer's name; then give the full date, entry title, blog title, and retrieval information.

Gautam, S. (2012, July 22). Structure of childhood tempera-
ments. *The mouse trap*. Retrieved from http://the-mouse-trap
.com/2012/07/22/structure-of-childhood-temperaments
/#comment-6470

41. entries in a wiki: Because wikis can be revised by anyone,
their content tends to change over time. It is important, therefore, to include your date of access in the References entry.
Wiki entries often have no single date of publication; if that's
the case, use *n.d.*

Code-switching. (n.d.). In *Wikipedia*. Retrieved January 17,
2013, from http://en.wikipedia.org/wiki/Code_switching

42. tweets: If the author's real name is known, provide it first,
followed by the author's screen name in square brackets. If
the author's real name cannot be determined, provide only the
screen name, without the square brackets. Include only the
date, not the time, of posting, and add *Twitter post* in square
brackets. Include the entire tweet.

Welch, J. [jack_welch]. (2012, October 5). Unbelievable jobs
numbers..these Chicago guys will do anything..can't
debate so change numbers [Twitter post]. Retrieved from
http://twitter.com/jack_welch

43. other Web references: In the case of online sources not
covered by the above, the same basic principles apply. Where
an author or editor is indicated, list by author; otherwise, list
by title. If the source is undated or its content likely to change,
you should include the date on which you accessed the material. Use square brackets to include information that will help
identify the source.

Brown University. (2006, May). Brown University. Women
writers project. Retrieved February 28, 2013, from http://
www.brown.edu/

44. maps or charts: Include the medium in square brackets.

Profile of book publishing and exclusive agency, for English language firms [Chart]. (2012). Statistics Canada. Retrieved
from http://www.statcan.ca/english/pgdb/arts02.htm

38d. APA Style Sample Essay Pages

Following are sample pages from an essay written in APA style. Note that the full essay, as well as additional sample essays in APA style, appear on the companion website associated with this book.

Among the details to notice in this reference system:

- Where two or more works by the same author are included in References, they are ordered by date of publication.

- APA style prefers author initials rather than first names.

- Only the first words of titles and subtitles are capitalized, except for proper nouns.

- The date appears in parentheses near the beginning of each entry in References.

- The in-text citation comes directly after the name of the author or after the end quotation mark. Often, these citations fall just before the period or comma in the surrounding sentence.

- If an in-text citation occurs within text in parentheses, commas are used to set off elements of the reference.

- When a work has appeared in an edited collection, information on the editors must be included in the reference.

- Authors' first and last names are reversed; note the use of the ampersand (&) in place of *and* between author names.

- Translators should be included where appropriate in the References list.

- Publisher as well as city of publication, including abbreviations for all states and provinces, should be given in References entries for print works.

- Months and publisher names are not abbreviated; the day of the month follows the name of the month.

- Online references include the date of publication or of last revision in parentheses immediately after the author's name. Note that, if a URL ends a reference entry, there is no period at the end of the entry.

top right-
hand corner
pagination
begins with
title page

Resistance to Vaccination:

A Review of the Literature

Jeremy Yap

Vancouver Island University

author's
name may
appear
either just
below the
title (as
shown) or
at the bot-
tom of the
page with
course and
instructor
information

Author note

This paper was prepared for Psychology 230,

taught by Professor J.B. Martin.

RESISTANCE TO VACCINATION   2

Abstract

In the past generation concern over the safety of vaccination against a variety of diseases has become common in North America, as well as in Britain and some other European countries. This paper reviews findings as to the safety of vaccines, as well as of their effectiveness in preventing the diseases they are designed to combat. It also explores the reasons for the now-widespread mistrust of vaccination, looking at the role played by the media, by health care professionals—and looking too at the findings of social psychologists. Finally, it asks what approaches may be most effective in increasing rates of vaccination; in all likelihood, the paper suggests, no single approach is likely to be enough.

separate page for the abstract

APA Style

title should be centred

Resistance to Vaccination:

A Review of the Literature

Since the late 1990s, vaccination has become highly controversial. This paper will review the literature on the subject, with a particular focus on the vaccination of children, by posing and responding to three key questions:

1. How effective is the practice of vaccination—and how safe?

2. Why have vaccination rates declined?

3. What are the best ways to increase rates of vaccination?

This is an area in which medical science must engage with the research findings of social psychologists; there is an urgent need to find effective solutions. The problems are sufficiently complex, however, that it seems unlikely that any single approach will be sufficient to resolve them.

How Effective Is the Practice of Vaccination—and How Safe?

There is overwhelming evidence on a variety of fronts that vaccination is one of the great triumphs of modern medical science. Thanks to the spread of vaccination, smallpox and polio have been eliminated in most of the world. The Centers for Disease Control and Prevention (2014) reports that diseases such as measles, mumps, and rubella, for which a combined

APA Style

vaccine has for generations been routinely given to children, are almost unknown in areas where vaccination is near-universal. The example of measles is an instructive one. Before the practice of vaccination was introduced, measles infected several million children every year in the United States alone, and killed more than 500 annually. After vaccination became common practice, measles almost entirely disappeared in North America—until recently. Now it is a threat once again in the United States and Canada—and not a threat to be taken lightly. According to the World Health Organization (2015), measles still kills over 100,000 worldwide each year; for 2012 the figure was 122,000.

Evidence for the effectiveness of vaccination is very strong in the case of polio and smallpox, and in the case of "childhood diseases" such as measles and rubella. There is also strong evidence that vaccination against influenza has been successful in bringing about significantly reduced rates of infection (Brewer et al., 2007). Importantly, though, the success of vaccination depends in large part on so-called "herd immunity." So long as approximately 95% or thereabouts of a population have been vaccinated, the incidence of a disease catching on in that population are negligible. When vaccination rates dip below that level, however, the risk for those who have

for citation of work with six or more authors use "et al."

RESISTANCE TO VACCINATION   5

not been vaccinated increases dramatically. Despite this, some communities where vaccination is readily available nonetheless have vaccination rates dramatically below the percentage required for herd immunity. In California, for example, where a 2015 outbreak of measles has received wide attention, Maimuna et al. (2015) have estimated that in the relevant population clusters vaccination rates have dropped below 50%.

What about the other side of the ledger? Have there been cases of patients suffering adverse effects after taking a vaccine? And if so, do the benefits of vaccination outweigh the risks? Here too the answers seem clear. Yes, there have been cases of adverse effects (notably, fever and allergic reactions for some individuals). But as Bonhoeffer (2007) and others have concluded, these are rare, and on balance vastly outweighed by the benefits of mass vaccination. Perhaps the broadest study of vaccines, their effectiveness, and their occasional side effects was that conducted by the Institute of Medicine (2011), which reviewed vaccines used against chickenpox, influenza, hepatitis B, human papillomavirus, measles, mumps, rubella, meningitis, and tetanus. Their conclusion was clear:

> Vaccines offer the promise of protection against a
> variety of infectious diseases ... [and] remain one
> of the greatest tools in the public health arsenal.

square brackets used for a word not in the original quotation

> Certainly, some vaccines result in adverse effects that must be acknowledged. But the latest evidence shows that few adverse effects are caused by the vaccines reviewed in this report. (p. 4)

Except in rare cases, then (as with certain individuals susceptible to severe allergic reactions), the benefits of vaccines clearly far outweigh the risks.

Why Have Vaccination Rates Declined?

centred headings for sections

Near the end of the last century, British medical researcher Andrew Wakefield and his colleagues (1998) published a study linking the vaccination of children against diseases such as measles, mumps, and rubella to increased incidence of gastrointestinal disease, and also to increased incidence of "developmental regression"—notably, autism. The study appeared in *The Lancet*, one of the world's leading medical journals, and had a major impact—but an entirely unfortunate one. News of the study's findings spread widely, with thousands of articles in the popular press in 2001 and 2002 questioning the safety of vaccination. Parents whose children suffered from autism started to blame vaccination, and many of them launched lawsuits.

It was not until six years later that serious doubts were publicly raised. Investigative journalist Brian Deer (2004)

APA Style

References

list of references alphabetized by author's last name

Belluz, J. (2015, February 7). Debunking vaccine junk science won't change people's minds. Here's what will. [Interview with B. Nyhan]. *Vox*. Retrieved from http://www.vox.com/2015/2/7/7993289/vaccine-beliefs

Bonhoeffer, J., & Heininger, U. (2007). Adverse events following immunization: perception and evidence. *Current Opinion in Infectious Diseases, 20*(3), 237–246. doi:10.1097/QCO.0b013e32811ebfb0

author initials used—not first names

Brewer, N. T., Chapman, G. B., Gibbons, F. X., Gerrard, M., McCaul, K. D., & Weinstein, N. D. (2007). Meta-analysis of the relationship between risk perception and health behaviour: The example of vaccination. *Health Psychology, 26*(2), 136–145. doi:10.1037/0278-6133.26.2.136

Chapin, A. (2015, February 13). How to talk to anti-vaxxers. *Ottawa Citizen*. Retrieved from http://ottawacitizen.com/opinion/columnists/how-to-talk-to-anti-vaxxers

Deer, B. (2004, February 22). Revealed: MMR research scandal. *The Sunday Times* (London). Retrieved from http://www.thesundaytimes.co.uk/sto/

El-Amin, A. N., Parra, M.T., Kim-Farley, R., & Fielding, J.E. (2012). Ethical issues concerning vaccination requirements. *Public Health Reviews, 34*(1), 1–20.

Retrieved from http://www.publichealthreviews.eu
/upload/pdf_files/11/00_El_Amin.pdf

Groopman, J. (2015, March 5). There's no way out of it.
[Review of the book *On immunity: An introduction*]. *The
New York Review of Books*, 29–31.

Haverkate, M., D'Ancona, F., Giambi, C., Johansen, K.
Lopalco, P. L., Cozza, V., & Appelgren, E. (2012, May).
Mandatory and recommended vaccination in the EU,
Iceland and Norway: results of the VENICE 2010
survey on the ways of implementing national vaccination
programmes. *Eurosurveillance*, *17*(22), 31. Retrieved from
http://www.eurosurveillance.org/ViewArticle
.aspx?ArticleId=20183

Institute of Medicine. (2011, August 25). Adverse effects of
vaccines: Evidence and causality. Report brief. Retrieved
from http://www.iom.edu/Reports/2011/Adverse-Effects-
of-Vaccines-Evidence-and-Causality.aspx

Kraft, P. W., Lodge, M., & Taber, C. S. (2015, March).
Why people "don't trust the evidence": Motivated
reasoning and scientific beliefs. *Annals of the American
Academy of Political and Social Science*, *658*(1), 121–133.
doi:10.1177/0002716214554758

for web-accessed material provide DOI whenever available

CONTENTS

39. CHICAGO STYLE

39a. About Chicago Style

The University of Chicago's massively comprehensive *Chicago Manual of Style* (17th edition, 2017), provides full information on two documentation systems: an author-date system of citation that is similar to APA style, and a traditional foot- or endnoting system. The latter, which this book refers to as Chicago Style, and which is often used in the history and philosophy disciplines, is outlined below. This chapter also includes, at the end, a short essay excerpt using Chicago Style documentation. Full sample essays in Chicago Style are available on the Broadview website. Go to sites.broadviewpress. com/writing/. You can also find additional information at Chicago Style's online site (www.chicagomanualofstyle.org).

In the pages that follow, information about electronic sources has been presented in an integrated fashion, with information about referencing hard copies of print sources presented alongside information about referencing online versions. General guidelines covering entries for online sources are as follows. Begin each note and bibliography entry for an electronic source as you would for a non-electronic source, including all relevant publication information that the source makes available. Then provide either the website's URL, followed by the usual end punctuation for the note or entry, or, if available, the source's digital object identifier (DOI): a string of numbers, letters, and punctuation, beginning with 10, usually located on the first or copyright page. If both a URL and DOI are available, provide only the latter; DOIs are preferred because they are stable links to sources, whereas URLs are often not permanent. If you need to break a URL or DOI over two or more lines, do not insert any hyphens at the break point; instead, break after a colon or double slash or before other marks of punctuation. Note that Chicago Style does not put angle brackets around URLs. Except when there is no publication or modification date available, Chicago Style

Chicago Style

does not require the addition of access dates for online material, but your instructors may wish you to include them. If so, put them after the URL or DOI, after the word *accessed*.

1. **notes:** The basic principle of Chicago Style is to create a note each time one cites a source. The note can appear at the foot of the page on which the citation is made, or it can be part of a separate list, titled *Notes*, situated at the end of the essay and before the bibliography. For both foot- and endnotes, a superscript number at the end of the clause in which the reference appears points to the relevant note:

- Bonnycastle refers to "the true and lively spirit of opposition" with which Marxist literary criticism invigorates the discipline.[1]

The superscript number [1] here is linked to the information provided where the same number appears at either the foot of the page or in the list of notes at the end of the main text of the paper:

> 1. Stephen Bonnycastle, *In Search of Authority: An Introductory Guide to Literary Theory*, 3rd ed. (Peterborough, ON: Broadview Press, 2007), 204.

Notice that the author's name is in the normal order, elements of the note are separated by commas, publication information is in parentheses, and the first line of the note is indented. The note ends with a page number for the citation.

In addition, all works cited, as well as works that have been consulted but are not cited in the body of your essay, must be included in an alphabetically arranged list, titled *Bibliography*, that appears at the end of the essay. The entry there would in this case be as follows:

Bonnycastle, Stephen. *In Search of Authority: An Introductory Guide to Literary Theory*. 3rd ed. Peterborough, ON: Broadview Press, 2007.

In the entry in the bibliography, notice that the author's name is inverted, elements of the entry are separated by periods, and no parentheses are placed around the publication information. Also, the entry is given a hanging indent: the first line is flush with the left-hand margin, and subsequent lines are indented. Notice as well that the province or state of publication is included in both notes and bibliography entries if the city of publication is not widely known.

In the various examples that follow, note formats and bibliography entry formats for each kind of source are shown together.

2. titles: italics/quotation marks: Notice in the above example that both the title and the subtitle are in italics. Titles of short works (such as articles, poems, and short stories) should be put in quotation marks. In all titles key words should be capitalized. For more details, see the Title of Source section in the chapter on MLA documentation above.

3. multiple references to the same work: For later notes referencing an already-cited source, use the author's last name, title (in shortened form if it is over four words long), and page number only.

> 1. Bonnycastle, *In Search of Authority*, 28.

If successive references are to the same work, you may omit the title of the work just cited to avoid repetition.[1]

> 1. Sean Carver, "The Economic Foundations for Unrest in East Timor, 1970–1995," *Journal of Economic History* 21, no. 2 (2011): 103.
> 2. Carver, 109.
> 3. Carver, 111.
> 4. Jennifer Riley, "East Timor in the Pre-Independence Years," *Asian History Online* 11, no. 4 (2012): par. 18, http://www.aho.ubc .edu/prs/text-only/issue.45/16.3jr.txt.
> 5. Riley, par. 24.

> Carver, Sean. "The Economic Foundations for Unrest in East Timor, 1970–1995." *Journal of Economic History* 21, no. 2 (2011): 100–121.

---

1   This recommendation represents a change from previous editions, which had recommended using *ibid.* (an abbreviation of the Latin *ibidem*, meaning *in the same place*) for successive references. The 17th edition discourages the use of *ibid*.

Riley, Jennifer. "East Timor in the Pre-Independence Years." *Asian History Online* 11, no. 4 (2012). http://www.aho.ubc .edu/prs/text-only/issue.45/16.3jr.txt.

4. page number or date unavailable: If an Internet document cited is in PDF format, the page numbers are stable and may be cited in the same way that one would the pages of a printed book or journal article. Many Internet page numbers are unstable, however, and many more lack page numbers. Instead, provide a section number, paragraph number, or other identifier if available.

2. Hanif Bhabha, "Family Life in 1840s Virginia," *Southern History Web Archives* 45, no. 3 (2013): par. 14. http://shweb.ut.edu/history/american.nineteenthc/bhabha.html (accessed March 3, 2015).

Bhabha, Hanif. "Family Life in 1840s Virginia." *Southern History Web Archives* 45, no. 3 (2013). http://shweb.ut.edu /history/american.nineteenthc/bhabha.html.

If you are citing longer texts from electronic versions, and counting paragraph numbers is impracticable, chapter references may be more appropriate. For example, if the online Gutenberg edition of Darwin's *On the Origin of Species* were being cited, the citation would be as follows:

• Darwin refers to the core of his theory as an "ineluctable principle."[1]

1. Charles Darwin, *On the Origin of Species* (1856; Project Gutenberg, 2001), chap. 26, http://www.gutenberg.darwin .origin.frrp.ch26.html.

Darwin, Charles. *On the Origin of Species.* 1856. Project Gutenberg, 2001. http://www.gutenberg.darwin.origin.frrp.ch26 .html.

Students should be cautioned that online editions of older or classic works are often unreliable; typically there are far more typos and other errors in online versions of literary texts than there are in print versions. It is often possible to exercise judgement about such matters, however. If, for example, you are not required to base your essay on a particular edition of Darwin's *Origin of Species* but may find your own, you will be far better off using the text you will find on the reputable Project Gutenberg site than you will using a text you might find on a site such as "Manybooks.com."

When there is no date for a source, include *n. d.*, as in the first example below. When there is no date for an online source, include your access date.

1. Thomas Gray, *Gray's Letters*, vol. 1 (London: John Sharpe, n. d.), 60.

2. Don LePan, *Skyscraper Art*, http://www.donlepan.com /Skyscraper_Art.html (accessed February 10, 2015).

Gray, Thomas. *Gray's Letters*. Vol. 1. London: John Sharpe, n. d.
LePan, Don. *Skyscraper Art*. http://www.donlepan.com /Skyscraper_Art.html (accessed February 10, 2015).

5. **two or more dates for a work:** Note that in the Darwin example above both the date of the original publication and the date of the modern edition are provided. If you are citing work in a form that has been revised by the author, however, you should cite the date of the revised publication, not the original, and use the abbreviation *rev. ed.* to indicate that the work has been revised.

1. Eric Foner, *Free Soil, Free Labor, Free Men: A Study of Antebellum America*, rev. ed. (New York: Oxford University Press, 1999), 178.

Foner, Eric. *Free Soil, Free Labor, Free Men: A Study of Antebellum America*. Rev. ed. New York: Oxford University Press, 1999.

6. **two or three authors:** If there are two or three authors, they should be identified as follows in the footnote and in the Bibliography. Pay attention to where commas do and do not appear, and note that in the Bibliography entry, only the first author's name is inverted. Put the names of the authors in the order in which they appear in the work itself.

4. Eric Alderman and Mark Green, *Tony Blair and the Rise of New Labour* (London: Cassell, 2002), 180.

Alderman, Eric, and Mark Green. *Tony Blair and the Rise of New Labour*. London: Cassell, 2002.

7. **four or more authors:** In the footnote name only the first author, and use the phrase *et al.*, an abbreviation of the Latin *et alia*, meaning *and others*. In the bibliography name all authors, as below:

11. Victoria Fromkin et al., *An Introduction to Language*, 4th Canadian ed. (Toronto: Nelson, 2010), 113.

Fromkin, Victoria, Robert Rodman, Nina Hyams, and Kirsten M. Hummel. *An Introduction to Language*. 4th Canadian ed. Toronto: Nelson, 2010.

8. **author unknown / corporate author / government document:** Identify by the corporate author if known, and otherwise by the title of the work. Unsigned newspaper articles or dictionary and encyclopedia entries are usually not listed in the bibliography. In notes, unsigned dictionary or encyclopedia entries are identified by the title of the reference work, e.g., *Columbia Encyclopedia*, and unsigned newspaper articles are listed by the title of the article in footnotes but by the title of the newspaper in the bibliography. Ignore initial articles (the, a, an) when alphabetizing.

6. *National Hockey League Guide, 1966–67* (Toronto: National Hockey League, 1966), 77.

7. "Argentina's President Calls on UK Prime Minister to Relinquish Control of Falkland Islands," *Vancouver Sun*, January 3, 2013, A9.

8. Broadview Press, "Questions and Answers about Book Pricing," Broadview Press, http://www.broadviewpress.com/bookpricing.asp?inc=bookpricing (accessed January 18, 2013).

9. Commonwealth of Massachusetts, *Records of the Transportation Inquiry, 2004* (Boston: Massachusetts Publishing Office, 2005), 488.

10. *Columbia Encyclopedia*, "Ecuador," http://bartleby.com/columbia.txt.acc.html (accessed February 4, 2013).

11. U.S. Congress. House Committee on Ways and Means, Subcommittee on Trade, *Free Trade Area of the Americas: Hearings*, 105th Cong., 1st sess., July 22, 1997, Hearing Print 105–32, 160, http://www.waysandmeans.house.gov/hearings .asp (accessed January 22, 2015).

Following are the bibliography entries for the preceding notes (notice that, because unsigned newspaper articles and articles from well-known reference works are not usually included in Chicago Style bibliographies, the *Vancouver Sun* and *Columbia Encyclopedia* articles are not included):

Broadview Press. "Questions and Answers about Book Pricing." Broadview Press. http://www.broadviewpress.com /bookpricing.asp?inc=bookpricing (accessed January 18, 2015).

Commonwealth of Massachusetts. *Records of the Transportation Inquiry, 2004.* Boston: Massachusetts Publishing Office, 2005.

National Hockey League Guide, 1966–67. Toronto: National Hockey League, 1966.

U.S. Congress. House Committee on Ways and Means. Subcommittee on Trade. *Free Trade Area of the Americas: Hearings before the Subcommittee on Trade.* 105th Cong., 1st sess., July 22, 1997. Hearing Print 105–32. http://www .waysandmeans.house.gov/hearings.asp (accessed January 22, 2015).

9. **works from a collection of readings or anthology:** In the citation for a work in an anthology or collection of essays, use the name of the author of the work you are citing. If the work is reprinted in one source but was first published elsewhere, include the details of the original publication in the bibliography.

6. Eric Hobsbawm, "Peasant Land Occupations," in *Uncommon People: Resistance and Rebellion* (London: Weidenfeld & Nicolson, 1998), 167.

7. Frederic W. Gleach, "Controlled Speculation: Interpreting the Saga of Pocahontas and Captain John Smith," in *Reading*

Chicago Style

Beyond Words: Contexts for Native History, 2nd ed., ed. Jennifer Brown and Elizabeth Vibert (Peterborough, ON: Broadview Press, 2003), 43.

Gleach, Frederic W. "Controlled Speculation: Interpreting the Saga of Pocahontas and Captain John Smith." In *Reading Beyond Words: Contexts for Native History*, 2nd ed., edited by Jennifer Brown and Elizabeth Vibert, 39–74. Peterborough, ON: Broadview Press, 2003.

Hobsbawm, Eric. "Peasant Land Occupations." In *Uncommon People: Resistance and Rebellion*, 166–90. London: Weidenfeld & Nicolson, 1998. Originally published in *Past and Present* 62 (1974): 120–52.

10. **indirect source:** If you are citing a source from a reference other than the source itself, you should include information about both sources, supplying as much information as you are able to about the original source.

- In de Beauvoir's famous phrase, "one is not born a woman, one becomes one."[1]

1. Simone de Beauvoir, *The Second Sex* (London: Heinemann, 1966), 44, quoted in Ann Levey, "Feminist Philosophy Today," *Philosophy Now*, par. 8, http://www.ucalgary.ca.philosophy.nowsite675.html (accessed February 4, 2015).

de Beauvoir, Simone. *The Second Sex*. London: Heinemann, 1966. Quoted in Ann Levey, "Feminist Philosophy Today," *Philosophy Now*, http://www.ucalgary.ca.philosophy.nowsite675.html (accessed February 4, 2015).

11. **two or more works by the same author:** After the first entry in the bibliography, use three hyphens to begin subsequent entries of works by the same author (rather than repeat the author's name). Entries for multiple works by the same author are normally arranged alphabetically by title.

Menand, Louis. "Bad Comma: Lynne Truss's Strange Grammar." *The New Yorker,* June 28, 2004. http://www.newyorker.com/critics/books/?040628crbo_books1.

---. *The Metaphysical Club: A Story of Ideas in America.* New York: Knopf, 2002.

12. **edited works:** Entries for edited works include the abbreviation *ed.* or *eds.* Note that when *ed.* appears after a title, it means "edited by."

> 5. Brian Gross, ed., *New Approaches to Environmental Politics: A Survey* (New York: Duckworth, 2004), 177.
> 6. Mary Shelley, *Frankenstein*, 3rd ed., ed. Lorne Macdonald and Kathleen Scherf, Broadview Editions (1818; Peterborough, ON: Broadview Press, 2012), 89.

> Gross, Brian, ed. *New Approaches to Environmental Politics: A Survey*. New York: Duckworth, 2004.
> Shelley, Mary. *Frankenstein*. 3rd ed. Edited by Lorne Macdonald and Kathleen Scherf. Broadview Editions. Peterborough, ON: Broadview, 2012. First published in 1818.

13. **translated works:** The name of the translator follows the work's title.

> 1. *Beowulf*, trans. R. M. Liuzza, 2nd ed. (Peterborough, ON: Broadview, 2012), 91.
> 2. Franz Kafka, "A Hunger Artist," *The Metamorphosis and Other Stories*, trans. Ian Johnston (Peterborough, ON: Broadview, 2015), 112.

> *Beowulf*. Translated by R. M. Liuzza. 2nd ed. Peterborough, ON: Broadview, 2012.
> Kafka, Franz. "A Hunger Artist." *The Metamorphosis and Other Stories*. Translated by Ian Johnston. Peterborough, ON: Broadview, 2015.

14. **e-books:** Electronic books come in several formats. The first of the two sample citations below is for a book found online; the second is for a book downloaded onto an e-reader.

> 4. Mary Roberts Rinehart, *Tish* (1916; Project Gutenberg, 2005), chap. 2, http://www.gutenberg.org/catalog/world/readfile?fk_files=1452441.
> 5. Lao Tzu, *Tao Te Ching: A Book about the Way and the Power of the Way*, trans. Ursula K. Le Guin (Boston: Shambhala, 2011), iBook Reader e-book, verse 12.

Lao Tzu. *Tao Te Ching: A Book about the Way and the Power of the Way*. Translated by Ursula K. Le Guin. Boston: Shambhala, 2011. iBook Reader e-book.

Rinehart, Mary Roberts. *Tish*. 1916. Project Gutenberg, 2005. http://www.gutenberg.org/catalog/world/readfile?fk_files=1452441.

15. **magazine articles:** The titles of articles appear in quotation marks. The page range should appear in the bibliography if it is known. (This will not always be possible if the source is an electronic version.) If no authorship is attributed, list the title of the article as the "author" in the footnote, and the magazine title as the "author" in the bibliography. Do not include page numbers for online articles.

2. Alan Dyer, "The End of the World ... Again," *SkyNews*, November/December 2012, 38.

3. "The Rise of the Yuan: Turning from Green to Red," *Economist*, October 20, 2012, 68.

4. Wendell Steavenson, "Two Revolutions: Women in the New Egypt," *The New Yorker*, November 12, 2012, http://www.newyorker.com/reporting/2012/11/12/121112fa_fact_steavenson.

Dyer, Alan. "The End of the World ... Again." *SkyNews*, November/December 2012, 38–39.

Economist. "The Rise of the Yuan: Turning from Green to Red." October 20, 2012, 67–68.

Steavenson, Wendell. "Two Revolutions: Women in the New Egypt." *The New Yorker*, November 12, 2012. http://www.newyorker.com/reporting/2012/11/12/121112fa_fact_steavenson.

16. **newspaper articles:** The basic principles to follow with newspaper articles or editorials are the same as with magazine articles (see above). Give page numbers in the note if your source is a hard copy rather than an electronic version, but indicate section designation alone in the Bibliography entry.

1. Konrad Yakabuski, "Many Looking for Meaning in Vice-Presidential Debate," *The Globe and Mail*, October 12, 2012, A3.

2. Claudia La Rocco, "Where Chekhov Meets Christopher Walken," *New York Times*, January 2, 2013, http://theater.nytimes.com/2013/01/03/theater/reviews/there-there-by-kristen-kosmas-at-the-chocolate-factory.html?ref=theater&_r=0.

La Rocco, Claudia. "Where Chekhov Meets Christopher Walken." *New York Times*, January 2, 2013, http://theater.nytimes.com/2013/01/03/theater/reviews/there-there-by-kristen-kosmas-at-the-chocolate-factory.html?ref=theater&_r=0.

Yakabuski, Konrad. "Many Looking for Meaning in Vice-Presidential Debate." *The Globe and Mail*, October 12, 2012, sec. A.

17. **journal articles:** The basic principles are the same as with magazine articles, but volume number, and issue number after *no.* (if the journal is published more than once a year) should be included as well as the date. Give page numbers where available. For online journal articles, provide the DOI, if available, rather than the URL.

1. Paul Barker, "The Impact of Class Size on the Classroom Behaviour of Special Needs Students: A Longitudinal Study," *Educational Quarterly* 25, no. 4 (2004): 88.

2. Maciel Santos and Ana Guedes, "The Profitability of Slave Labour and the 'Time' Effect," *African Economic History* 36 (2008): 23.

3. Thomas Hurka, "Virtuous Act, Virtuous Dispositions," *Analysis* 66, no. 1 (2006): 72.

4. Ruth Groenhout, "The 'Brain Drain' Problem: Migrating Medical Professionals and Global Health Care," *International Journal of Feminist Approaches to Bioethics* 5, no. 1 (2012): 17, doi: 10.2979/intjfemappbio.5.1.1.

Barker, Paul. "The Impact of Class Size on the Classroom Behaviour of Special Needs Students: A Longitudinal Study." *Educational Quarterly* 25, no. 4 (2004): 87–99.

Groenhout, Ruth. "The 'Brain Drain' Problem: Migrating Medical Professionals and Global Health Care." *International Journal of Feminist Approaches to Bioethics* 5, no. 1 (2012): 1–24, doi: 10.2979/intjfemappbio.5.1.1.

Hurka, Thomas. "Virtuous Act, Virtuous Dispositions." *Analysis* 66, no. 1 (2006): 69–76.

Santos, Maciel, and Ana Guedes. "The Profitability of Slave Labour and the 'Time' Effect." *African Economic History* 36 (2008): 1–26.

18. **films and video recordings:** Include the director's name, the city of production, the production company, and date. Add the medium of publication if the film is recorded on DVD or videocassette.

> 5. *Memento*, directed by Christopher Nolan (Universal City, CA: Summit Entertainment, 2000), DVD.

> 6. *Beasts of the Southern Wild*, directed by Behn Zeitlin (Los Angeles: Fox Searchlight Pictures, 2012).

> *Beasts of the Southern Wild*. Directed by Behn Zeitlin. Los Angeles: Fox Searchlight Pictures, 2012.
> *Memento*. Directed by Christopher Nolan. Universal City, CA: Summit Entertainment, 2000. DVD.

19. **television broadcasts:** Start with the title of the show; then give the episode number, broadcast date, and network. Include the names of the director and writer.

> 1. *Mad Men*, episodes no. 53–54, first broadcast March 25, 2012, by AMC, directed by Jennifer Getzinger and written by Matthew Weiner.

> *Mad Men*. Episodes no. 53–54, first broadcast March 25, 2012, by AMC. Directed by Jennifer Getzinger and written by Matthew Weiner.

20. **sound recordings:** Include the original date of recording if it is different from the recording release date, as well as the recording number and medium.

1. Glenn Gould, performance of *Goldberg Variations*, by Johann Sebastian Bach, recorded 1981, CBS MK 37779, 1982, compact disc.

Gould, Glenn. Performance of *Goldberg Variations*. By Johann Sebastian Bach. Recorded 1981. CBS MK 37779, 1982, compact disc.

21. **interviews and personal communications:** Notes and bibliography entries begin with the name of the person interviewed. Only interviews that are broadcast, published, or available online appear in the bibliography.

7. Louise Erdrich, interview by Bill Moyers, *Bill Moyers Journal*, PBS, April 9, 2010.

8. Ursula K. Le Guin, "Beyond Elvish," interview by Patrick Cox, *The World*, podcast audio, December 13, 2012, http://www.theworld.org/2012/12/beyond-elvish/.

9. Willie Nelson, "The Silver-Headed Stranger," interview by Andrew Goldman, *New York Times Magazine*, December 16, 2012, 12.

10. Herbert Rosengarten, telephone interview by author, January 17, 2015.

Erdrich, Louise. Interview by Bill Moyers. *Bill Moyers Journal*. PBS, April 9, 2010.

Le Guin, Ursula K. "Beyond Elvish." Interview by Patrick Cox. *The World*. Podcast audio. December 13, 2012. http://www.theworld.org/2012/12/beyond-elvish/.

Nelson, Willie. "The Silver-Headed Stranger." Interview by Andrew Goldman, *New York Times Magazine*, December 16, 2012, 12.

22. **book reviews:** The name of the reviewer (if it has been provided) should come first, as shown below:

1. Brian Leiter and Michael Weisberg, "Do You Only Have a Brain? On Thomas Nagel," review of *Why the Materialist Neo-Darwinian Conception of Nature Is Almost Certainly False*, by Thomas Nagel, *The Nation*, October 22, 2012, http://www.thenation.com/article/170334/do-you-only-have-brain-thomas-nagel.

Leiter, Brian, and Michael Weisberg. "Do You Only Have a Brain? On Thomas Nagel." Review of *Why the Materialist Neo-Darwinian Conception of Nature Is Almost Certainly False*, by Thomas Nagel. *The Nation*, October 22, 2012. http://www.thenation.com/article/170334/do-you-only-have-brain-thomas-nagel.

23. **blog posts:** Begin with the author's name, if there is one.

1. Karen Ho, "What Will Gioni's Biennale Look Like?," *The Art History Newsletter*, July 20, 2012, http://arthistory newsletter.com/.

Ho, Karen. "What Will Gioni's Biennale Look Like?" *The Art History Newsletter*. July 20, 2012. http://arthistory newsletter.com/.

24. **websites:** Unless the website title is also that of a book or periodical, do not put the site's title in italics. If possible, indicate when the site was last updated; otherwise, include your date of access.

1. The Camelot Project. University of Rochester, last modified December 21, 2012, http://www.lib.rochester.edu/camelot /cphome.stm.

The Camelot Project. University of Rochester. Last modified December 21, 2012. http://www.lib.rochester.edu /camelot/cphome.stm.

25. **online videos:** Include the author or principal performer, length of the video, and date of posting, if available, as well as the medium and its source.

1. Great Ape Trust, "Kanzi and Novel Sentences," YouTube video, 1:43, January 9, 2009, http://www.youtube.com /watch?v=2Dhc2zePJFE.

Great Ape Trust. "Kanzi and Novel Sentences." YouTube video, 1:43. January 9, 2009. http://www.youtube.com /watch?v=2Dhc2zePJFE.

26. **tweets:** As of this book's press time, Chicago Style recommends that a tweet be described fully in the essay's text, as in the first example below. Following that is, as an alternative, Chicago Style's suggested format for a Twitter feed note citation. There is as yet no guidance for formatting a bibliography entry for a tweet, but one would not go far wrong in following Chicago Style's general guidelines for Web source entries; a suggested example is given in what follows.

• Jack Welch (@jack_welch) quickly lost credibility when, on October 5, 2012 at 5:35 a.m., he tweeted that the U. S. Bureau of Labor had manipulated monthly unemployment rate statistics in order to boost the post-debate Obama campaign: "Unbelievable jobs numbers..these Chicago guys will do anything..can't debate so change numbers."[1]

> 1. Jack Welch, Twitter post, October 5, 2012, 5:35 a.m., http://twitter.com/jack_welch.

> Welch, Jack. Twitter post. October 5, 2012, 5:35 a.m. http://twitter.com/jack_welch.

39b. Chicago Style Sample

A sample of text with citations in Chicago style appears below. Note that a full sample essay in Chicago style appears on the adjunct website associated with this book.

Chicago Style

Urban renewal is as much a matter of psychology as it is of bricks and mortar. As Paul Goldberger has described, there have been many plans to revitalize Havana.[1] But both that city and the community of Cuban exiles in Florida remain haunted by a sense of absence and separation. As Lourdes Casal reminds us,

> Exile
>
> is living where there is no house whatever in
> which we were ever children ...[2]

The psychology of outsiders also makes a difference. Part of the reason Americans have not much noticed the dire plight of their fifth-largest city is that it does not "stir the national imagination."[3] Conversely, there has been far more concern over the state of cities such as New Orleans and Quebec City, whose history and architecture excite the romantic imagination. As Nora Phelps has discussed, the past is in itself a key trigger for romantic notions, and it is no doubt inevitable that cities whose history is particularly visible will engender passionate attachments.[4] And as Stephanie Wright and Carole King have

---

1. Paul Goldberger, "Annals of Preservation: Bringing Back Havana," *The New Republic*, January 2005, 54.

2. Lourdes Casal, "Definition," trans. Elizabeth Macklin, *The New Yorker*, January 26, 1998, 79.

3. Witold Rybczynski, "The Fifth City," review of *A Prayer for the City*, by Buzz Bissinger, *New York Review of Books*, February 5, 1998, 13.

4. Nora Phelps, "Pastness and the Foundations of Romanticism," *Romanticism on the Net* 11 (May 2001): par. 14, http://users .ox.ac.uk/~scato385/phelpsmws.htm (accessed March 4, 2009).

detailed in an important case study,[1] almost all French-speaking Quebecers feel their heritage to be bound up with that of Quebec City. (Richard Ford's character Frank Bascombe has suggested that "New Orleans defeats itself" by longing "for a mystery it doesn't have and never will, if it ever did,"[2] but this remains a minority view.)

Georgiana Gibson[3] is also among those who have investigated the interplay between urban psychology and urban reality. Gibson's personal website now includes the first of a set of working models she is developing in an attempt to represent the effects of psychological schemata on the landscape.[4]

---

1. Stephanie Wright and Carole King, *Quebec: A History*, 2 vols. (Montreal: McGill-Queen's University Press, 2014).

2. Richard Ford, *The Sportswriter*, 2nd ed. (New York: Random House, 1995), 48.

3. Georgiana Gibson, *Cities in the Twentieth Century* (Boston: Beacon, 2015).

4. Gibson, Homepage, accessed March 4, 2015, http://www.geography.by/u.edu/GIBSON/personal.htm.

The bibliography relating to the above text would be as follows:

Bibliography

Casal, Lourdes. "Definition." Translated by Elizabeth Macklin. *The New Yorker*, January 26, 1998, 79.

Ford, Richard. *The Sportswriter*. 2nd ed. New York: Random House, 1995.

Gibson, Georgiana. *Cities in the Twentieth Century*. Boston: Beacon, 2015.

---. Homepage. http://www.geography.by/u.edu/GIBSON /personal.htm (accessed March 4, 2015).

Goldberger, Paul. "Annals of Preservation: Bringing Back Havana." *The New Yorker*, January 26, 2005, 50–62. http:// www.findarticles.com.goldberg.p65.jn.htm (accessed March 4, 2009).

Phelps, Nora. "Pastness and the Foundations of Romanticism." *Romanticism on the Net* 11 (May 2001). http://users.ox.ac .uk/~scato385/phelpsmws.htm (accessed March 4, 2009).

Rybczynski, Witold. "The Fifth City." Review of *A Prayer for the City*, by Buzz Bissinger. *New York Review of Books*, February 5, 1998, 12–14.

Wright, Stephanie, and Carole King. *Quebec: A History*. 2 vols. Montreal: McGill-Queen's University Press, 2014.

Among the details to notice in this reference system:

- Where two or more works by the same author are included in the bibliography, they are normally arranged alphabetically by title.

- All major words in titles and subtitles are capitalized.

- Date of publication must appear, where known. Provision of your date of access to electronic materials may be helpful, but is not required.

- Commas are used to separate elements within a footnote, and, in many circumstances, periods separate these same elements in the bibliographic entry.

- When a work has appeared in an edited collection, information on the editors must be included in both the first note and the bibliographic reference.

- First authors' first and last names are reversed in the bibliography.

- Translators must be noted both in footnotes and in the bibliography.

- Publisher as well as city of publication should be given.

- Months and publisher names are not abbreviated.

- The day of the month comes after the name of the month.

- Online references should *not* include the revision date but may include the date on which you visited the site (access date).

CONTENTS

40. CSE STYLE

The Council of Science Editors (CSE) style of documentation is commonly used in the natural sciences and the physical sciences. Guidelines are set out in *Scientific Style and Format: The CSE Manual for Authors, Editors, and Publishers*, 7th ed. (2006). The key features of CSE style are outlined below, and short sample essays using the three formats of the CSE documentation system follow at the end of this section.

In-text Citation: Citations in CSE style may follow three alternative formats: a **citation-name** format, a **citation-sequence** format, or a **name-year** format.

In the **citation-name** format, a reference list is compiled and arranged alphabetically by author. Each reference is then assigned a number in sequence, with the first alphabetical entry receiving the number 1, the second the number 2, and so on. Whenever you refer in your text to the reference labelled with number 3, for example, you use either a superscript number 3 (in one variation) or the same number in parentheses (in another).

- The difficulties first encountered in this experiment have been accounted for, according to Zelinsky[3]. However, the variables still have not been sufficiently well controlled for this type of experiment, argues Gibson[1].
- The difficulties first encountered in this experiment have been accounted for, according to Zelinsky (3). However, the variables still have not been sufficiently well controlled for this type of experiment, argues Gibson (1).

In the **citation-sequence** format, superscript numbers (or numbers in parentheses) are inserted after the mention of any source. The first source mentioned receives number 1, the second number 2, and so on.

- The difficulties first encountered in this experiment have been accounted for, according to Zelinsky[1]. However, the variables still have not been sufficiently well controlled for this type of experiment, argues Gibson[2].

- The difficulties first encountered in this experiment have been accounted for, according to Zelinsky (1). However, the variables still have not been sufficiently well controlled for this type of experiment, argues Gibson (2).

Reuse the number you first assign to a source whenever you refer to it again.

In the **name-year** format, you cite the author name and year of publication in parentheses:

- The key contributions to the study of variables in the 2000s (Gibson et al. 2008; Soames 2009; Zelinsky 2007) have been strongly challenged in recent years.

For two authors, list both, separated by *and* only; for more than two authors, give the first author's surname, followed by *et al.*

List of References: Citations in CSE style must correspond to items in a list of References.

In the **citation-name** format, entries are arranged alphabetically and assigned a number.

1. Gibson DL, Lampman GM, Kriz FR, Taylor DM. Introduction to statistical techniques in the sciences. 2nd ed. New York: MacQuarrie Learning; 2008. 1254 p.
2. Soames G. Variables in large database experiments. J Nat Hist. 2009; 82: 1811–41.
3. Zelinsky KL. The study of variables: an overview. New York: Academic; 2007. 216 p.

In the **citation-sequence** format, the references are listed in the sequence in which they have been cited in the text.

1. Zelinsky KL. The study of variables: an overview. New York: Academic; 2007. 216 p.
2. Gibson DL, Lampman GM, Kriz FR, Taylor DM. Introduction to statistical techniques in the sciences. 2nd ed. New York: MacQuarrie Learning; 2008. 1254 p.
3. Soames G. Variables in large database experiments. J Nat Hist. 2009; 82: 1811–41.

In the **name-year** format, the references are listed alphabetically, and the year of publication is given prominence.

Gibson DL, Lampman GM, Kriz FR, Taylor DM. 2008. Introduction to statistical techniques in the sciences. 2nd ed. New York: MacQuarrie Learning. 1254 p.

Soames G. 2009. Variables in large database experiments. J Nat Hist. 82: 1811–41.

Zelinsky KL. 2007. The study of variables: an overview. New York: Academic. 216 p.

The basic principles of the system are the same regardless of whether one is citing a book, an article in a journal or magazine, a newspaper article, or an electronic document. Here are the main details.

Author names in the References list are all inverted, with initials given instead of full first names. Initials have no periods after them, and no commas separate them from surnames. If a source in the References list has two to ten authors, include all of them; do not include *and* at any point in the list. For more than ten authors, give the names of the first ten, with *and others* following the last one listed.

Capitalize all major words in the titles of periodicals (journals, magazines, and newspapers). For books and articles, capitalize only the first words of the title, as well as any proper nouns. Abbreviate journal titles according to standardized guidelines. You can find the accepted abbreviation of a journal title at the Genamics JournalSeek site online (http://journalseek.net/); enter the journal's full title into the *Search Title* field.

Entries for books include the city of publication, the publisher, and the date of publication.

Entries for periodical articles should include the date: for journal articles, give the year; for magazine articles, give the year and month (abbreviated); for newspaper articles, give the year, the month (abbreviated), and the day.

For online sources, include all of the publication information that you would for print sources. Add *[Internet]* after the book or periodical title. The position of the date of access (e.g., *cited 2013 Feb 13*) varies according to which format you use. Give the URL after *Available from:*, and then, if there is one, the DOI (digital object identifier—a string of numbers, letters, and punctuation, beginning with *10*, usually located on the first or copyright page). Do not put a period at the end of a DOI or a URL (unless it ends with a slash).

40a. CSE Style Samples

The following is written using the **citation-sequence** format.

Over the centuries scientific study has evolved into several distinct disciplines. Physics, chemistry, and biology were established early on; in the nineteenth and twentieth centuries they were joined by others, such as geology and ecology. Much as the disciplines have their separate spheres, the sphere of each overlaps those of others. This may be most obvious in the case of ecology, which some have claimed to be a discipline that makes a holistic approach to science respectable[1]. In the case of geology, as soon as it became clear in the nineteenth century that the fossil record of geological life would be central to the future of geology, the importance of connecting with the work of biologists became recognized[2]. Nowadays it is not surprising to have geological research conducted jointly by biologists and geologists (e.g., the work of Newton, Trewman, and Elser[3]). And, with the acceptance of "continental drift" theories in the 1960s and 1970s, physics came to be increasingly relied on for input into discussions of such topics as collision tectonics (e.g., Pfiffton, Earn, and Brome[4]).

The growth of the subdiscipline of biochemistry at the point of overlap between biology and chemistry is well known, but many are unaware that the scope of biological physics is almost as broad; Frauenfrommer[5] provides a helpful survey. Today it is not uncommon, indeed, to see research such as the recent study by Corel, Marks, and Hutner[6], or that by Balmberg, Passano, and Proule[7], both of which draw on biology, chemistry, and physics simultaneously.

Interdisciplinary scientific exploration has also been spurred by the growth of connections between the pure sciences and applied sciences such as meteorology, as even a glance in the direction of recent research into such topics as precipitation[8] or cratonising[9] confirms. But to the extent that science is driven by the applied, will it inextricably become more and more driven by commercial concerns? Christopher Haupt-Lehmann[10] thinks not.

The citations above would connect to References as follows:

References

1. Branmer A. Ecology in the twentieth century: a history. New Haven: Yale UP; 2004. 320 p.

2. Lyell C. Principles of geology. London: John Murray; 1830. 588 p.

3. Newton MJ, Trewman NH, Elser S. A new jawless invertebrate from the Middle Devonian. Paleontology [Internet]. 2011 [cited 2015 Mar 5]; 44(1): 43–52. Available from: http://www.onlinejournals.paleontology.44 /html doi:10.1136/p.330.6500.442

4. Pfiffton QA, Earn PK, Brome C. Collision tectonics and dynamic modelling. Tectonics 2012; 19(6): 1065–94.

5. Frauenfrommer H. Introduction. In: Frauenfrommer H, Hum G, Glazer RG, editors. Biological physics third

international symposium; 1998 Mar 8–9; Santa Fe, NM [Melville, NY]: American Institute of Physics. 386 p.

6. Corel B, Marks VJ, Hutner H. The modelling effect of Elpasolites. Chem Sci 2013; 55(10): 935–38.

7. Balmberg NJ, Passano C, Proule AB. The Lorenz-Fermi-Pasta-Ulam experiment. Physica D [Internet]. 2005 [cited 2015 Mar 7]; 138(1): 1–47. Available from: http://www.elseviere.com/locate/phys

8. Caine JS, Gross SM, Baldwin G. Melting effect as a factor in precipitation-type forecasting. Weather Forecast 2010; 15(6): 700–14.

9. Pendleton AJ. Gawler craton. Reg Geo 2001; 11: 999–1016.

10. Haupt-Lehmann C. Money and science: the latest word. New York Times 2001 Mar 23; Sect. D:22 (col 1).

Among the details to notice in the citation-sequence format of the CSE style:

- The entries in References are listed in the order they first appear in the text.

- Unpunctuated initials rather than first names are used in References.

- The date appears near the end of the reference, before any page reference.

- Only the first words of titles are capitalized (except for proper nouns and the abbreviated titles of journals).

- When a work has appeared in an edited collection the names of the editor(s) as well as the author(s) must appear in the reference.

- Publisher as well as city of publication should be given.

- Months and journal names are generally abbreviated.

- References to electronic publications include the date of access as well as date of publication or latest revision.

- Names of articles appear with no surrounding quotation marks; names of books and journal titles appear with no italics.

Here is the same passage with the CSE **name-year** format used:

Over the centuries scientific study has evolved into several distinct disciplines. Physics, chemistry, and biology were established early on; in the nineteenth and twentieth centuries, they were joined by others, such as geology and ecology. Much as the disciplines have their separate spheres, the sphere of each overlaps those of others. This may be most obvious in the case of ecology, which some have claimed to be a discipline that makes a holistic approach to science respectable (Branmer 2004). In the case of geology, as soon as it became clear in the nineteenth century that the fossil record of geological life would be central to the future of geology, the importance of connecting with the work of biologists became recognized (Lyell 1830). Nowadays it is not surprising to have geological research conducted jointly by biologists and geologists (e.g., Newton, Trewman, and Elscr 2011). And, with the acceptance of "continental drift" theories in the 1960s and 1970s, physics came to be increasingly relied on for input into discussions of such topics as collision tectonics (e.g., Pfiffton, Earn, and Brome 2012).

The growth of the subdiscipline of biochemistry at the point of overlap between biology and chemistry is well known, but many are unaware that the scope of biological physics is almost as broad; Frauenfrommer (1998) provides a helpful survey. Today it is not uncommon, indeed, to see research such as the recent study by Corel, Marks, and Hutner (2013) or that by Balmberg, Passano, and Proule (2005), both of which draw on biology, chemistry, and physics simultaneously.

Interdisciplinary scientific exploration has also been spurred by the growth of connections between the pure sciences and applied sciences such as meteorology, as even a glance in the direction of recent research into such topics as precipitation (Caine, Gross, and Baldwin 2010) or cratonising (Pendleton 2001) confirms. But to the extent that science is driven by the applied, will it inextricably become more and more driven by commercial concerns? Christopher Haupt-Lehmann (2001) thinks not.

The citations above would connect to References as follows:

References

Balmberg NJ, Passano C, Proule AB. 2005. The Lorenz-Fermi-Pasta-Ulam experiment. Physica D [Internet] [cited 2015 Mar 7]; 138(1): 1–47. Available from: http://www.elseviere.com/locate/phys

Branmer A. 2004. Ecology in the twentieth century: a history. New Haven: Yale UP. 320 p.

Caine JS, Gross SM, Baldwin G. 2010. Melting effect as a factor in precipitation-type forecasting. Weather Forecast. 15(6): 700–14.

Corel B, Marks VJ, Hutner H. 2013. The modelling effect of Elpasolites. Chem Sci. 55(10): 935–38.

Frauenfrommer H. Introduction. In Frauenfrommer H, Hum G, Glazer RG, editors. 1998 Mar 8–9. Biological physics third international symposium. Santa Fe, NM [Melville, NY]: American Institute of Physics. 386 p.

Haupt-Lehmann C. 2001 Mar 23. Money and science: the latest word. New York Times; Sect D:22 (col 1).

Lyell C. 1830. Principles of geology. London: John Murray. 588 p.

Newton MJ, Trewman NH, Elser S. 2011. A new jawless invertebrate from the Middle Devonian. Paleontology [Internet] [cited 2015 Mar 5], 44(1). 43–52. Available from: http://www.onlinejournals.paleontology.44 /html doi:10.1136/p.330.6500.442

Pendleton AJ. 2001. Gawler craton. Reg Geol; 11: 999–1016.

Pfiffton QA, Earn PK, Brome C. 2012. Collision tectonics and dynamic modelling. Tectonics. 19(6): 1065–94.

Among the details to notice in the name-year reference system:

- The entries in References are listed in alphabetical order by author.
- Unpunctuated initials rather than first names are used in References.
- The date appears immediately after the author name(s) at the beginning of the reference.
- The in-text citation comes before the period or comma in the surrounding sentence.
- Only the first words of titles are capitalized (except for proper nouns and the abbreviated titles of journals).
- When a work has appeared in an edited collection the names of the editor(s) as well as the author(s) must appear in the reference.
- The word *and* is used for in-text citations of works with more than one author—but not in the corresponding reference list entry.
- Publisher as well as city of publication should be given.
- Months and journal names are generally abbreviated.

- References to electronic publications include the date of access as well as the date of publication or latest revision.
- Names of articles appear with no surrounding quotation marks; names of books, journals, etc. appear with no italics.

Here is the same passage again, this time using the CSE **citation-name** format:

Over the centuries scientific study has evolved into several distinct disciplines. Physics, chemistry, and biology were established early on; in the nineteenth and twentieth centuries they were joined by others, such as geology and ecology. Much as the disciplines have their separate spheres, the sphere of each overlaps those of others. This may be most obvious in the case of ecology, which some have claimed to be a discipline that makes a holistic approach to science respectable[2]. In the case of geology, as soon as it became clear in the nineteenth century that the fossil record of geological life would be central to the future of geology, the importance of connecting with the work of biologists became recognized[7]. Nowadays it is not surprising to have geological research conducted jointly by biologists and geologists (e.g., Newton, Trewman, and Elser[8]). And, with the acceptance of "continental drift" theories in the 1960s and 1970s, physics came to be increasingly relied on for input into discussions of such topics as collision tectonics (e.g., Pfiffton, Earn, and Brome[10]).

The growth of the subdiscipline of biochemistry at the point of overlap between biology and chemistry is well known, but many are unaware that the scope of biological physics is almost as broad; Frauenfrommer[5] provides a helpful survey. Today it is not uncommon, indeed, to see research such as the recent study by Corel, Marks, and Hutner[4] or that by Balmberg,

Passano, and Proule[1], both of which draw on biology, chemistry, and physics simultaneously.

Interdisciplinary scientific exploration has also been spurred by the growth of connections between the pure sciences and applied sciences such as meteorology, as even a glance in the direction of recent research into such topics as precipitation[3] or cratonising[5] confirms. But to the extent that science is driven by the applied, will it inextricably become more and more driven by commercial concerns? Christopher Haupt-Lehmann[6] thinks not.

The citations above would connect to References as follows:

References

1. Balmberg NJ, Passano C, Proule AB. The Lorenz-Fermi-Pasta-Ulam experiment. Physica D [Internet]. 2005 [cited 2015 Mar 7]; 138(1): 1–47. Available from: http://www.elseviere.com/locate/phys

2. Branmer A. Ecology in the twentieth century: a history. New Haven: Yale UP; 2004. 320 p.

3. Caine, JS, Gross SM, Baldwin G. Melting effect as a factor in precipitation-type forecasting. Weather Forecast 2010; 15(6): 700–14.

4. Corel B, Marks VJ, Hutner H. The modelling effect of Elpasolites. Chem Sci 2013; 55(10): 935–38.

5. Frauenfrommer H. Introduction. Frauenfrommer H, Hum G, Glazer RG, editors. Biological physics third international symposium; 1998 Mar 8–9; Santa Fe, NM [Melville, NY]: American Institute of Physics. 386 p.

6. Haupt-Lehmann C. Money and science: the latest word. New York Times 2001 Mar 23; Sect. D:22 (col 1).

7. Lyell C. Principles of geology. London: John Murray; 1830. 588 p.

8. Newton MJ, Trewman NH, Elser S. A new jawless invertebrate from the Middle Devonian. Paleontology [Internet]. 2011 [cited 2015 Mar 5]; 44(1): 43–52. Available from: http://www.onlinejournals.paleontology.44/html doi:10.1136/p.330.6500.442

9. Pendleton AJ. Gawler craton. Reg Geo 2001; 11: 999–1016.

10. Pfiffton QA, Earn PK, Brome C. Collision tectonics and dynamic modelling. Tectonics 2012; 19(6): 1065–94.

Among the details to notice in the citation-name format of the CSE style:

- The entries in References are numbered and listed in alphabetical order according to author.

- Unpunctuated initials rather than first names are used in References.

- The date appears near the end of the reference, before any page reference.

- Only the first words of titles are capitalized (except for proper nouns and the abbreviated titles of journals).

- When a work has appeared in an edited collection the names of the editor(s) as well as the author(s) must appear in the reference.

- Publisher as well as city of publication should be given.

- Months and journal names are generally abbreviated.

- References to electronic publications include the date of access as well as date of publication or latest revision.

- Names of articles appear with no surrounding quotation marks; names of books and journal titles appear with no italics.

GLOSSARY OF USAGE

accept/except: *Accept* is a verb meaning to receive something favourably; *except* is a conjunction meaning *not including* or *but*. ("All the members of the Security Council except China voted to accept the proposal.")

advice/advise: *Advice* is the noun, *advise* is the verb. ("We advised them to proceed, but they did not take our advice.")

affect/effect: *Effect* is normally used as a noun meaning result. *Affect* is normally a verb meaning *cause a result*. ("There is no visible effect; perhaps nothing we can do will affect it.") Note, however, that *effect* may also be used as a verb meaning *put into effect*, as in "The changes were effected by the committee."

all right: Two words.

allusion: See *illusion*.

a lot: Two words.

already/all ready: When used as an adverb, *already* is one word. ("They were all ready to do the job, but he had already done it.")

alternately/alternatively: *Alternately* means *happening in turn, first one and then the other*; *alternatively* means *instead of*. Be careful as well with the adjectives *alternate* and *alternative*.

altogether/all together: One word when used as an adverb to mean *completely* or *entirely*. ("He is not altogether happy with the result." "They were all together for the picnic.")

among: See *between*.

amoral/immoral: An *amoral* act is one to which moral standards do not apply; an *immoral* act, on the other hand, is one that goes against a moral standard.

anybody/anyone: See pages 65–66, 116–17.

anyone: One word unless it is followed by *of*.

anyways/anywheres: There is never a need for the *s*.

assure/ensure/insure: To *assure* someone of something is to tell them with confidence or certainty; to *insure* (or *ensure*) that something will happen is to make sure that it does; to *insure* something is to purchase insurance on it so as to protect yourself in case of loss.

because of the following reasons: See page 21.

beg the question: To *beg the question* is to take for granted the very thing to be argued about. In recent years the phrase has been widely used to mean *invite the question*.

between/among: Use *among* if it's among three or more.

can/may: *Can* is used to refer to ability, *may* to refer to permission. ("He asked if he might leave the room.")

capital/capitol: *Capitol* refers to an American legislative building or a Roman temple; *capital* can refer to wealth, to the city from which a government operates, or to the top of a pillar; it may also be used as an adjective to mean *most important* or *principal*.

change: You <u>make</u> a *change* (not *do* a change).

childish/childlike: The first is a term of censure, the second a term of praise.

classic/classical: As adjectives, *classic* means of such high quality that it has lasted or will last for a long time, and *classical* means *pertaining to ancient Greece and Rome* or, particularly when speaking of music, *written in a traditional style*. ("Sophocles was a great classical author; his plays are acknowledged classics.")

climatic/climactic: Weather is not the most exciting part. ("Climatic projections concerning average temperature are often inaccurate." "He spilled his drink at the most climactic moment in the movie.")

compliment/complement: To *compliment* people is to praise them, and a *compliment* is the praise; to *complement* something is to add to it to make it better or complete, and a *complement* is the number or amount needed to make it complete. ("None of the divisions had its full complement of troops, and the troops were complimented on the good job they had done despite being short-staffed.")

comprise/compose: The whole *comprises* or includes the various parts; the parts *compose* the whole.

conscience/conscious/consciousness: To be *conscious* is to be awake and aware of what is happening, whereas *conscience* is a part of our minds that tells us what is right or wrong to do. ("Her conscience told her not to steal the chocolate bar.")

continual/continuous: If something is *continuous* it never stops; something *continual* is frequently repeated but not unceasing. ("He has been phoning me continually for the past two weeks.")

could of: A corruption of *could have*.

council/counsel; **councillor/counsellor:** A *council* is a group of officials, and a *councillor* is a member of that group. *Counsel* is advice or, in the special case of a lawyer, the person offering advice. In other situations the person offering *counsel* is a *counsellor*.

couple: The phrase *a couple of* should be avoided in formal writing. In informal English, be sure to include *of* after *couple*.

definite/definitive: If something is *definite* then there is no uncertainty about it; a *definitive* version of something fixes it in its final or permanent form.

deny/refute: To *deny* something is to assert that it is not true; to *refute* it is to prove conclusively that it is not true. ("After weeks of denying the allegations he was finally able to produce evidence to refute them.")

discrete/discreet: *Discrete* means separate or distinct, whereas *discreet* means prudent and tactful; unwilling to give away secrets. ("The Queen is renowned for being discreet.")

disinterested/uninterested: A *disinterested* person is unbiased; uninfluenced by self-interest, especially of a monetary sort. If one is *uninterested* in something, one is bored by it.

each: See pages 82–83, 116–17.

effect: See *affect*.

e.g./i.e.: The abbreviation *e.g.* is short for *exemplum gratia* ("example given"; or, in the plural *exempli gratia*, "examples given"). It is sometimes confused with the abbreviation *i.e.*, which is short for *id est* ("that is to say").

elicit/illicit: *Elicit* is a verb; one elicits information about something. *Illicit* is an adjective meaning illegal or not approved.

emigrate/immigrate: To *emigrate* is to leave a country; to *immigrate* is to move to it. ("More than 10,000 emigrants from the United States became immigrants to Canada last year.")

enthuse/enthusiastic: *Enthuse* is a verb; *enthused* is its past participle. The adjective is *enthusiastic*. ("Everyone was enthusiastic about the movie.")

everybody/everyone: See pages 65–66, 116-17.

everyday/every day: One word when used as an adjective to mean "daily," but two words when used to mean "each day." ("Brushing your teeth should be part of your everyday routine." "She comes here every day.")

everyone: One word unless it is followed by *of*.

explicit/implicit: Something *explicit* is stated in precise terms, not merely suggested or implied. By contrast, something *implicit* is not stated overtly.

farther/further: *Farther* refers to physical distance, *further* to time or degree. ("We do not have much farther to go." "The plan needed further study.")

flaunt/flout: To *flout* is to disobey or show disrespect for; to *flaunt* is to display very openly. ("The demonstrators openly flouted the law.")

forget: To *forget* something is to fail to remember it, not to leave it somewhere. ("I left my book at home" or "I forgot to bring my book" but not "I forgot my book at home.")

forward/foreword: You find a *foreword* before the other words in a book.

good/well: The most common of the adjective-for-adverb mistakes. ("He pitched very well today.") See pages 88–89.

hardly: *Hardly* acts as a negative; there is thus no need to add a second negative. ("They claim that you can hardly tell the difference.")

historic/historical: *Historic* means *of sufficient importance that it is likely to become famous in history* (a historic occasion). *Historical* means *having to do with history* (historical research).

hopefully: Traditionalists argue that the correct meaning of the adverb *hopefully* is *filled with hope*, and that the use of the word to mean *it is to be hoped that* is therefore incorrect. Others argue, plausibly, that many other adverbs may function as independent comments at the beginning of a sentence ("Finally, ..." "Clearly, ..." "Obviously, ...") and that there is no good reason for treating *hopefully* differently. Using *hopefully* to mean *it is to be hoped that* should not be regarded as a grievous error—but it is a form of English usage that will upset many instructors.

illusion/allusion: An *allusion* is an indirect reference to something; an *illusion* is something falsely supposed to exist. ("Her poem makes many allusions to Shakespeare.") Also, when you make an *allusion*, you are alluding to something.

in/into/throughout/within: Whereas *in* typically indicates a particular location, *into* implies motion, and *throughout* implies omnipresence. *Within* and *in* are not interchangeable; *within* should be used only in certain contexts involving extent, duration, or enclosure.

increase: Numbers can be *increased* or *decreased*, as can such things as production and population (nouns which refer to certain types of numbers or quantities). Things such as *houses*, however, or *books* (nouns which do not refer to numbers or quantities) cannot be *increased*; only the number of houses, books, etc. can be *increased* or *decreased*, *raised* or *lowered*.

infer/imply: To *imply* something is to suggest it without stating it directly; the other person will have to *infer* your meaning. ("This sentence implies that the character is not to be trusted.")

irregardless/regardless: There is no need for the extra syllable; use *regardless*.

is when/is where: Avoid these expressions when defining something. ("Osmosis occurs when...," not "Osmosis is when....")

its/it's: *Its* is an adjective meaning *belonging to it*. *It's* is a contraction of *it is*—a pronoun plus a verb. ("It's true that a coniferous tree continually sheds its leaves.")

later/latter: *Later* means afterwards in time, whereas the *latter* is the last mentioned of two things.

lay/lie: You *lay* something on the table, and a hen *lays* eggs, but you *lie* down to sleep. In other words, *lie* is an intransitive verb; it should not be followed by a direct object. *Lay*, by contrast, is transitive. ("That old thing has been lying around for years.")

lend/loan: In formal English *loan* should be used only as a noun; *lend* is the verb. ("He was unwilling to lend his sister any money.")

less/fewer: Use *less* only with uncountable nouns; use *fewer* with anything that can be counted. ("This checkout is for people buying fewer than twelve items.")

liable/likely: Do not use *liable* unless you are referring to possible undesirable consequences. ("It is liable to explode at any moment.")

like/as: In formal writing use the conjunction *as* to introduce a clause—not the preposition *like*. ("He looks like his father." "He looks as his father did at his age.")

literally: A *literal* meaning is the opposite of a figurative or metaphorical meaning. Do not use *literally* simply to emphasize what you are saying.

loose/lose: *Loose* is normally used as an adjective meaning *not tight*; *lose* is always a verb. ("The rope has come loose." "He began to lose control of himself.")

may be/maybe: One word when used as an adverb to mean *possibly*, but two words when used as a verb. ("Maybe he will arrive later tonight." "He may be here later tonight.")

may of: A corruption of *may have*.

might of: A corruption of *might have*.

mitigate/militate: To *mitigate* something is to make it less harsh or severe ("mitigating circumstances"); to *militate* against something is to act as a strong influence against it.

must of: A corruption of *must have*.

neither: See pages 116–17.

none: See pages 116–17.

nor: Use in combination with *neither*, not in combination with *not*. When using *not* use *or* instead of *nor*. ("She does not drink or smoke." "She neither drinks nor smokes.")

nothing/nobody/nowhere: These words should not be used with another negative word such as *not*. With *not* use *anything*, *anybody*, *anywhere*. ("He could not do anything about it.")

passed/past: "She *passed* me on the street," and "I *passed* her a note," but "that was all in the *past*."

per cent/percentage: If you use *per cent*, you must give the number. Otherwise use *percentage*. ("The percentage of people who responded was very small.")

persuade: If one does not succeed in making people believe or do what one wants, then one has not *persuaded* or convinced them, but only *tried* to persuade them.

precede/proceed: To *precede* is to come before; to *proceed* is to go forward. ("Once the students understood that *G* precedes *H* in the alphabet, they proceeded with the lesson.")

prescribe/proscribe: To *prescribe* something is to recommend or order its use; to *proscribe* something is to forbid its use.

principal/principle: *Principal* can be either a noun or an adjective. As a noun it means *the person in the highest position of authority in an organization* (e.g., a school principal) or *an amount of money*, as distinguished from the interest on it. As an adjective it means *first in rank or importance*. ("The principal city of northern Nigeria is Kano.") *Principle* is always a noun; a principle is *a basic truth or doctrine*, *a code of conduct*, or *a law describing how something works*. ("We feel this is a matter of principle.")

protest: You *protest* something (not protest against it).

quote/quotation: *Quote* is the verb, *quotation* the noun. ("The following quotation illustrates the point.")

real/really: *Real* is the adjective, *really* the adverb. ("She was really happy.")

reason is because: Use *that* instead of *because* to avoid redundancy. ("The reason may have been that they were uncertain of the ally's intentions.")

respectively/respectfully: *Respectively* means *in the order mentioned*; *respectfully* means *done with respect*. ("Green Bay, Denver, and San Francisco are, respectively, the three best teams in the league.")

sensory/sensuous/sensual: Advertising and pornography have dulled the distinction among these three adjectives; *sensual* is the one relating to sexual pleasure.

set/sit: *Set* means *to place something somewhere.*

short/scarce: If people are *short* of something, that thing is *scarce.* ("Food is now extremely scarce throughout the country.")

should of: A corruption of *should have.*

since (1): As a time word, *since* is used to refer to the <u>point</u> at which a period of time began ("since six o'clock," "since 2008"). *For* is used to refer to the <u>amount</u> of time that has passed ("for two years," "for centuries"). ("He has been with us for three weeks" or "He has been with us since three weeks ago.")

since (2): Watch for ambiguity involving *since* meaning *because,* and *since* meaning *from the time that*; "Since he crashed his car he has been travelling very little" could mean either "Because he crashed his car..." or "From the time that he crashed his car...."

so: *So* should not be used in formal writing as an intensifier in the way that *very* is used. ("He looked very handsome," not "He looked so handsome.")

some/someone: With negatives (*not, never,* etc.) *any* is used in place of *some.* ("He never gives me any help.")

somebody/someone: See pages 116–17.

stationary/stationery: *Stationary* means not moving; *stationery* is what you write on. ("The cars were stationary.")

suppose/supposed: Be sure to add the *d* in the expression *supposed to.* ("We are supposed to be there now.")

sure and: In formal writing always use *sure to,* not *sure and.*

than/that: *Than* is the one used for comparative statements ("more than we had expected").

than/then: *Than* is used in comparisons, whereas *then* denotes time.

thankful/grateful: We are *thankful* that something has happened and *grateful* for something we have received. ("I am very grateful for the kind thoughts expressed in your letter.")

that/which: See page 134.

they/there/their/they're: Four words that are confused perhaps more frequently than any others. *They* is a pronoun used to replace any plural noun (e.g., books, people, numbers). *There* can be used to mean *in* (or *at*) *that place*, or can be used as an introductory word before various forms of the verb *to be* (*There is, There had been*, etc.). *Their* is a possessive adjective meaning *belonging to them*. Beware in particular of substituting *they* for *there*. ("There were many people in the crowd," not "They were many people in the crowd.")

tiring/tiresome: Something that is *tiring* makes you feel tired, though you may have enjoyed it very much. Something that is *tiresome* is tedious and unpleasant.

to/too/two: *Too* can mean *also* or be used to indicate excess (*too many, too heavy*); *two* is of course the number. ("She seemed to feel that there was too much to do.")

try and: In formal writing always use *try to*, not *try and*. ("He had agreed not to try to convert them.")

unexceptional/unexceptionable: *Unexceptional* means *ordinary, not an exception*; if something is *unexceptionable*, then you do not object (or *take exception*) to the thing in question.

unique/universal/perfect/complete/correct: None of these can be a matter of degree. Something is either unique or not unique, perfect or imperfect, and so on, never *very unique* or *quite perfect*.

use/used: Be sure to add the *d* in the expression *used to*. ("This neighbourhood used to be very different.")

valid/true/accurate: An *accurate* statement is one that is factually correct. A combination of *accurate* facts may not always give a *true* picture, however. *Valid* is often used carelessly and as a consequence may seem fuzzy in its meaning. Properly used it can mean *legally acceptable*, or *sound in reasoning*; do not use it to mean *accurate, reasonable, true*, or *well-founded*.

weather/whether: *Whether* the *weather* will be good or bad is hard to predict.

were/where: *Were* is of course a past tense form of the verb *to be*, while *where* refers to place.

where: Do not use *where* for *that* (as in *I read in the paper where the parties are tied in popularity*).

whose/who's: *Whose* means *belonging to whom*; *who's* is a contraction of *who is*.

would of: A corruption of *would have*.

your/you're: *Your* shows possession, *you're* is a contraction of *you are*.

Additional Material Online
Exercises on words that may cause confusion and on other points of usage may be found at **sites.broadviewpress.com/writing**. Click on **Exercises** and go to **"Words and Usage."**

CORRECTION KEY

Correction Key

Ab	Faulty abbreviation
Adj	Improper use of adjective
Adv	Improper use of adverb
Agr	Faulty agreement
Amb	Ambiguous
Awk	Awkward expression or construction
Cap	Faulty capitalization
D	Faulty diction
Dgl	Dangling construction
Frag	Fragment
lc	Use lowercase
Num	Error in use of numbers
‖	Lack of parallelism
P	Faulty punctuation
Ref	Unclear pronoun reference
Rep	Unnecessary repetition
R-O	Run-on
sp	Error in spelling
SS	Faulty sentence structure
T	Wrong tense of verb
∽	Transpose elements
∨	Wrong verb form
Wdy	Wordy
∜	Add apostrophe or single quotation mark
⌒	Close up
⌄	Add comma
ℓ	Delete
∧	Insert
¶	Begin a new paragraph
No ¶	Do not begin a new paragraph
⊙	Add a period
⌄⌄	Double quotation marks
#	Add space

INDEX

INDEX

Entries in **bold** are to words, not topics.

From the Publisher

A name never says it all, but the word "Broadview" expresses a good deal of
the philosophy behind our company. We are open to a broad range of academic
approaches and political viewpoints. We pay attention to the broad impact book
publishing and book printing has in the wider world; we began using
recycled stock more than a decade ago, and for some years now we have used
100% recycled paper for most titles. Our publishing program is
internationally oriented and broad-ranging. Our individual titles often
appeal to a broad readership too; many are of interest as much
to general readers as to academics and students.

Founded in 1985, Broadview remains a fully independent company owned by
its shareholders—not an imprint or subsidiary of a larger multinational.

For the most accurate information on our books (including information on
pricing, editions, and formats) please visit our website at www.broadviewpress.
com. Our print books and ebooks are also available for sale on our site.

broadview press

www.broadviewpress.com

The interior of this book is printed on 30% recycled paper.

30%

PERMANENT